THE CONTRARY VIEW

Notes from an Odd Country
Penguin Modern Poets 23
Ingestion of Ice-cream and Other Poems
A Skull in Salop and Other Poems
Discoveries of Bones and Stones and Other Poems
Sad Grave of an Imperial Mongoose
Collected Poems 1924–1962
Poems and Poets
Poems of Walter Savage Landor (*editor*)
A Choice of Robert Southey's Verse (*editor*)
A Choice of Thomas Hardy's Poems (*editor*)
A Choice of William Morris's Verse (*editor*)
Concise Encyclopedia of Modern World Literature (*editor*)
Faber Book of Popular Verse (*editor*)
Unrespectable Verse (*editor*)

For children

The Cherry Tree: An Anthology of Poems (*editor*)
Rainbows, Fleas and Flowers: A Nature Anthology (*editor*)
Looking and Finding
Shapes and Creatures
Shapes and People
Shapes and Stories (*with Jane Grigson*)
Shapes and Adventures (*with Jane Grigson*)
O Rare Mankind
Poets in their Pride

THE CONTRARY VIEW

Glimpses of Fudge and Gold

GEOFFREY GRIGSON

ROWMAN AND LITTLEFIELD
Totowa, New Jersey

First published in the United States 1974
by Rowman and Littlefield, Totowa, N.J.

First published in the United Kingdom 1974 by
The Macmillan Press Ltd

Library of Congress Cataloging in Publication Data

Grigson, Geoffrey, 1905–
    The contrary view.

    1.   English literature—Addresses, essays, lectures.
2.   American literature—Addresses, essays, lectures.
I.   Title.
PR99.G6878   809   73–21736
ISBN 0–87471–152–5

Printed in Great Britain

In gratitude to Karl Miller, who
was diversely the best of literary
editors

Contents

Preface

Old convicts learn caution. When they face the bench again and the bench ask if they have anything to say for themselves, the old recidivists must know that some remarks, or some excuses, could be distinctly dangerous.

This writer with a record will take a risk, all the same. He will start off by saying that he is offering his readers a book of light reading. Sniff from the bench. Well, he adds, not long-winded reading: it isn't necessary to be long-winded or heavy about poems and poets, about books and authors. The bench confers. Becoming reckless now, this writer blurts that many of the pieces are not long-winded because they began – as book reviews. The word is out. 'And haven't you written yourself against collecting book reviews? In this collection don't you even slate another writer for collecting his reviews?'

But look at the situation. There was a time when the professional man of letters could earn his keep (and satisfy his desire to estimate) in long bursts of several or many thousand words. He could argue. Now he must more often dogmatize, in short space, since long critical articles cannot be in demand with editors who conduct short periodicals. It used to be said – I remember T. S. Eliot writing to this effect – that space was a *sine qua non* for marshalling a serious literary argument. Yet it should be possible to write with effect in a few hundred words – even if that makes the writer more open to inconsistency or repetition; which are not the worst of offences. And isn't it allowable that even short notes may be threaded on a writer's continuing and developing and changing interests, conveying his views with the aid of sufficiently attractive illustration from the work he is discussing?

The Contrary View is a title which suggests contradiction, if not contrariness. It would be boring never to contradict, but I hope the view revealed will be positive, in spite of expectations. I look for a special independence (and dependence), a special freedom (and obedience) in good writing, mostly to be found, for various reasons, in poetry, which is my favourite concern. I offer a blend, too, of the familiar and the unfamiliar in these mixed glimpses of fudge and gold. For a reason it would be altogether too grand to call historical (perhaps autobiographical would be the word) I have included two pieces, one at the beginning, one nearly at the end, which bring underlying convictions and sentiments and keepings up to the surface.

GEOFFREY GRIGSON

Acknowledgements

A number of pieces in this collection were first published in the *Times Literary Supplement*, the *New Statesman*, the *Spectator*, *Encounter*, the *Guardian*, the *Listener*, the *Observer*, *Country Life*, and the *Sunday Times*. 'The Poet Who Did Not Care for Life' is a shortened version of the 1973 annual birthday lecture to the Thomas Hardy Society.

Disliking the Gentlemen
of England

Isn't it time a rejoinder and a corrective to the Martin Greens
– born in the late Twenties, poor family, Oxford, Cambridge
or Redbrick – were advanced by someone who happens to be
older, though he objects in a life and literary way to much
the same things? Someone who comes – as many thousands
of his readers must do – out of the milieu which the Martin
Greens so dislike, distrust and condemn? I shall try. And I
see that as I go along I must declare – though not at all out of
egoism – my interest, or at any rate my keepings, one by one,
if Mr Green, flushed by the reception of his book,[1] is not to
think it the old act of the con man. So first –

Age and Origins. Far away from Martin Green, I am in
what is optimistically or evasively called late middle age. I
was born in 1905. I should now be acquiescent. No matter
what I may object to or condemn, I descend from Martin
Green's detested eunuch class of sensibility and discrimina-
tion, the Gentlemen, my father a parson of the Church of
England who had his niche (though without much justification in land) in *Burke's Landed Gentry.* My ancestry – of
which I have been conscious with some pleasure and perhaps
cynicism as well – is modest, rural, clerical, medical, legal,
minor squirearchy, graduates of Cambridge (where I have a
son) generation by generation back to the sixteenth century.
From a footnote in a historical journal I learn that my great-
grandfather, after whom I am named, successfully used his
powers as trustee of a Norfolk charity (in 1777) to rent all its
lands to himself. But I do not think – on other evidence – that
he was a bad man.

Education. Self-educated, but with a grounding in prep
schools, a minor, averagely repellent 'public' school (classics,

[1] *A Mirror for Anglo-Saxons*, by Martin Green (1961).

against a defeated will for biology and botany), and then Oxford. As for my own family, I have children who have been educated neither at state schools nor 'public' schools, but at a co-educational progressive school (though some such schools are now tending to become reserves for the retarted or delinquent children of the managerial sector).

Livelihood. I have inherited nothing, except a share, a few hundred pounds, in the scanty proceeds of a Victorian marriage settlement. I have earned, independently; have held some – but very few – offices of profit under what Christopher Isherwood once named the Poshocracy. I earn from a country parish – Martin Green's Old World rurality – because I was bred in a country parish, and prefer it for recreation, exercise, isolation, work, and economy. I live, yes, under a thatched roof, because I was unable to afford a tiled one. Very well, the thatch is now being removed. I have had to write much that I am sorry to have written, whether from weakness of character or weakness of talent. I have *tried* in doing so not to curry favour too often with prejudice or do dirt on existence.

Politics and Religion. Labour, always; and no religion. I cannot believe there is a God because my father did – but then he was born in 1845 – or because John Betjeman does, or because God beliefs have been vehicles of value, and demonstrably useful to my human race. I dislike priests (no, I did not dislike or despise my father) in so much as most of them are witch-doctors, now of low degree, supporting with feebleness and equivocation a system no longer tenable intellectually. I am conscious with Malraux, for example, that I belong to the first culture which does not know, and admits that it does not know, the significance of man – though I should put this differently and say that I belong to the first culture which knows that the family of life is an accident of chemistry.

Papers habitually read. Yes, *The Times*, in part because I take shall I say a tonal delight in 'XYZ writes . . .' on the obituary page, and partly because I like to know what poshocrats are up to in thought and prejudice before they make that page; but also because I welcome news about, for example, the discovery of nettle cloth in a Stonehenge barrow.

The *News Chronicle*,[2] because there is not an intelligent socialist daily. At weekends the *Tribune*, with misgiving at its frothiness; the *New Statesman*, partly from pious habit; the *Spectator*, partly because it sees truth now and then, and also prints my poems; the *Observer*, partly – although as a wit has observed, one always expects to find the editor in the front hall at the loom, initiating classes in home weaving – because the drivelling spirit of Garvin has been so long exorcized, and it would rather print the comments of Martin Green than the memoirs of a bird-watcher; the *Sunday Times*, because it now and then contains a brilliant review; the *Sunday Express*, to observe the lack of conscience in Mr Green's lower middle class.

Select Culture Heroes. Neither Colonel Lawrence nor D. H. Lawrence (though I wept at D. H. Lawrence's death, and wrote probably the only leading article it occasioned in the whole British press). Neither Eliot nor Leavis. No, but on a list liable to diminution or addition, Auden, and Wyndham Lewis. Aksakov, Leskov, and Babel, Ralegh, George Herbert, Dryden, Coleridge, Hopkins (much for his letters and journals). Bruegel, Poussin, Hokusai, Corot. I suspect I should add to these Tu Fu, Wen-i-to and Pasternak, if I could read their poems other than in translation. All these Heroes to be understood more as works than persons.

If Auden, Babel, Bruegel, Wen-i-to, Pasternak, and perhaps Hokusai, are loosely describable as Left, all the others on this list are loosely describable as Right. Vis-à-vis their essence, their art, this distinction would be both temporal and puerile.

Select Detestations. Unswervingly and for very long, the Establishment. It is not a word I care to use, but the existence of the things so indicated is ridiculed only by its acolytes and menials. It is also a moral term, and they might as well deny the existence of good, bad, love, hatred, justice; though to isolate a pure strain of Establishment virus might not be easy. It can de described in other ways. It is *In* vis-à-vis *Out* (which I know suggests envy). I do not assent to ideas of the Establishment as a conspiracy or as something entirely recognized

---

[2] Now defunct. Also when this was written the *Guardian* had not become a national paper.

by its constituting groups or individuals. It is a condition; inevitable in all societies, even 'primitive' ones, I imagine. All the same I detest the various products above ground (to alter the biological metaphor) of the Establishment's huge subterranean mycorrhizal system, whether saprophyte or parasite. I detest writers who when found out as writers, can fall back on being gentlemen (or on being of the working class, on being non-gentlemen). I detest writers sustained only by the purple they succeed to, only by the literary-social position in which they find themselves – there are plenty of these – by the accident of birth. I detest – there are plenty of these too – young women or young men of the Establishment or the Poshocracy (these two are not quite the same) who have no talents and are yet placed in culture jobs, a case, to borrow from Coleridge, of favours for the already endowed and undeserving being robberies of the unendowed and the deserving.

Extreme Detestations. I detest with a conviction equal to Martin Green's, and I think for the same reasons, those groupings he has named of writings or activities – Priestley to Snow, *The Confidential Clerk* to C. S. Lewis, above all Betjeman–Waugh, all symbols or items of a convenient shorthand. Realizing that black and white seldom exist in separated purity I have attempted for a long while, not to deny, but to control and keep private my distaste for *some* of the now more prominent of these symbolic manifestations, whether the Betjeman antic in poetic nostalgia, so much an insular product, or public Christianity (too different from Herbert's, or Christopher Smart's, for my observer's approbation), or syrup lavished with maximum coverage by way of journalism or television on the sentimental loves and joke-loves of the Establishment. No good. Years ago I refused to publish poems by Betjeman in *New Verse*. My built-in shock-proof Establishment detector (apologies to Hemingway for the image) was right about the poems, broadly, though I think some of them are to be admired and enjoyed. I am told the poet retaliated by standing somewhere on the body of the Uffington White Horse – the backside, no doubt – and cursing me; though I have survived.

Present-day Class. I consider that I belong to no class.

I have, of course, some inevitable trappings, accent (which is often a matter of verbal aesthetic, after all), carriage, certain tastes, etc., the personality, like the body, having its birthmarks. But I endeavour neither to speak, think, feel nor act, in anything that matters, from a position of class.

Here it is I quarrel with Martin Green, who does, I think, speak deliberately from a condition of another class or another class origin. There are many thousands of us of all ages from mine to Martin Green's, and of my class origin, who prefer, and disdain, and condemn as he does, more or less, but with a freedom consciously acquired. He is luckier, too, than those of my age. Time has clarified the issues for him; and when others discerned the infection decades ago, the possibilities of publishing the fact, or being listened to, were small. I am amused – and pleased – to see how much one of us who was vocal, W. H. Auden (origin: professional sensibility class, medicine, clergy, correct suburb and rurality, 'public' school, Oxford. Named after a not generally known Anglo-Saxon saint) now reappears in so to say translation – and this in spite of the long, long critical vendetta carried on against his poems by that champion of Mr Green's decency, F. R. Leavis.

> And over the Cotswolds now the thunder mutters:
> 'What little of the truth your seers saw
> They dared not tell you plainly but combined
>   Assertion and refuge
> In the common language of collective lying.'

It is that language the artist at any rate has to discard – or the polemicist, I might say to Martin Green, there being more collectives than one. Each – I emphasize each – writer or artist of every kind has to come through: let us have a classless Auden out of the professional middle class, a classless John Clare out of the working class, writing classless poems, allowing that words can have their independence.

If someone points for example at Wyndham Lewis, and says 'Gentleman, Right Winger, Fascist', my first reply is 'Artist, Writer, Fighter for mental freedom': I answer or reiterate that Wyndham Lewis has been a culture hero of mine, not only because I knew him, and know what the charges against him of intellectual brutality are worth, but because with admirable defiance he pronounced and maintained, against everyone, the 'literary-social Establishment' included, that art is 'a constant stronghold of the purest human consciousness'.

Writers and painters and the rest – no, as many as possible of all of us – have to come through as much and as often and as near as we can to a pure human consciousness. It is time that the Martin Greens and many others stopped – I don't say using that word 'Establishment', which is so much more than a concept of class – but stopped looking for a pure consciousness, and conscience too, anywhere except in those individuals who endeavour to possess it freely, whoever they are, originating in whatever class, with whatever affiliations.

It is naïve to think that such are, have been, ever will be in good supply, or in control, in any society; that they will ever be dominant in governing, in teaching, in practising the arts; though in each department they should keep together, and not sniff, and sniff and sniff, and snarl at the tail-end of each other's class origin. Also I doubt if they are in fact to be discovered in any higher ratio in Martin Green's preferred America, surely a society not less confused or less corrupt or more pure, or allowing more opportunity of moral action, than our own, *our* Establishment or no (though undoubtedly it can give higher academic salaries, and higher advances and royalties, and magazine fees).

P.S. About the success of Betjeman's poems, 'the greatest popular success of the century for poetry in England', Martin Green is wrong. Their success is not even remotely near that of A. A. Milne's poems in *When We Were Very Young*; though with respect to Mr Betjeman's encomiasts I cannot see a pronounced difference between the skill of one and the other; and though I admit this is merely to correct Mr Green's illustration, not the argument he illustrates.

1961

Hendren–Rhododendron

I want! I want! What does John Betjeman want? What most of us regret and yearn for and love and despise and reject, in the middle classes. The vanished ease, the vanished security, the vanished self-confidence, expressed in the lawns, the laurels, the laurustinus, the purple glass on the stairs, the mahogany, the starched surface over the unacknowledged and angry lust, the crunch of wheels on the drive, the poets, the albums, the Besant and Rice and the Edna Lyalls in the revolving bookcase.

It is in that sense that I am going to write about his new poems.[1] I must not repeat that they are delightful, that they are better written.

Tasteful variations about the delight they give, about their 'remarkable wit' and their Victorian element and so on, will flourish in the natural weekly habitats of ecstasy and repetition. Of course, I agree about John Betjeman's merit (although I am a convert – an uneasy convert, not a cradle-admirer).

I could just say that butterflies – it is true – can best be admired if they are not dismantled; but it will not destroy these poems if we do dismantle them just a bit. I like to know, myself, that Purple Emperors, while they enjoy the sun at the top of the oak tree, also come down to feed on the stoats and decaying jackdaws nailed to the trunk. So if I risk brushing some of the iridescence off Mr Betjeman – well, you do not need to go on. It will do you no good, all the same, to evade this matter, just as it will do Americans and Mr Lehmann's drab proletarians no good to sneer at Betjeman as a poetaster and a pasticheur. If Betjeman is pastiche (he is) – so are we. But you do not get rid of us by saying that we ape the past, or that we do not exist. And so these poems are not only about the drawing-rooms of our childhood, they

[1] *Old Lights for New Chancels*, by John Betjeman (1940).

remind us of the actual poetry on the shelves of the drawing-
room, of all poetry between Stephen Phillips and Crabbe.
When I read the first of them,

> *Floruit, floret, floreat!*
>   *Cheltonia's children cry.*
> I composed those lines when a summer wind
>   Was blowing the elm leaves dry . . . ,

I wondered whose cadence I was hearing, and I found it
reminded me of the cadence of the Rev. R. S. Hawker, who
is certainly one of Mr Betjeman's smaller favourites (as, indeed, he is one of mine). So we could go on, dissecting, track-
ing, fixing upon prototypes – though that would be pedantry,
because part of what ambiguous John Betjeman intends is
this: that in spite of Eliot and Herbert Read, we and he
should *feel at home*, should feel ourselves, by the sound and
the properties, back by the loose-cover of the armchair, by
which, in 1909, we learnt '*Up the airy mountain, down the
rushy glen*'. Of course, then, Mr B. finds 'hardly any pleasure
in the Elizabethans', in those alien, mannered, precise,
enamelled poets with their codpieces, etc.

> Hide, Oh hide those hills of Snow
>   Which thy frozen bosome bears,
> On whose tops the Pinks that grow
>   Are of those that April wears.

What have those hills to do with Cheltenham, or with the
'Conifer county of Surrey approached/Through remarkable
wrought-iron gates'? What on earth have they to do with
Holy Trinity, Sloane Street, or Norham Gardens, or Bosie?
The quatrain might as well be written in Middle English or
O.H.G. No, it was in church, in J. B. Dykes, in the blessing on
Sunday night under the oil lamps, in the sighing A-a-a-men,
in Meredith ('lovely are the curves of the white owl sweeping'), in Matthew Arnold, in wagonettes, in *Hearth & Home*,
in Van Heems and Wheeler (the clerical tailors), in *Burke's
Landed Gentry*, that John Betjeman, and the great class he
amusedly and ambiguously champions and so acutely understands, felt secure and happy. Mr Betjeman has taken sides.

For this reason he is not a satirist, but a critical partisan. Too many people have let the side down.

> See the strength of her arm, as firm and hairy
>   as Hendren's;
> See the size of her thighs, the pout of her lips
>   as, cross,
> And full of a pent-up strength, she swipes at
>   the rhododendrons,
>   Lucky the rhododendrons –

That is keeping the side up. And *this* – in Westminster Abbey – is letting the side down, is why the side is down, down, down indeed:

> Now I feel a little better,
>   What a treat to hear Thy Word,
> Where the bones of leading statesmen
>   Have so often been interr'd.
> And now, dear Lord, I cannot wait
> Because I have a luncheon date.

Mr Betjeman is a Christian and no doubt, with Prior and Praed, a Conservative, but a knowing Christian and a knowing Conservative:

> 'Forgive me, aren't we talking rather loud?
> I think I see a woman praying there.'
> 'Praying? The service is all over now
> And here's the verger waiting to turn out
> The lights and lock the church up. She cannot
> Be Loyal Church of England. Well, good-bye.
> Time flies. I must be going. Come again.
> There are some pleasant people living here,
> I know the Inskips very well indeed.'

I am sure that if you asked, he would call himself a Christian *high* enough not to know the Low Church Inskips (Law Officer, Lord Chancellor, Low Church Sir Thomas Inskip will require a note from Mr Betjeman's twenty-first-century editor) and not to justify Mammon by mingling it with God; and he would call himself a Conservative of the Professions – the Clergy, the Doctors, the Barristers, the Army and Navy –

a Conservative of no rights without duties, and not a Conservative of Commerce; and because in this way Mr Betjeman *knows* his own moribund side, he is such a good poet.[2] He lets go. He admits and solidifies the obscene fear of death (the death we are *in*):

> He liked old City dining-rooms,
>   Potatoes in their skin.
> But now his mouth is wide to let
>   The London clay come in.

He admits frequently – and solidifies – the obscene lust for the forbidden flesh of the adolescent girl:

> Get down from me! I thunder there,
>   You spaniels! Shut your jaws!
> Your teeth are stuffed with underwear,
> Suspenders torn asunder there
>   And buttocks in your paws.

Here, then, are cameos and velvet gowns, and conifers, and Liddon's Sermons and *Tract XC*, the cooking smell from the basement, the pennies laid out on the dining-room mantelpiece for the offertory bag, the snobbish interest in the aristocracy and the Manor House. Here also I smell Dickens enjoying the gas-lit wickedness he was afraid to go through with, Reade enjoying the tanking of female lunatics in the asylum, Chadwick revelling in the cesspits and corpses of Holborn. Approving and disapproving, but *yearning for it all*, late and early, John Betjeman completes his comi-tragic pastiche even in appearance. He writes like Hawker and like Newbolt, he silhouettes himself on the frontispiece (a pretty resemblance to Rupert Brooke), he puts a Pickering anchor on the title-page, then wraps his poems, label and cloth, in an 1835 casing.

[2] This was written in 1940, and readers will detect from the last piece and from pieces to come, that I have not been exactly faithful to this early view. The question was whether this slyly serious pasticheur would succumb poetically to his own charm and to the image of him which his admirers were forming, with consequent changes in his verse. Now we might ask, how seriously are the arts taken when the class jester is made into the court poet?

Remarkable. It is the word, all right. And no wonder that, for his skill and the familiarity of his way, John Betjeman has now become a fashionable poet. Many want in the way that he does. Fewer recognize the wistful futility of wanting, or recognize the imperfection of the object of desire; and therefore the fashion for Betjeman will produce – indeed it has already produced – much queer jinks in matters of religion-and-architecture-and-art-and-journalism and personal behaviour. Late entrants into the fringe of the Middle Class of the Professions (see Miss Marrible on gentlemen in Trollope's *Vicar of Bullhampton*) who never enjoyed its security or grew up in the authentic dregs of its tradition, will crawl after the continual dew of Mr Betjeman's blessing. They do not see, as Betjeman, I think, does, how inevitably the old park of the Middle Class is now becoming a rubbish dump where the rats slip round the ragwort and the hip-baths and the old dummy figures labelled *Sitwell* and *Blunden*. But when fashion is pushed away, when all this fawning, if pathetic, is reckoned ridiculous and is dismissed, there remains, all right, the bamboo-tea-table solidity of these poems. Here we are in the second of the new wars. In the world at last the dangerous hunchback rides the powerful motor-bike with the overhead valves; so the ladder is in place on the crescent moon and Mr Betjeman – I want! I want! – continues the impossible ascent.

And yet – oh, to hell with necrophiliac John Betjeman, to hell with these poems, to which I will not genuflect any further, though I will not pull the ladder away.

1940

The Mildly Monstrous

1. *When Hoo, Exactly, Was Very Young?*

Once, oh once, did not the Public find its voice in the Poet? Once – but not now, O Apollo – weren't new poems sold, in the largest numbers? *Lalla Rookh*, and *Childe Harold*, and *Idylls of the King*, and *Poems and Ballads* (and *Proverbial Philosophy*)?

Then T. S. Eliot came; and poetry changed to modern; and did not sell.

As such facts are recited (often, if not quite so often as heretofore), how is it that no one remembers Alan Alexander Milne? How is it that no one is asked, in Advanced Level English, even in the Tripos, to estimate the influence upon 'Now I'm engaged to Miss Joan Hunter Dunn' of

> Hush! Hush! Whisper who dares!
> Christopher Robin is saying his prayers?

A. A. Milne was a poet – he wrote poems, shall I say, no less than John Betjeman, or Eliot; or William Empson. Undeniably *When We Were Very Young*, his most successful book, is filled with poems. Undeniably these poems have sold (and are selling still). Few other poems in English have sold so enormously. They were published – two years after *The Waste Land* – in the autumn of 1924: they have been reprinted (this is the fact) fifty-six times in thirty-four years.

This poet was born to a Scottish prep school master, in London, in 1882, six years before our Mr Eliot was born in St Louis, Missouri. He was educated (nothing 'wrong' about his education) at Westminster School and Trinity College, Cambridge; and soon enough, after editing the *Granta*, the undergraduates' magazine, he was helping to edit *Punch* in its least aggressive and most evasive days. This young man knew the electric fences of the interest in which he was now involved, his master J. M. Barrie, his editor R. C. Lehmann. At what college – let us give an example – should we then have expected something, or someone, so unmanly as a *chess* blue? At an 'inferior' college, to which the better-born sons did not go. 'This is the ballad of Edward Bray', A. A. Milne began a poem, in *Punch*, on the chess match between the universities of Oxford and Cambridge,

Captain of Catharine's, Cambridge Blue.

Exactly so, the 'wrong' college, not King's, not Trinity.

With his own *curriculum vitae*, his own dye of the Posh-ocracy, in the Squeamish Age (in which St Loe Strachey, editor of the *Spectator*, led a deputation to the Home Secretary asking him to ban *Ann Veronica* by H. G. Wells), Milne's later poems of *When We Were Very Young* were in tune, precisely.

The nature of the best-seller has to do with the nature of a class, its prime interest is one of sociology, not literature; which is the fun of such books. The readers have mattered most of all, and it is not difficult to be sure of the readers who have found a voice in A. A. Milne, to be sure of the readership (and the sociological writership) to which he belonged. From the poems you need only to deduce the keepings of Christopher Robin, and Percy, and John, and Mary Jane, and Emmeline, and James James Morrison Morrison Weatherby George Dupree.

The poems intimate that these children are of good family – at least up to the Forsyte standard. They have nannies and nurseries (*passim*). Maids are also in attendance – though not butlers (see *The Wrong House*).

Their homes, in London, are in the right squares, are not too grand and not too mean. Their families keep dogs, and are kind to uncles, aunts, and animals other than dogs; and display an embryo interest in bird-watching. Their daddies know about trout, mayfly, and expensive rods, their mamas about trugs and delphiniums. When they are not very ill, they are attended by frock-coated white-haired family doctors. They are Church of England – could a dissenting child or a Presbyterian child say 'Thank you, God, for my nice new

braces'? They are accustomed, with a full staff, to seaside
holidays (I think in North Cornwall), in a rented house:

When we got home, we had sand in the hair,
In the eyes and the ears and everywhere.

Their world is Us, and the Other People. Those of the
Other People who sell in shops or work with their hands
(Jonathan Jo the gardener) are a little queer, and perhaps
need washing (see *Bad Sir Brian Botany*), but they must be
treated with consideration; which averts revolution. Bad
Sir Brian blipped 'the villagers' on the head with his battle-
axe and kicked them into the pond, and into the ditches, and
under the waterfall. But observe that the treatment simply
made Bad Sir Brian renounce his title, his battle-axe, and his
spurred boots, which he threw into the fire; after which he
'goes about the village as B. Botany, Esquire'. He has become
one of Us. The class structure is repaired, and improved.

Conclusions? We may now be sure that of these children
the males are earmarked for the better schools, then the
better colleges, high on the river (*mens mediocris in corpore
sano*), at one of the 'two' universities; and that male and
female they come of families comfortable, secure, self-certain,
somewhat above the middle of the middle class.

Are the poems for other children of such homes? No, rather
than yes. Children, in my experience, of every generation
since and including the Twenties, have found the poems
nauseating, and fascinating. In fact, they were poems by a
parent for other parents, and for vice-parental nannies – for
parents with a war to forget, a social (and literary) revolution
to ignore, a childhood to recover. *When We* – We – *Were
Very Young* the book is named, after all, indicating its aim;
which, like the aim of all natural best-sellers, was not entirely
explicit, one may assume, in the author's consciousness.

Here mamas of the middle way, and fathers, and nannies,
those distorting reflectors of the parental ethos, could be sure
of finding Innocence Up to Date. Little Lord Fauntleroy –
here he was, stripped of frills and velvet (as we can tell by
the splendid insipidity of the accompanying drawings) for
modern, sensible clothes; heir, after all, to no peerage, but
still the Eternal Child. No hint in these poems of children

nasty, brutish and short, as *Struwelpeter* or Hilaire Belloc made them (or as they are being re-established in newspaper cartoons).

Are there ever tantrums, as these nice children say 'cos', and 'most', and 'nuffin'', and 'purfickly', and 'woffelly', in their nice accent?

> *What* is the matter with Mary Jane?
> She's perfectly well, and she hasn't a pain.

If there are tantrums, it is rice pudding again; but not the child psyche, not infant sexuality, not Freud, who had now entered the pure English world. (In fairness, though, I must admit a touch of complex in Christopher Robin when he signs off with his prayers –

> *God bless Mummy.* I know that's right.
> Wasn't it fun in the bath to-night?
> The cold's so cold, and the hot's so hot.
> Oh! *God bless Daddy* – I quite forgot.

But no doubt this came of independent observation.)

The innocence of *When We Were Very Young* – of course it chimes with the last tinkle of a romantic innocence which by the Twenties had devolved to whimsy. Christopher Robin comes trailing the tattiest wisps of a glory soiled by expectation and acceptance. The clouds have gone grey. The Child, in spite of Westminster and Trinity, is all too much at last the Father of the Man. And whenever the Child's impresario allowed an entr'acte, it came in parallel modes of the expected and decayed – daffodowndillies and the last fairies (inherited from the more fanciful – and sinister – inventor of Peter Pan), Twinkletoes upon the apple leaves, the Lake King's daughter on the water-lilies, cave ancients tapping at golden slippers for dainty feet, bluebells, and backbirds' yellow bills.

For some Poets Who Don't Sell, these poems for people towards the top with children beneath the age of literary consent have the qualities of rhythm, shape, economy, and games with words – good qualities, after all. Would it be too ponderous to say as well that they were poems for a class of middle to top people who had lost their intellectual and cultural nerve, who expected of right things which they had not earned, and who had scarcely looked a fact in the eye for fifty years? It might be too ponderous. But it would be true.

And sometimes out it comes in the charming sick, in the actual stuff, with an ironic unconsciousness. As Christopher Robin says, imagining himself on a desert island instead of his holiday coast of Cornwall, in the land of Betjeman:

> And I'd say to myself as I looked so lazily
>   down at the sea:
> There's nobody else in the world, and the world
>   was made for me.

A few days after A. A. Milne died the editor of *The Times* had occasion in his paper (which had just given Milne an obituary not very kind, though much longer, and kinder, than the one it had allowed years before to D. H. Lawrence) to write, in his role as 'Oliver Edwards', on Modern Poetry. He admitted to wondering often, 'heretically, whether, where Mr T. S. Eliot is concerned, Old Possum will not outlive Alfred Prufrock' – hand in hand, no doubt, with Christopher Robin, Hoo, and Pooh. At any rate, more than 745,000 copies of *When We Wewe Very Young* have been sold. And it is in the bookshops still.

2. *The Wind in the Willows*

Kenneth Grahame was born a century ago, on 8 March 1859. He became Secretary of the Bank of England, published his three principal books, *The Golden Age* in 1895, *Dream Days* in 1898, and *The Wind in the Willows* in 1908, dying at last, a sad and successful master of royalties, in 1932.

For his centenary Peter Green has written this very curious life,[1] having inserted himself as an industrious millipede under the loose bark and discovered there damp things which are not at all pleasant, which are saddening, yet are very fascinating, and will some of them be (I hope) offensive to Tops and Climbers nesting in what is left of the Great Lie.

How did this bankers' chief employee come to write *The Wind in the Willows*, so good a thing in spite of itself, or of himself?

[1] *Kenneth Grahame, 1859–1932*, by Peter Green (1959).

About many Victorian and Edwardian artists of every kind there is a frightening fact, first of all, which Mr Green recognizes: they were subject to an extra degree of that unfreedom to which we are all subject or to which we subject ourselves for a variety of reasons. Compulsive goblins ate into their lives. The spirit's features stiffened into the social grin. How do we avoid, I mean how should we avoid wearing that false smile? How can we train ourselves into being a true witness upon oath?

By luck, partly; by not enduring, to begin with, a childhood such as Kenneth Grahame's. Law, money, and Scotland with an eye on South Kensington was Grahame's family milieu. His mother died when he was five. His father, a Scotch lawyer, took to drink, abandoned his children, and died in poverty in France.

So Grahame began with severe doses of the great Victorian liquorice powder of Dependence – upon uncles and aunts. He was schooled in Oxford, he wished to go to the university, and was all too sharply reminded of Dependence, that moral conditioner, when his controlling uncle said no. So he was found a gentleman clerkship at the Bank, suffering what his brisk biographer calls one of his ugly splits between hope and fulfilment, dream and reality.

The child 'without the proper equipment of parents'. No independence. No love also of Olympian elder relatives. How do you escape? You don't. But in two ways you try – ways at first successive, which may then alternate or be simultaneous. You retreat to ideal situations, into fantasy, dream days, golden ages, the sound of the wind in the Thames willows of Cookham Dene, where Grahame lived as a child. You emerge, you advance, you work at the Bank, you eye the Olympians and the Tops, and acquire their characteristics. Retreat, advance; advance, retreat.

Layer by layer, visible in the cruel strip-without-tease forced upon him in his centenary account, this Galsworthian victim of disparate temptations, disparate goblins, becomes eventually that Blank Face with handlebar moustaches which stares out of later photographs; inwardly the ambivalently kind, uneasy, and not wholly conscious satirist of *The Wind in the Willows*.

A globule of being refuses destruction. Grahame, a large fawn with a startled look, is the country lover, the Open Roader, the Cornish holiday-maker, the devotee of a sexless Pan (Peter). He presides at sing-songs at Toynbee Hall, that egregiously symbolic centre of self or class justification. 'I divide', he says, 'the whole population of Europe into English people and blacks.' He is advanced in the Bank. He is Tory, but also Utopian. He conforms, and he escapes, though not entirely. He conforms, and he resorts to satire, but the satire is covert. And clay-hearted Tops and mud-masked Olympians recognized in *Dream Days* and *The Golden Age* that child's-eye truth which – once – shone in themselves.

For a good way Mr Green's long book drives on a flattening tyre, with spurts of knowingness and pedantry which are nearly ridiculous. 'As Mr David Daiches observed . . .', 'Mr Lionel Trilling takes this point further . . .', 'As Mr Eliot says . . .' (though they are never observing or saying anything about Kenneth Grahame).

But then the appalling narrative takes charge energetically of Mr Green and Mr Green's, alas, myriad clichés. At forty, after a bad illness, the Secretary of the Bank entangles himself with a girl – decidedly – of thirty-seven, half courted, half parried by him in letters of the most glucose baby talk. She is an elfette, an elfin art-adorer, who had been a little girl friend of Tennyson, Mark Twain and Sir John Tenniel (her stepfather, a Lord in Appeal, one is glad to note, inappropriately sends Kenneth Grahame, at Fowey, where he is recuperating in the company of that spongy middleman of literature Quiller-Couch, a copy of Balzac's *Droll Stories*).

They marry, in 1899. Sex intrudes into courtly love, and as hurriedly withdraws (on Grahame's side); though a sickly child is born, half-blind, who is idolized and idealized, forced into Rugby, then Eton, removed, and tutored into Oxford; where he kills himself on the railway line near Port Meadow.

The Wind in the Willows of 1908 arises from stories told to this strange child; and is Grahame's last retreat, from his wife, this time, into the mixed realisms of the ideal, before dragging on towards death through a marriage of two isolations.

The globule of real being asserts itself in a myth of universal elements wrung out of a life of compromise, New World

against Old. Now against Golden Age, Car against Caravan.
Here are the good River-Bankers (who are also gentle Thread-
needle Street bankers?): over there, on the wrong side of the
River, are the unwashed Stoats of the Wild Wood. Here is
Toad, who forgets loyalty to caste and lets down the side, and
drives cars; but he is at once, says Mr Green, the irresponsible
landed *rentier* (the renegade bank director?) and the victim
of society's pursuit of the nonconformist, the heterodox.

There are no real escapes. Poor Rat conforms and yields.
He sucks his pencil and scribbles at poetry instead of going
South. Grahame conforms and yields, and scribbles his myth;
and Mole shuts the door, like any House Master, any Director,
any senior diplomat, or senior administrator of the British
Broadcasting Corporation or the British Council, glad to see
the cure has begun.

At what cost the globule of being has maintained itself!
And what a life situation, what a trap, was required to
squeeze the civet out of the civet cat, or to extrude the odd
pearl of Mr Toad (whom A. A. Milne was rapidly to soften
into a still more acceptable oddity): I do not think Mr Green's
analysis can be contradicted. He may write rather badly, but
extracting grubs from under the bark of the old British Oak
he gives us another perfect sample of the extent and the cost
of our lie, which has so long used schools and universities,
not to liberate, but to justify. I commend the sample to those
who would change the games of birding and churching to the
sceptical man's game of son-and-parent watching, on Satur-
days, in the nearest tea-shop to a greater 'public' school.

I must report two other things from Mr Green. In 1898 a
director of the Bank of England bought *The Golden Age*,
thinking it had to do with bimetallism. In 1908 the *Times*
reviewer said of *The Wind in the Willows*: 'As a contribution
to natural history, the work is negligible.'

1958–9

3. *Disneydust – for 240,000,000 Viewers*

It is an odd book, Richard Schickel's *Walt Disney*,[2] and
when you reflect on it, the subject is odd as well, for exactly
what is, or was, Walt Disney, who is now dead, or so we are
told?

If you say Walt Disney – though I suppose the words are
pronounced less often now that cinema-going has declined –
you mean less a person than evanescent figures capering and
talking on a screen. You leave the cinema, and these figures
vanish, they are so unreal or so impersonal, from your mind
or your memory; or they leave behind no more than a general
impression of squeak and squawk, Mickey, Minnie, Donald
Duck, Porky Pig, and so on, down to the Disneyization of
The Jungle Book, the vulgarization, the Americanization (but
is that fair?) of Kipling and Mowgli and Shere Khan.

A vanishing sequence, a vanishing trick, for instant entertainment? Was Walt Disney real, or a brand name? A personal fact, or a Mouse Factory (as the earlier Disney
organization was known to Disney employees)?

I am almost surprised to discover from this book that he
was; that he was once born – in Chicago, in 1901; that he
actually died, in 1966. FOUNDED AN EMPIRE ON A
MOUSE, said the *New York Times* in an obituary headline –
Miki Kuchi in Tokyo, Mikel Mus in Athens. Behind the
empire, behind the foundation, behind the figure (according
to Walt Disney Productions) that every new Disney offering
is seen by 240,000,000 viewers throughout the world, Mr
Schickel's difficulty has been to find, cage, and offer the man.
That he fails to do so more or less (no help came to him from
the Mouse Factory or from the Mouse factor's family) he
might agree to be the substance of his book, though a someone called Walt Disney for short does appear in a photograph
– and looks quite normal – on the back of the jacket. At any
rate Mr Schickel does not cage an artist, or a person it would
be very interesting to meet or talk to, or listen to, next Satur-
day morning – supposing he could be made to talk. He finds
instead a man so ordinary as to be almost invisible except in

[2] *Walt Disney*, by Richard Schickel (1967).

terms of profit. One journalist – but journalists will say anything – said about Walt Disney after he died, that he had
been 'a twentieth-century Cellini who supervised the mining
of his own gold'.

But Cellini is not ordinary, he is not difficult to find, he did
make objects with his own hands, he did set himself down on
paper, in his own writing, in a sparkling autobiography.
Whereas Disney – well, as much as anything real or human
emerges, somewhere at the back of a huge technological,
profit-making kingdom, somewhere at the back of a house
style in mice, ducks, et cetera, was a little-big mid-western
go-getter. Go-getting was his natural objective, for which he
was not so very exceptionally equipped. He had nothing to
trade except a residue, less of childishness, or something
which sounds so pleasant, than of childish fixation at a certain
mental age. He arrived out of failure almost accidentally.
Once arrived, he hung on, he organized, he showed extreme
efficiency in exploiting technological inventions. He knew,
he loved, he was a monomaniac about the fixation, the arrest,
the lack of development he had to offer: he made it join up
with technology. Dollars were also the required outcome, and
dollars came.

Disney identified himself with his own mouse. He was
ignorant, ill-educated, incurious. 'Culture' seemed to him an
unAmerican word. He disliked art, which 'he often equated
with obscenity'; and in the house-style of his movies, he or
his Mouse Factory, his Magic Kingdom, provided art de-
individualized, a kind of sweet coffee without caffein, art
with the art removed – the mouse, the duck, the pig, the
fawn for those whose idea of mouse, duck, pig or fawn is not
enforced by ever having observed or regarded such a creature.

He liked to be thought Mr Clean. He liked to be thought
avuncular – 'Call me Walt' – though he was ill at ease, and
was apt to stare through visitors as if afraid of being found
out in his ordinariness, as if 'fascinated by the sight of something very small and ugly at the back of your head'. He was
stingy, in the affairs and salaries of Mouse Factory or Magic
Kingdom, he was sneaky around the office, he was mildly
anti-semitic, in a mild way he was a supporter of Barry
Goldwater and Governor Reagan.

The author is a little horrified. He calls Disney or Disney-ism 'a kind of rallying point for the subliterates of our society', a 'microcosm of modern America'. He says: 'In this most childlike of our mass communicators I see what is most childish and therefore most dangerous in all of us who were his fellow Americans.'

A bit too serious, I would rejoin. Of course there are grown-ups who read comics, or look at them; and comics are the Disney offering, simply comics-plus-electronics, comics with an extra large circulation, on the screen – and then off, out, forgotten, as I say, as if nothing had ever capered there.

They have no 'magic', except animation and voices; I doubt if their fans, even if there are 240,000,000 of them in the world, not all children, are really being seduced from a Grimm, a Perrault, a Tolkien they would otherwise enjoy – or from Leonardo, or from pictures by Douanier Rousseau, or Mirò. I doubt if they do any harm. And if Disney movies all caught myxamatosis and disappeared I suspect there would still be exactly the same number of potential Disneyists. But that is no reason for not looking through Mr Schickel's eye, in this book, on to his own countrymen.

One detail I must mention, slightly contradicting my assertion that there was no 'magic' in Disneyism. Nursing his mental age, his fantasy-fiction, knowing what he was about and what he wanted, Disney was not inclined to change or to keeping up with the times. But Disney movies did make more and more use 'of what has come to be known in the trade as *Disneydust*, those sparkly highlights that burst from any object touched by any magic wand in any Disney ani-mated film . . . Walt was known to have liked this effect.'

I may be snootily indifferent to Mouse Factory products (danger, debasement, entertainment and all), as to the rattles I used to rattle in my cot, but Disneydust I do rather like: it is as if something 'genuine' came through for once in a scarcely debased form, as if on the Missouri farm where he spent much of a hard, harsh childhood (his father failed and had to sell up), he once – only once – managed to get hold of some Christmas sparklers, and light them in the dark.

Uses of Pasternak

Which do you prefer, Pasternak or the 'Pasternak affair'?
Reading his poems and *Dr Zhivago*, or reading about the way
Pasternak was treated by the chuck-out men of Moscow's
official orthodoxy? These are proper questions, though perhaps I should turn in some perplexity to Mr Conquest and
ask *him* which of the two he prefers; and also what it was,
really and underneath, which moved him to assemble this
book?[1]

It is an outline, with documents, of the whole nastiness,
from the immediate results of the publication of *Zhivago* in
Italy to the recent sentencing of Pasternak's friend Olga
Ivinskaya for receiving *Zhivago* royalties introduced from the
West. What puzzles me is whether – according to his main
title – Robert Conquest wishes to exhibit the 'courage of
genius', or whether – according to his sub-title – his chief
intent is to give a 'report' on the 'literary and political significance' of the affair. Is he illuminating genius or having a cold
swipe at Moscow?

I should think, on the documents, that the affair might be
very shortly summarized in this way: that Pasternak, a great
poet of moral and historical insight and bravery, behaved as
such a man should behave, though with some naïvety, and
that Moscow officialdom, literary-political and political,
behaved stupidly and monstrously in accord with its system,
though a little less stupidly and monstrously than might have
been expected. Also that the West, not a little shamelessly
and hypocritically, contributed more to the filthy muddle,
the misery, the cruelty, and the stupidity than Robert
Conquest, for one, is prepared to admit.

[1] *Courage of Genius*, by Robert Conquest (1961).

Pasternak seemed naïve in expecting that *Dr Zhivago*
would or could be accepted as a book above politics, or at
least that it could or would be realized that, in his own words,
he had 'borne witness as an artist'. Not to accept or realize
either truth suited both the cold Western warriors and the
Russian orthodox. It was specifically as a poet and a novelist
that Pasternak was awarded the Nobel Prize by the Swedish
Academy, after *Zhivago* had been refused publication in
Russia, after it had been published in the West and after the
trouble of the Union of Soviet Writers against Pasternak had
begun. Mr Conquest uses a good many pages to say that this
was in no way a political or ideological counter-award, and
to prove that, on his standing as a European poet, Pasternak
was in any case fit – but of course he was – to receive the
prize. It is possible to be too innocent about the Swedish
Academicians. They must have known that *Zhivago* had
already been delightedly announced and reviewed and
advertised and regaled as an anti-Soviet masterpiece, so that
five minutes' thought could (or should? – but that is another
matter) have convinced these good gentlemen that if in such
circumstances they gave the prize to Pasternak, then far from
assuring and underwriting his economic and creative future,
they might be killing him, or at any rate making it certain
that if he wasn't killed, he would be all the more harassed,
injured, and humiliated. They could have waited and given
him the award another year, if by then the shemozzle had
died away or died down. But they didn't, and some day it
should be explained why they didn't.

Just before I opened Mr Conquest's documentary-cum-
commentary on these matters, I happened to have been
reading De Quincey's *Savannah-la-Mar*. 'God smote
Savannah-la-Mar' and its children with an earthquake, and
the Dark Interpreter explained to De Quincey that earth-
quakes and sorrow were the fierce ploughshares of God's
agriculture, necessary for stirring the stubborn soil of the
strange children of Earth, so that they might understand.
O.K. for God, maybe. But it seems to me that in making the
award the Swedish Academicians, if they weren't acting more
than the least little human bit politically or ideologically,
were all too grandly playing the Dark Interpreter's God – and

damn the consequences to mere living Pasternak; or else that they were all too naïvely acting as God proposing and God disposing, in a supposedly innocuous vacuum of perfect Soviet goodness, sweetness and understanding.

Pasternak was clearly in two minds before very long, between immediate pleasure at the award and gathering contempt, not of the Swedish Academy, but of the Western journalistic furore (which Mr Conquest hardly documents at all, though why?). To have been made an earthquake victim for the ultimate instruction of the mysterious children of the Earth may in the end have given satisfaction to this great man; but he knew that he was being used as well ('I could not imagine that I would be in the centre of such a political campaign as started to be fanned around my name in the West', Pasternak to Khrushchev, 1 November 1958. 'Do people buy *Dr Zhivago* because it is a good book or only because they think it is anti-Communist?' – Pasternak to an interviewer, 30 September 1959). I would put it to Mr Conquest, and Mr Conquest's readers, that he also is using Pasternak, not as clearly or shoddily or sensationally as some people in the West have used him, not as clearly as some of the politicians and cold warriors, but still using him, ambiguously.

In Moscow, where they think it right and good that a political leader in his eighty-first year should be humiliated and reduced to tears in public, how are they likely to treat an aberrant someone so little as a great poet? We know; and know also that mankind, wherever we like, London, Moscow, New York, always produces its brash literary dung beetles and ichneumon flies, its conforming and performing establishmenteers; know as well that Moscow's establishmenteers differ only in being organized by the disciplines of ideology and fear, so that they have a power more totally and brutally of inflicting literary death or castration, or actual death.

Do we need a book – like Mr Conquest's – to tell us that, again? Possibly. Even then I would urge on Mr Conquest that someone else should have compiled it – that the proper duty of an English poet who has the good fortune to know Russian, towards the poet Pasternak, and ourselves, is to translate Pasternak, or to write about his writing so as to make it better understood and more widely effective. It would be less profitable, but more honourable. It is certainly what Pasternak would have preferred; and he would have been sorry to observe a *poet* declining into a propagandist, and doing the Russian thing in reverse, i.e. subscribing (though from the opposite pole of fear instead of desire) to that ludicrous notion of Communists that the most 'total' system has the power of embracing everything of consequence in life immutably, and for all time. It was part of Pasternak's distinction to reject that shallowness – with every danger to himself.

II

The great acclaim for *Dr Zhivago* was fishy, I have always thought. It had more to do with the division between East and West than with appreciation or the virtues of the novel; which isn't to say that it lacked virtues, or that Pasternak was anything other than – I nearly said a great writer, but I would rather say a great poet. In another small book[2] he is the poet – the poet writing about life in letters to other poets or others who understood poetry; and I notice that the acclaim, by contrast, has been rather cool. Pasternak might be amused, might be relieved. I can imagine him saying: 'Well, I am dead. I am no longer news. The sensation is over. This time I have not been smuggled out of Russia, and you can read me as I was, without the hullaballoo of oppression and the Cold War: you have a better chance to see me as a witness to less transitory affairs in these letters to Georgian friends and poets you have never heard of.'

I shall not bother about the circumstances of these letters, but I should like to say just why I looked forward to them. They were announced some months ago, last autumn, together with quotations in advance. This man, who maintained his integrity in danger, spoke in one of these preliminary extracts of the happiness of his life, which had been full 'of such quiet concentrated meaning' – 'What was the chief and fundamental thing about it? The example of my father's work, love of music and Scriabin, two or three

[2] *Letters to Georgian Friends*, by Boris Pasternak (1968).

chords in my own writing, night in the Russian countryside, the revolution, Georgia.' I was taken by the way 'night in the Russian countryside' came into that list; and in so much Russian literature, present as well as past, a warming and infinitely taking element is such an 'attitude towards the earth' (Pasternak's words in another of these letters), an attitude not at all cuckoo, not at all sentimental, but lyrical, sane, and balanced.

Could an English writer put 'night in the countryside' into such a list? If he did now, he would probably be a sentimental writer, a nostalgic writer. England in 1966 feels smaller than it is, distance has contracted, the urban sense has expanded, until it pervades modern England inescapably. It is good that in modern ideologically controlled Russia a writer can still talk, as Pasternak does, of his 'attitude towards the earth and poetry', of 'the feeling of loyalty to life . . . and to nature', and can still write: 'I do not believe in anything very big in size or in anything of which there is very much. Women give birth to people, not to Cyclopses.'

I would have been inclined to call this book 'Women Give Birth to People', rather than 'Letters to Georgian Friends'. Its spirit is that the people, the children, born from women, grow into a world and a life, and that life must not be insulted or despised or rejected: other people have to live it, other people are one's friends. In one letter Pasternak remembers Vronsky in *Anna Karenina*, who buys canvases, pencils, brushes, paints, in order to paint pictures – 'but somehow nothing seems to come right, either the mood is wrong or the weather is not good enough'. And with this he compares 'a man mad about painting who contracts tuberculosis because of his dedication to art'. He goes on: 'It is this gentlemanly, amateurish, idle attitude towards the whole world of self-sacrifice and hard work, which I know so well and to the service of which I am devoted, that surprises and repels me. I saw something in life that had some connection with great men.'

Again and again the reader of these letters will find sentences which exhibit the loving seriousness and greatness of the writer. He loves potentiality. 'Love of the future is for me as much a constant and intimate thing as love of a woman, and I cannot do without it.' Wonder is necessary to him, to all of us, he writes: 'One must write wonderful things, make discoveries and see to it that wonderful things happen to you. That is life. The rest is rubbish.' He does not, like a sentimentalist, separate nature and man: 'The significant thing that excites one in nature and in the world of men has so far' – here is wonder again, and potentiality – 'not been given a name and is still waiting for a definition. It is indeed this waiting that is so exciting, like a still unsolved problem or a flare hanging in the sky in expectation of the moment of action.'

How extraordinary that last image out of war (Pasternak was for a time, in his mid-fifties, a war correspondent), implying rather action for life, not action for killing. Always in these letters the accented thing is fullness of becoming, fullness of being. No turning off into the dead-ends of eccentricity. Poetry must have its fullness. He speaks of some of his poems as second-rate 'because they are only tender and musical, whereas poetry ought, in addition to music, to contain painting and meaning'.

He never whines, never complains in these letters – and obviously wants no one else – no Kremlinologist, for instance – to whine or complain on his behalf: 'On my return home portents of dangers and sufferings awaited me. But everywhere in the world one has to pay for the right to live on one's own naked spiritual reserves.'

I was moved by his attitude to women, blending a confession of personal inadequacy and timidity in respect of them, with a deep regard for their 'place in life'; which brings him back again to himself and the earth: 'I am a realist who has a thorough knowledge of the earth not because, like Don Juan, I have frequently had a lot of fun with women on earth, but because since childhood I have gathered pebbles from under her feet on the path she has trodden.' (I wonder if I am right in thinking that an apparent tone of sentimentality in that last sentence is due rather to translator's English than to Pasternak's Russian?)

In the end it is seriousness, earnestness – not a boring or priggish quality in its right nature – which marks the extraordinariness of this man. I remember something written by

another realist of earth, our own Gerard Manley Hopkins,
that 'a kind of touchstone of the highest or most living art is
seriousness; not gravity, but the being in earnest with your
subject – reality'. Happiness for Pasternak was serious –
'happiness as it should be – serious, profound, fathomless,
and sad', work was serious: 'I am a man who is accustomed
to his day being filled with work as it is filled with the sun
and the sky.' He wrote that active, industrious, persevering
as he might be, he was not a man to take steps; there was a
feminine, passive streak in himself. Then this sentence: 'Just
as I have given myself up several times into the hands of life
and into the hands of serious work, so, in the long run, all that
is left to me is to give myself up into the hands of death.
That is all my programme.'

Splendid to be allowed to know such a man, so concerned
with the unselfish function of himself, splendid that he has
left his life behind him to such a degree. I would call *Letters
to Georgian Friends* one of those books to be read again and
again at intervals, every good passage marked, as a test of
one's own life and understanding of it; reflecting in the mean-
time that there are other, unpleasant ways of using an author
of genius who happens to have lived under the hammer and
the sickle.

1968

A Captured Unicorn

A symbol is inert, or it lacks entity, acquiring effect according to the way it is employed or the keepings of the employer. A phoenix painted by bird-watching Mr Peter Scott would inevitably, it is to be feared, have some of the characteristics of a goose. Let us consider the characteristics of a unicorn presented by Miss Iris Murdoch,[1] by whose novels I find myself little entranced.

The hunt of this unicorn is over. She sits (a rare unicorn in the habiliments of a she) guarded inside her fence, healed of her wounds in a house (a Victorian castle) near the sea, in what is an evident derivative of Burren – if a little reality may be intruded – a district in County Clare of naked limestone and naked dolmens and rarest flowers, bordering not only the grinding and variable ocean, but a boggy, exceptionally sour extent of coal measures.

By a kind of inversion, various virgins, male and female, lay their heads upon the lap of this unicorn, who is blonde, young, beautiful, blousy, rich, and named Hannah Crean-Smith, owner of the circumambient lands. She should be free, think the virgins from outside who have forgotten their unicorn lore and have not yet come by an understanding of Gaze Castle, to escape. She stays in her room, where the flowers are not the customary tall orchids of the unicorn, purple against the white flank, but pampas grass and dried honesty in two brass pots. The worshippers approach, virgins and guardians and ex-huntsmen, finding her with bare feet, not as purely, unambiguously white as the religious-cum-sexual unicorn of the Middle Ages, but with her love-inviting face a little sallow, her hair a little tousled, her fingernails not quite clean, defiling whiteness with whiskey and the yellow of cigarettes.

With a newly-employed virgin from England, not yet

[1] *The Unicorn*, by Iris Murdoch (1963).

initiated, she reads the *Cimetière Marin*; and significance
gathers.

Ce toit tranquille, où marchent des colombes,
Entre les pins palpite, entre les tombes.

This hired virgin is told – of course she laughs, at first –
that 'all the people round here are related to the fairies'. Her
employer appears fey (the word is used), the circumstances
appear more and more weird (the word is frequently used).
This virgin 'feared the rocks and the cliffs and the grotesque
dolmen and the ancient secret things'. She tried bathing, but
the sea wasn't always peacock blue, but angry on the narrow
foreshore of pebbles under the black cliffs (and was in any
case, if she had known it at this stage, full of salmon, which
are the souls of the living about to force their valiant way up
the falls, through a different element, to God in the salmon
pool, in contrast to certain goldfish guarded from the herons
by wire up in the castle gardens). She observed also in things
said by her employer – said by the captured unicorn inside
the fence – 'a startling possessive savagery . . . oddly at
variance with the accustomed *douceur*', having yet to realize
the force in the sharp weapon which grows out of the head
of this beast, and the difficulty and dangers which had
attended the hunt, and having yet to hear this unicorn
described as a murderess and a whore, having yet to hear
from her, in the recesses of her enclosure, 'a sort of howl,
the scarcely human cry of a soul in agony', or to see the
salmon stranded on the hillside by the bursting of the big
waters.

The queen-wasp in the heart of this papery nest (if one
may change from a unicorn to a wasp) turns out to be the
guilt of the devotees. I shall not swear to that; but if I should
be wrong, I don't think it will matter, because I shall swear
meanwhile to some of the ways in which the symbolisms are
deployed or planted *entre les tombes*, or as the tombs
approach in the incessant downpour of Irish, or universal,
rain.

Fey or fated to return to the ordinary realm from this
'psychological masquerade', this 'vampire play', the virgins
or guardians who are manipulated in this novel may be

described, I think, as characters lifted by Miss Murdoch –
not for the first time – from any serial in a woman's magazine
and then animated in the manner of Walt Disney (though
one must imagine animations who are allowed to be whores,
virgins, perverts, masochists, sadists, etc.), touching them
with a little whimsicality from the late James Stephens.

How are they environed? By *things* which intervene, as if
animated once more by Disney or drawn by Rackham, oil
lamps which murmur, gates which resist, lawns which wait to
see what someone will do, rocks which struggle from the soil,
waves which destroy themselves, a sea which transmits the
beating of its heart to the cliffs.

How, in this wrigglesome milieu, do they encounter? By
sudden histrionic jumps. 'It was Pip Lejour, and he was
carrying a shotgun.' 'Good morning all! The loud voice
behind him made Effingham jump.' Or by a drop into
bathos, as when two of the faithless virgins are about to
copulate by God's pool, fretted under the sunset by the now
rising salmon: 'Denis, tell me, how many girls have you
had?'

How do they act? They 'cast roguish glances' at each
other, or 'submit utterly', or are 'awakened by a murmur of
voices'.

How do they talk – or *converse*? 'Wildly', or they 'speak
wearily, contemptuously', or they say 'I'll be bound!' or
'Effingham, she is destroyed'.

Indeed, though this mightn't be quite the novel for the
sixth form, one could go through it in class substituting, *ad
infinitum*, 'forehead' for 'brow', 'tomorrow' for 'on the mor-
row', 'upset' for 'troubled', 'nothing had happened' for 'all
was as before', 'boy' for 'lad', 'go away' for 'flee'.

I should myself go most of the way with William Empson
in the claim he made the other day that in poetry – and prose
– we have had enough symbolism and should take to argufy-
ing instead. At any rate when I try a novel by Miss Murdoch
I realize how easily the 'cool element' of prose or of fiction
can make extra-special extra-pretentious fudge out of symbolism. Fiction goes on a long time. Symbolic fiction succeeds, if
at all, not by the symbols deployed, but by involving them in
one's substance, and then keeping hold with the greatest

power and literary circumspection. For Miss Murdoch's substance I can say very little. With a kind of effect she does drive its vulgarity along.

1963

Skoal to the Stanchless Flux, or the Worst of Henry Miller

To call a selection 'The Best' of an author's work is dangerous. What happens if much or even some of the best turns out by usual standards to be bad? What has one then to think of his second best, or his average?

This selection,[1] divided into stories, accounts of places, portraits, literary essays, and aphorisms, is taken from twenty years of Henry Miller's writing; and the selector, Lawrence Durrell, as a friend and partisan introduces Henry Miller with ominous caveats which may also be taken as defences or evasions. Henry Miller, says Mr Durrell, 'is rather a visionary than merely a writer'. He suspects that his 'final place' will be among 'those towering anomalies of authorship like Whitman or Blake who have left us, not simply works of art, but a corpus of ideas which motivate and influence a whole cultural pattern'.

These defensive expressions ('not simply works of art,' not 'merely a writer') are used in a remarkably old-fashioned way to avoid a settling of relationships with 'art'. In 'good art' – does this have to be repeated? – there can be no humble residue of 'simply art' after the ideas have been detached for separate glorification. The artist's necessary 'style', the necessary 'fine writing' which elevates him and distinguishes him, is nothing etiolated or narrow, but is the substance, the total, the whole word-structure, emotive and intellective, of his alertness, honesty, freshness, and earnest professionalism; and Henry Miller's 'style' in that whole sense through page after page of this 'best' does nothing but sprawl in easily demonstrable clumsiness, slackness, and rant. The case against him is not at all one of disliking or condemning obscenity; and in this 'best' the obscene is at any rate dis-

[1] *The Best of Henry Miller*, edited by Lawrence Durrell (1960).

counted, and only occasional, and (since the censors still prowl around) by no means Miller at his most shocking or terrifying. The case is simply one of writing badly.

What would justify the mention of Blake, Whitman, and Henry Miller as a trio? Blake could be slack. Whitman could rant (so could Melville, or De Quincey, or Donne or Ralegh or any other of the Great Exclaimers). Suppose, all the same, that Mr Durrell were to edit a 'best' of Blake or Whitman. In either one plenty of particular idea is involved in their passages of 'the roll, the rise, the carol, the creation'. If the writer were Whitman, his best would include the nobler items of vision from *Specimen Days*; if he were Blake, his best would certainly include some of the keenest of his marginal aphorisms. But could such a best include writing of this order (chosen by Mr Durrell for the aphoristic section, from Henry Miller's *Time of the Assassins*):

> It is a dilemma of the first magnitude, a dilemma fraught with the highest significance. One has to establish the ultimate difference of his own peculiar being and doing so discover his kinship with all humanity, even the very lowest. Acceptance is the key word. But acceptance is precisely the great stumbling block. It has to be total acceptance and not conformity.

This is not an exceptional sinking, and a cool look shows Henry Miller, in spite of virtues of gaiety and gulping bonhomie, to be a lost addict of the weak or auxiliary verb, of *is* and *has*, and of *with* and *like*, a master of endless flow sweeping along the nearest word, and of clichés which are loyal to him no less in high than low excursions:

> Here the redwood made its last stand. At dawn its majesty is almost painful to behold. That same prehistoric look. The look of always. Nature smiling at herself in the mirror of eternity.

In high moments he ejaculates high nonsense: 'Now it is all snow and lice, with the great band of Orion slung round the ocean's crotch' (felt upon first encountering Dostoevsky – from *Black Spring*). In lower moments – for instance, the Automotive Passacaglia from *The Air-Conditioned Nightmare* on the waywardness of cars – Mr Miller no more than reincarnates the winsome crochet of an E. V. Lucas or a Robert Lynd. He believes – not always a surely constructive thing for the writer to do – he believes in his ideas ('Back of every creation, supporting it like an arch, is faith. Enthusiasm is nothing: it comes and goes. But if one *believes*, then miracles occur'); better to test than believe. He is obsessed ('To write one has to be possessed and obsessed'). But like believing, obsession can insist that snot is chrysoprase. Nor does the tone strengthen when the tap ('I'm here as a pleni-potentiary from the realm of free spirits') begins to deliver with more than usual gush Mr Miller's often good but never original gospel of self-liberation and of reconciliation by total confession. Good gospelling can be delivered second-hand through dull mouths, and good sentiments appear on Christmas cards, after all.

II

A correspondence between two writers, over many years, is likely to be about writing, and its substance, up to a point; this long 'private correspondence',[2] now made public, began in 1935, with an ecstatic piece of fan-mail from Lawrence Durrell, Corfu, to Henry Miller, Paris – Durrell having just read *Tropic of Cancer*. The correspondence starts the way it continues. *Tropic of Cancer* is

> a howling triumph from the word go . . . it really gets down on paper the blood and bowels of our time . . . turns the corner into a new life which has regained its bowels. . . . I love its guts . . . to see every whim-wham and bagatelle of your contemporaries from Eliot to Joyce dunged under. . . . It finds the way out of the latrines at last. Funny that no one should have thought of slipping out via the pan during a flush, instead of crowding the door. . . . It's man-size, and goes straight up among those books . . . which men have built out of their own guts . . . skoal to the stanchless flux.

Do I disapprove, morally, in quoting this? No. I point only to a persistent view of writing as flux, or loose shitting, or

[2] *A Private Correspondence*, by Lawrence Durrell and Henry Miller (1963).

vomit, or womb-moulding, or a confusion of bowel-process
and womb-process – on both sides of the correspondence,
though particularly on Durrell's. The prose of Thomas Nash
is 'one long dysentery of delight', prose has 'visceral rhythms',
a major book by Miller should 'vomit without any sign of
effort', Anais Nin's *House of Incest* 'squeezes itself into sudden malleable shapes and colours', Nin, Miller, etc., are
'specialists in plasm, germ-plasm, mind-plasm, ecto-plasm,
soul-plasm'. L.D. in one of his books hasn't used 'the minera-
logical material of the form-worshippers', he has employed
'the live, plastic material of the womb'. When *Tropic of
Capricorn* is published, H.M. ejaculates a pleased 'Ho Ho!
So I have become the public emmerdeur No. 1. Hurrah.'

A 'life' rejection of 'art', of imagination as structure, is a
conviction and a sympathy (loosely) tying together the two
sides of the correspondence. 'Perfectionism' is rejected, there
is no control except the end of the (writing) paper and the
automatic closing of the backside muscles. Miller on Balzac:

> Thank God he didn't waste time in perfecting himself.
> When I hear him speak to Georges Sand, that speech in
> which he tells her what he intends to accomplish, what
> life means to him, and so on, I get down on my knees to
> him and I say, Old bugger, I'm for you, right or wrong,
> whether you're a misfire genius or a perfectionist. Any-
> thing you say or do goes. Do you know what he said to that
> prick, Georges Sand? He said 'Literature! but, my dear
> lady, literature doesn't exist. There is life, of which politics
> and art are part. And I am a man that's alive, that's all – a
> man living his life, nothing more.

That is the Miller line about writing; and, though diminished
by a little later sense and caution as the correspondence proceeds, the Durrell line. What you eat, you digest, and
evacuate, slackening the sphincter. Two comments are fair.
Although by Bruegel's proverb those who eat fire shit sparks,
in general the pat – cow-pat or man-pat, or in particular the
Miller-pat – isn't much of a shape, even when it grows cold
and hardens; though if you lift it up, you do find Bruegelian
or Bosch-like life squirming on the under side, among the
white grass or white dandelion leaves. Also evacuation with

only the crudest control does explain the super-abundant presence in the man-pat book (Miller-pat, and Durrell-pat, or Durrell-pat poem) of undigested gobs of verbiage and cliché.

Another thing, the mixed process in these letters of combating possible criticism or dislike is either abuse or self-abuse, either Ya! or congratulation of selves, either the bloody public, bloody reviewers, bloody English, bloody prissies (which is funny at times: 'I part my hair in the middle, adjust the horn-rimmed lenses and settle like a Catholic homosexual at the master's feet'), or 'In everything you do you are the great man of your age', reminding one of Shakespeare, Pascal, Valéry, Freud. In fact there is plenty of rhetoric, and no realness, no uncluttered liberated vision or touch about these letters, which jump the estimate of the future, and strike me as very much by two who haven't emerged from the often squalid, stunted, amateur self-importance of little magazines:

> We must . . . print everybody, good or bad. Then in exchange they will print us for better or for worse. Then we shall get into all the anthologies and finally into Westminster Abbey, so help us. Cheers chaps.

Letters are personal: personally, biographically, this correspondence is often fun. Knowing neither of them, it enables me to imagine the person Durrell as an effing pre-Christian leprechaun collecting words and poems –

> Out of the gorse
> Came a homosexual horse –

and the person Miller as a card, effing and evacuating cheerfully, without ageing, through the years and the exclamation-marked pages of this correspondence.

But is it persons we are being asked to meet, or writers, ordinary neighbours in the world, or artists? Or besotted with decades of life-peddling, if we root for Miller as the Great Writer, aren't we (that 'we' including Mr Durrell, his chief rooter) advancing a confusion of our age – that living it up, strong, long, or free, is making, or *writing*?

1963

Leavis against Eliot

In the November number of *Commentary*,[1] the admirable review sponsored by the American Jewish Committee, Mr Leavis (I refuse to employ the term Doctor for a man of letters) has at last made a turn against T. S. Eliot from which there is no retreat. He has finally – for himself – 'revalued' Eliot's criticism. It is an article in which a long affair of selective homage or rather of attraction and repulsion crystallizes at last into contempt. Also it is one – for which reason it deserves examination – curiously exceeding the better limits of critical disagreement or exchange.

A simple genuflection is first made to Eliot (in terms from Eliot), as 'the man of genius who, after the long post-Swinburnian arrest, altered expression'. Eliot's altered expression, in his poems, 'won attention for the criticism'; and Mr Leavis then takes a long look at 'Tradition and the Individual Talent', and decides that in fact this essay, which is the leg of Eliot's critical reputation, 'is notable for its ambiguities, its logical inconsequences, its pseudo-precisions, its fallaciousness, and the aplomb of its equivocations and its specious cogency'.

The special stick he selects is the famous statement that 'the more perfect the artist, the more completely separate in him will be the man who suffers and the mind which creates'. We are then invited to think, *per contra*, upon Tolstoy or D. H. Lawrence (mark the crescendo, as a wit remarked on hearing – not quite accurately – that Ezra Pound's child was named Homer Shakespeare Pound); upon Shakespeare, or George Eliot or Mark Twain. 'What pressure, what need, we ask, explained this earnestness of intellectual subtlety devoted in so strenuous a play of trenchancy, confusion, and inconsequence, to absolving the artist from the need to have lived?'

Ask we may, and Mr Leavis may ask; but exactly in what

[1] November 1958.

directions, and how far, and in what terms, should he force
the answer?

Suppose Mr Leavis made the question a rhetorical one,
which inferred that the artist in Eliot – or Eliot inside the
critic – had not lived. That would be fair dealing. Fair
enough (perhaps) to go, as he does now and has done before,
a little further, and express some doubt about Eliot's inner
turmoils – to consider the essay on *Hamlet* in *The Sacred
Wood*, which 'reduces that tragedy to a matter of an in-
expressible emotional state, one of disgust, occasioned in
Hamlet by his mother', and then to ask, after various glances
(including one at the relationship of Harry, in *Family
Reunion*, to his creator), if in this critic there are not failures
of critical intelligence caused by 'a pressure of disordered
inner life, of emotion he fears and distrusts and cannot understand'.

But Mr Leavis jumps on. This T. S. Eliot, who does not
like sex, who has attitudes towards life of 'disgust and fear
and rejection' (a charge Mr Leavis first made in rebutting
Eliot on Lawrence in 1934), has done so and so. In support
all his so and sos, his acts, his misdemeanours are paraded.
His value-judgements have been shaky. He has been a
disastrous judge of his contemporaries. He has backed
Wyndham Lewis (to whose opinion of Eliot as a critic hiding
'in a volatilized hypostasization of his personal feelings' Mr
Leavis seems indebted), he once admitted Hugh Walpole to
the *Criterion*, he found virtue in Kipling, absurdly and
orthodoxly overestimated Virginia Woolf, spoke well to the
French of David Garnett, and assisted unforgivably as a
fairy godmother at the literary birth or christening of
W. H. Auden. Given in different ways to such modish conventionality Mr Eliot has approved Ker the scholar only
because Ker belonged to 'a select social-literary world', and
Charles Whibley the scholar only because Whibley was 'a
current social literary value in an English social world of the
"best people"'. And after all, even T. S. Eliot proves to have
been affined to the caucus of Cambridge–Bloomsbury (in
spite of backing Wyndham Lewis, who quite positively was
not affined to Bloomsbury); and Bloomsbury also were his
fairy godchildren Mr Auden and Mr Stephen Spender; and

such younger and unworthy friends of Mr Eliot also knew him as Tom. And coterie defeated the desirable possibility of a critical élite; and standards were betrayed; and Mr Eliot revised his strictures on Milton (which had been accepted by Mr Leavis) only 'for the reassurance and ingratiation of a British Academy public', and when he reprinted the revision which Mr Leavis had criticized, he did not of course mention the criticisms of Mr Leavis, or the name Leavis at all.

Worst of all, Lawrence, and again Lawrence. Mr Eliot has not spoken up for Lawrence. And Cambridge–Bloomsbury (including Mr Garnett) has not spoken up – or has not spoken up loudly enough – for Lawrence. And Wyndham Lewis did not speak up for Lawrence. And some friends and members of Cambridge–Bloomsbury were educated at Eton; and coterie and breeding have triumphed; and such items are all evidence for, or factors in, 'the radically destructive thing' about Mr Eliot – 'that he should have fallen so short of achieving the consciousness that one thinks of as necessary to the great creative writer', who hasn't fitted the template of behaviour constructed for him by Mr Leavis.

In case the last should seem an unfair remark, I should say I have much sympathy with Mr Leavis – up to a line, and in general rather than in all of his particulars. Mr Eliot's criticism is open to criticism, and much of his attitude may fairly strike one as both comic and dismaying. And of course Mr Leavis is right when he says that the spirit of coterie is opposed to the spirit of élite. And of course one may dislike, so far as it exists, or so far as it interferes, a social-literary 'Establishment'. Only élites, it has escaped Mr Leavis's attention, seldom exist in human or critical history. We may extract or construct our élites posthumously from the coteries; which are inevitable and are apt to include in themselves good, mediocre, and bad. 'Bloomsbury', so far as it was definable, has seemed to many of us, including Wyndham Lewis, who was its arch-enemy, not the least damaging of coteries intellectually and creatively. But to be sure may we not extract from Bloomsbury E. M. Forster, and G. E. Moore, and even Mr Eliot the Poet, if Mr Leavis is correct in placing him there in years past as a member or a fellow-first-class-travelling-associate?

Not only does Mr Leavis always expect too much of the human condition, always demand impossible perfection, and then exclaim in moral disgust when that perfection is not obtained; not only does he look for villains, and victims and occasions to abuse: he fails as well to look strictly in his own direction, at his own expressed preferences, his own tastes, his own coterie. Of course we should like a proper 'consciousness' in all critics, consciousness of their peculiar drive to subtract or to promote; we should like every critic 'to discipline his personal prejudices and cranks, tares to which we are all subject, in the common pursuit of true judgement' – to quote a passage from Eliot which Mr Leavis admired. But Mr Leavis, if I may be allowed to say so, is not quite so interesting a figure as Mr Eliot. Few of us have been so impelled to scrutinize him, or to examine the back numbers of *Scrutiny* for all of his own value-judgements, his own slips, his own odd assessments of the living. Yet it will be borne in upon the most casual that Mr Leavis is no more the free critical intelligence than Mr Eliot. The most casual reader of his books will have noticed pique, for example, and a not always very amiable or dignified lack of control over his own tares.

Would he expect one now to look closer, to reply in kind? Much as Mr Graham Greene now proposes to write an authorized private life of Mr John Gordon, the moralizing Nosey Parker of the weekend press, should one reply in kind by writing an unauthorized private character study of Mr Leavis? Should one inquire, for example, in order to correct his critical deviations, into the relation of his physical stature and his psyche? I have never met Mr Leavis; but is he tall and impressive, or short and insignificant? Is his health poor, his breath bad? Does he wear an open shirt? Was he bullied as a child? Or snubbed as an undergraduate (see 'Keynes, Lawrence and Cambridge' in *The Common Pursuit*)?

If Bloomsbury was a compact of 'gentlemen', can Mr Leavis's clique have been composed of critics and others who feel that they are not 'gentlemen'? Is Mr Leavis thus psychologically or socially underprivileged?

If Mr Eliot came to his conventionality from St Louis, Mo., has Mr Leavis come to his own set of conventions from

the conventicle? As a teacher who is neither a scholar nor a
'creative writer' (see 'Mr Eliot and Milton' in *The Common
Pursuit*), can it be that while Mr Leavis thinks little of
scholars, he is jealous of 'creative writers', who think little of
him? If the fault of Mr Eliot's criticism may be ascribed by
Mr Leavis to a sexual disgust which he postulates with a
considerable impertinence in Mr Eliot, may the absurdities
of Mr Leavis's overestimate of D. H. Lawrence be ascribed –
who knows without an investigation? – to some sexual shortcoming, some special puritanism, some lack of 'life' in himself, for which he seeks a cure or compensation in Lawrence,
so fully engaged – or so hysterically engaged – in 'life'?
Whom does Mr Leavis call Tom or Morgan? Who calls him
Frank?

And so on, if one thought it necessary to explain that
manifest degree of unconsciousness and unfreedom in Mr
Leavis's criticism, that frequent lack of pure astringency, of
the properly humane and the heartfelt, which twists his
attitude, that cliché-ridden tortuosity, indeed and pomposity,
of a style badly imitated from Henry James, which does not
manage to conceal in his writing, after all, a small mind,
brooding and vengeful, and a frequent barbarity of taste.

1959

Lou Andreas-Salome

One doesn't often come across a more extraordinary, more fascinating, yet I suppose in some ways, or to some people, more repellent character than Lou Andreas-Salome, whose life is now recounted by H. F. Peters.[1] She belonged to the world of letters in Central Europe – Zürich, Berlin, Vienna – before and after the disasters of 1914 to 1918, not the world of average letters, but the world of the greatest men, from Nietzsche, in her strange youth, to Freud, in her still strange decline. She was beautiful, she was intelligent, she was a queer specimen of the *femme fatale*, fit for the museum of the class. I can well imagine her being denounced in the Middle Ages – by angry, affronted men and angry, jealous, affronted women – as a witch, and tortured accordingly, and burnt *à petit feu*. As it was, she did the torturing, even the burning.

But to begin nearer the beginning. This woman, whom English and American readers will know of as the object of adoring poems by one of the greatest of modern poets, Rainer Maria Rilke, was Russian, born in Petersburg in 1861, youngest child of a Russian general. It was as if some very strangely feathered creature, some fire-bird, burning, disappearing, reappearing, unattainable, was born to a correct English brigadier at Camberley, or more exactly to an elderly field-marshal with the correct town-house and manor house. She adored her father, who died when she was on the verge of womanhood, she was adored by her brothers; she was adored – and this was especially relevant – by a Dutch evangelical pastor in Petersburg, who was her tutor in philosophy, married, years older than herself, who seems to have jolted her into a prolonged virginity – though she adored him, in her way – by making it clear that his adoration was far more than 'spiritual'.

[1] *My Sister, My Spouse*, by H. F. Peters (1963).

She felt in a dream of unreality. 'Have you ever seen St Petersburg in a White Night?' she wrote afterwards. 'In June, for example, when it remains bright as daylight. . . . It looks unreal. Everything is light and colourless. Everything seems to float. Are you made of granite, one says to St Isaac Cathedral, are you not light as if made of grey paper, one says.' In her unreality, she wanted to be free and real. She wanted the 'roots of life', yet the unreality she had known was her childhood presided over by her father, the godlike, partial, adored, protective old general. 'She escaped those harsh confrontations with reality that are the lot of most children. As far as she knew, life was a perennial spring and the world a garden for children to play in. The sense of loss she felt when she was finally forced out of it, stayed with her all her life.' That is her biographer's explanation: her passionate search for reality – and all that it entailed – 'was her longing to re-enter the lost paradise of her childhood'.

Well, it is something many of us wish to regain – but without being Lou von Salome. All was worse for her when her father died, and with him her belief in God. Her mother took this child of opened mind and maturing beauty, elegant, vital, quick, piquant (and marked, I would suspect, by that most intoxicating, captivating – and infrequent – of all qualities, grace of movement) to Zürich, where she was told by one of the most eminent Zürich theologians that her daughter was no more and no less, in her innermost being, than a diamond, hard, sharp, sparkling, unflawed.

She determined not to go back to Russia. She had ideas of intellectual freedom, of an intellectual, studious, spiritual *ménage à trois*, the other two being a young philosopher Paul Rée and Nietzsche, then in his late thirties (Nietzsche first met Lou Salome in St Peter's, in Rome, in a side chapel in which Rée 'had discovered a quiet corner . . . where he could work undisturbed on his new book in which he wanted to prove the non-existence of God').

It would be unfair to the reader – and this book deserves many readers, deserves every reader capable of feeling the enigmas of personality – to give more than a skeleton of all that followed. In a moment off guard she seems to have kissed Nietzsche on a hill above the grey granite-edged Lago di Orta. The three of them were photographed in a Victorian (yet all too savage) tableau: Lou in a small cart, with – yes – a whip in her hand, Nietzsche and Rée harnessed to the cart. She drove Nietzsche to distraction and despair and to terrible bitterness against women in *Thus Spake Zarathustra*, she lived with Rée, a strict brother-and-sister partnership, in Berlin, the distracted Rée in the end committing suicide by throwing himself from a cliff where he and Lou had had some of their happiest times. Maintaining her freedom, she married a Göttingen professor, again on a strict, lasting, and for him agonizing basis of brother and sister (his attempted suicide had swayed her into the marriage).

In her early thirties, a successful writer, undiminished in beauty and sparkle, this woman whom Nietzsche had described as having 'the character of a cat, a beast of prey that pretends to be a domestic animal', this woman out of Ibsen's plays (she wrote a book on Ibsen's women), overcame the death of her father and the passion of the Dutch minister and philosophy tutor, and took to the normalities of love, first, it seems, with a Russian compatriot, with whom she lived for some time in a high Alpine hut, the two of them delighting to walk barefooted together through the wet, flower-filled mountain grass, then – for years – with a Viennese physician, and for a three-year interval with Rilke. Rilke was then twenty-two, Lou Salome thirty-six.

One of Lou's friends described the trait which ruled her – you might not guess this so far – as an 'extreme readiness toward life, a humble and courageous holding herself open to its joys and woes, a fascinating mixture of masculine earnestness, childlike light-heartedness and feminine ardour'. Rilke said that she changed him as a poet, that a great reality emanated from her, everything she touched, reached, and saw *existed*. He met her, and 'things arose. I learned to distinguish animals and flowers. Slowly and with difficulty I learned how simple everything is and I matured.' There was more barefoot walking, and watching deer in the early light. There is a poem by Rilke in which her words are altars on her young poet's quiet shore, as they sit in a dark summer-house watching the summer evening light of a Bavarian landscape:

I love you. You're sitting in a chair, your cool
　　white hands asleep as in a bed.
My life is lying like a silver spool
　　within your hands. Release my thread.

I was reminded of the young D. H. Lawrence in Bavaria
with Frieda Weekley, and the poems he wrote, and of their
walk over the Alps to Sterzing.

Yet Lou Salome left Rilke, as she left others. She said that
'a woman is like a tree longing for the lightning that splits it,
and yet always like a tree that wants to grow'. In the end,
she dived deeper and systematically into life as a psycho-
therapist, a true witch-doctor of high degree, a healer of
others, as if in atonement, trained by life and more directly
by Freud, who 'gave her one of the five rings he had made
for his most trusted friends'.

How wonderful a woman, a daughter of the Sun (Circe
among her flowers and streams could have given fine instruction to a poet), and how glad one might be not to have encountered her – except in this book and Rilke's poems and
letters; and how willingly one would have succumbed!

1963

Leopardi's Hump

In the museum at Albi there is a sketch of Toulouse-Lautrec (by himself) wearing lemon-yellow trousers and a red shirt. A hygienic sketch, since it reinstates the artist who drew with tenderness and grace and strength, and displaces our journalistic biographical image of the freak whose legs never grew. To read Leopardi as he should be read I feel that we have in the same way to expunge or greatly reduce the celebrated hump, and with it perhaps something of the horror of his restricted and despondent years in the family palace at Recanati. It is better, with posterity to face, to have worn your hump internally and invisibly; and I have had my vision or version of Leopardi cleared by discovering from the Marchesa Origo[1] that Leopardi, one day when he was seventeen, looked in the mirror and 'realized that he was a hunchback' – in other words that seven years of incessant close-eyed reading in his father's library had produced, gradually, less of a hunchback's natal hump than 'a slight curvature of the spine'. The curvature also told on his health and led to him dying under the dry shoulder of Vesuvius (after writing 'La ginestra' and 'Il tramonto della luna') when he was no more than thirty-nine. But it did not make him into the Leopardi poet any more than his short legs made Toulouse-Lautrec into the Lautrec artist. In any case, his hump or curvature was composite, was circumstantial as well as physical, was also his terrible mama and his isolation in that hilltop town of Recanati which he both loved because he came to consciousness there, and hated because it imprisoned him.

In his own lifetime, after he had escaped at last from Recanati and his parents, Leopardi had to speak against this theory of the hump. One Italian of his day detected in his

[1] *Leopardi: Selected Prose and Verse*, translated by Iris Origo and John Heath-Stubbs (1966).

poems, when they were published in 1831, only 'a little
Count, singing like a frog of Cephisus and crying *There is no
God, because I am a hunchback. I am a hunchback, because
there is no God.*' A similar charge was made in a review of
his *Operette Morali*, stinging Leopardi to exclaim that whatever his troubles may have been, he had always had 'enough
courage not to try to lighten their burden either by frivolous
hopes of an alleged felicity' – all such were illusions – 'or by
a cowardly resignation'. He insisted that his view of destiny
was his own: he advised his readers to concentrate on reply-
ing to his remarks and his arguments rather than accusing
his infirmities in a way which he described as weak and
vulgar; and the advice still holds when we read those objects
in liberation which are Leopardi's poems, vehicles of a 'total
disenchantment' and of discovering that those illusions he
had once considered to be the 'only true and substantial
things in our existence' were themselves illusory.

As prolegomenon to the poems most of this book in the
'Oxford Library of Italian Classics' is made up of extracts
which Iris Origo has chosen from the very considerable – but
not always very interesting – extents of Leopardi's prose. I
was a little disappointed, even bored, by many of the extracts,
which are sometimes arid and stuffy, and sometimes too
rhetorical, though interest at once quickens when Leopardi
directly answers to some stimulus, is concerned directly with
his estimates of genius or poetry, or when he comments on
his own, or on the human, situation; when he watches the
moon, for instance, which becomes the risen or the setting
moon of his poems; when he hears a man singing on his way
home from work (a favourite image); when he has visions of
infinity – 'Lying beside a hayrick at S. Leopardo towards
dusk watching a peasant coming towards me from the
horizon'; or when he remarks 'Although I am only twenty-
seven and therefore young in body, yet I observe that my
spirit has not only used up its youth, but has advanced' – and
this was a condition of his insight – 'a long way into old age'.

One note from his huge commonplace book, written down
when he was twenty-two, particularly fits his own poems:
that works of genius, 'even when they vividly show the
nothingness of things, and plainly represent and convey to us

the inevitable unhappiness of life, even when they express the most terrible despair', always console disillusioned and despairing readers, reawakening their enthusiasm, and giving them back life, for a while, 'even if it is only death' that such works describe or represent.

Apply this to Hardy, and to others. But the consolation resides in the movement and the form.

When the reader of this selection comes at last to the poems after the prose, or rather to the translations by John Heath-Stubbs, alongside the Italian, he is more likely to be depressed than comforted or excited. He will discover a curiosity of backwardness. The quality of translation drops to zero. The translator declares that Leopardi's language is 'highly literary and allusive'. That may be so; but it is also very often simple and direct, styled in an activating way by a master who thought about words, working by a simultaneity of its directness and a broad horizontal nobility of rhythm, holding Leopardi's white moons in the space of his celestial infinities above woods, mountains, and the sea.

Contrariwise this translator, seeming to lack an English of his own, goes to work with a poesy word-book. He turns black to *sable*, white to *pale*, look to *behold*, flow to *flood*, passed into *passed away*; writing now as Shakespeare or Elegy Gray, now as Keats, now as Wordsworth, now as Edgar Allen Poe or Tennyson–Malory, now as *Hymns Ancient and Modern* or Patience Strong, never as Stubbs or Stubbs–Leopardi. Particulars are generalized, actives weakened into passives, repetitions disregarded, brevities elongated. 'This wound' becomes 'a very grievous wound', 'without wind' becomes 'and no wind blows'; 'all other sound is mute' is borrowed to say 'everything is silent', and so on. A pity, if a curiosity. I never expected to see poems of such ruthless benediction (which by bad luck never have been well translated) translated, in these decades, into such falsity.

1966

Jesuit Hopkins: Violets Knee-deep

I am not convinced that religion – at least in its particular Christian form – remains the primary interest of the best poems by Gerard Manley Hopkins, or of Hopkins himself as a puzzle in poetic biography. Hopkins was distinguished by a particular talent for making poems, a peculiar responding power we can call, however obviously, the power of being moved to wonder and joy; which he could not allow to rip without inquiry into what it might signify and what might be the best way of using life and sensation. In the eighteen-sixties such a responding power still led 'naturally', or normally rather, to theology, to the still apparently valid or inescapable centre. As for George Herbert in the sixteen-twenties –

> I once more smell the dew and rain,
>   And relish versing: O my only light,
>   It cannot be
>   That I am he
>   On whom thy tempests fell all night

– so still for Hopkins in the eighteen-seventies; and on that account I am sceptical about the closing implication of Father Thomas's book[1] – that Hopkins the poet, no less than Hopkins the priest, was the product of fourteen years of rigorous remoulding as a Jesuit.

Per contra, the question – the more opposite or basic question – I find too infrequently asked is what Hopkins meant, to the dotted *i*, by likening himself to Walt Whitman. 'I always know in my heart Walt Whitman's mind to be more like my own than any other man's living.' However

[1] *Hopkins the Jesuit*, by Alfred Thomas, S.J. (1969).

limited his knowledge of Whitman (and of Whitman's homosexuality, which is another possible link between the two),
he had certainly read 'You shall no longer take things at
second or third hand, nor look through the eyes of the dead,
nor feed on the spectres in books', and

> Prais'd be the fathomless universe,
> For life and joy, and for objects and
>   knowledge curious.

In that kinship I suppose you have the unique core of this
man, present and active in him before he ever encountered
Liddon – or Newman. But as well he was scrupulously intelligent, with as fine a judgement in his strong sensuality as
ever belonged to any poet. Perhaps in a Jacobean or Carol-
ingian climate he might have taken greater risks than could
easily be taken in the English climate of the eighteen-sixties
or seventies. Even then he could see the danger in being a
Whitman or a Hugo. Rather than expand like those two great
storms and deep calms, he subjected himself to years of the
severest training one could know.

The training is described in *Hopkins the Jesuit*. He enters
the novitiate of the Jesuit order at twenty-four, in 1868.
Then follow his philosophate, his theologate (ending with his
ordination as priest in 1877), and his tertianship, the final
stage of probation, which came to an end in 1882, when he
vowed himself, then aged thirty-eight, to perpetual poverty,
chastity, and obedience. In less than seven years he was
dead.

No other account of Hopkins explains in such detail the
daily life of a probationary Jesuit. The aim of the society is
'personal sanctification, and the sanctification of one's neigh-
bour', the method is attaining self-conquest, obedience, and
humility. Remembering Whitman or Hugo (Hopkins was
severe against both of them), the process is contraction rather
than expansion; or, from our ordinary point of view, the
willing surrender to a kind of martyrdom. Incongruously I
think of St Lawrence on his griddle asking to be turned over
so that both sides of him could be cooked.

The first of his greater poems erupt from Hopkins over a
fairly short period during his theologate at St Bruno's College,

in Denbighshire, 'on a pastoral forehead of Wales', in 1876–7, after nine years of this tough self-subjection; it was as if Hopkins, months, then weeks short of his ordination, had satisfied himself with a full theologic justification for those ecstasies in nature which still lifted him off his feet in spite of everything. He could have dedicated his new poems much as Herbert dedicated the poems of *The Temple*, that they were his, yet not his,

> Lord, my first fruits present themselves to thee;
> Yet not mine neither: for from thee they came,
> And must return. Accept of them and me,

and with justice Father Thomas places before his first chapter a comment Hopkins made on the rigour of the second phase of his training, at Stonyhurst in 1871 – 'This life here though it is hard is God's will for me as I most intimately know, which is more than violets knee-deep'. Yet I cannot make myself agree that these Jesuit probationary years decisively formed Hopkins as a poet. Formed is too big or total a word – shaped, possibly, inclined, directed, concentrated; not formed. And shaped, perhaps, only in a limited way, for it is possible that Hopkins as Hugo, Hopkins as Whitman, Hopkins at risk, would have been a greater, grander, more voluminous poet altogether, if with flaws corresponding to the elevations.

From Father Thomas's book one does discover at any rate the millstones which Hopkins passed between. Another convert and Jesuit of Hopkins's day is quoted on the training of young Jesuits in the necessary 'sacrifice of their own will and judgement', in the cultivation of blind obedience so that they did what they were told, and judged obediently that what they were told was the best thing possible for them, by divine ordinance. I would regard Hopkins's survival, as a poet, through the probationary years, as a marvel of interior constitution. Many poems he had written Hopkins burnt before he became a Jesuit. Then he wrote next to no poems for seven years, by resolution, since writing poems, he said, did not belong to his profession. One has the spectacle of a poet abating his natural proclivity, and yet, as he admits, having at least the echo of a new rhythm haunting his ear (the

rhythm realized in 1876 in *The Wreck of the Deutschland*);
he suppresses, he cannot kill. *Hopkins the Jesuit* rather
stupefied me with its accumulation of dust and detail, but it
does add very much to his biography.

Gerard Manley Hopkins: The Poet as Victorian,[2] on the
other hand, adds only to that ennui now endlessly produced
by academics whose talents for criticism and appreciation do
not reach beyond the lecture-room. To consider X, Y or Z
mainly as a Victorian might have its use substractively, as
long as the critic validly wished to discover how much a poet
penetrated to himself, in spite of his period (see Hopkins on
Purcell:

> It is the forgèd feature finds me; it is the
>   rehearsal
> Of own, of abrúpt sélf there so thrusts on, so
>   throngs the ear.)

This collegial critic seems to wish, invalidly, to embroil
Hopkins in the fashion for Victoriana now promoted by
smart justifiers of sado-masochistic hypocrisy, trendy dealers
in Victorian pictures or antiques or bygones, and joky (or
earnest) architectural sentimentalists. Even that is not
managed with dexterity. For instance it doesn't do to harp
on this poet's 'Pre-raphaelite' concern for nature: the point
is the startling difference on the matter between this poet of
the abrupt self and the Pre-raphaelites or Ruskin, as it might
be the point to illuminate, let us say, the difference between
the hard style of Hopkins and the soft style of Arnold in his
'Dover Beach'. Judge of Professor Johnson on his statement
that a drawing by Hopkins might be a Holman Hunt or
'even' a Ford Madox Brown (painter, we are told, of *The
Blind Girl*, which is by Millais) or that Hopkins 'can sometimes evoke a brightly lit and shaded landscape *more vividly
than the painter-poet Dante Rossetti*' (whose vivid and
characteristic landscapes, in verse or paint, are to be discovered where, except in this profesor's fancy?).

1969

[2] *Gerard Manley Hopkins: The Poet as Victorian*, by Wendell
Stacy Johnson (1968).

Of Asphodel, that Greeny Flower

Mary Cassatt once remarked to Renoir that the technique of his painting was too simple for the public, they wouldn't like it; to which Renoir replied: 'Don't worry. Complicated theories can always be thought up *afterwards*.'

This can be applied in reverse, not to simple but simpleton work – for instance, to some of Mondrian's paintings and most of William Carlos Williams's poems. Either Mondrian or Williams in a moment of frankness or of self-illumination might have said: Our simpleton-works are vehicles of theory: we can trust others to read the art or the poetry into them afterwards.' In passing I guess this covers many more of the products of our muddled time. In for a pound as for an ounce I should extend it to most of Ezra, and most of Eliot after 'The Hollow Men', I should hazard that the production of theory-art is – or was – in their cultural situation tempting to Americans. The unprejudiced observer in the U.S.A. may have observed the way European norms of grace, developed from or through the Renaissance, have disappeared in such things as doors, panels, mouldings, windows, façades, may have observed a brutish unproportion in domestic fittings. Knops debased, and never a nightingale –

How could her delicate dirge run democratic,
Delivered in a cloudless moundless place
To an inordinate race?

There have been two ways out, according to taste and ability: a looking, now and then, eastward, or a Williams-like defiance, a stay-at-home insistence on a theoretic value which can be extracted from one's shortcomings. Most of the poems of William Carlos Williams have been assemblages of lengths, short lengths as a rule (though they may continue

for pages), of inert language. If in his imagism or 'phraseism'
one came across such sudden life-illuminations as are to be
found in the best seventeen-syllable poems by the Japanese
or in Quasimodo's *Ed è subito sera,* how pleasurable it could
be. Cold arrested phrases, cut and trimmed, have generally
emerged from his deep-freeze: their form is partly the
accident of a sub-zero temperature. So in his actual 'Pictures
from Brueghel', ten great pictures are paraphrased, or
selected from, with quite surprising obviousness and banality.
'Brueghel saw it all', 'This horrible but superb painting',
'The over-all picture is winter', 'The whole pageantry of
the year'. This is *not* – and by a very long way – a Bashō
saying

> The mushroom:
>   from an unknown tree, a leaf
>   sticks to it.

Actually the Simple Simon misses (I apologize for using
once more this too favourite phrase from Hopkins, but how
it fits *our* need) the roll, the rise, the carol, the creation, because they are beyond his scope. Theoretically he may justify
himself and may appear to be rejecting them, because in the
past the r, the r, the c and the c have stunk so when they
went wrong. So the Simple Simon's art theory isn't without
some use as an example – even if a pretentious one – of
the need to avoid pretension or as a dulled emptiness of
order criticizing, *ipso facto,* a rhetorical emptiness of the
chaotic.

But there is a better reason for acquiring this volume[1] of a
poet who has been little praised or published in England
(rather to our credit for once). It includes, in three short
books and a coda, what I believe to be Williams's one
splendid poem, 'Asphodel, that Greeny Flower', which was
first published nine years ago. It is a love poem, to his wife.
It is suddenly as if he had looked into Sidney and noticed the
injunction – which isn't a bad one, after all – 'Fool, said my
Muse to me, look in thy heart and write'. Williams looked and
defroze, before his death in 1963, and his words kept shape.

[1] *Pictures from Brueghel and Other Poems,* by William Carlos
Williams (1963).

Honesty and a flood of feeling made something of his man-
nerism and a symbol, as well as rhythm, took charge:

> Of asphodel, that greeny flower,
>   I come, my sweet,
>   to sing to you.

That greeny flower (see the *Odyssey*) belongs to Persephone
and death. He pressed asphodel, forebodingly, in a flower-
book when he was a boy; and if he brings it to his wife, it
also illuminates, it also celebrates life, imagination, and love:

> Asphodel
>   has no odor
>   save to the imagination
> But it too
>   celebrates the light.
>   It is late
> but an odor
>   as from our wedding
>   has revived for me
> and begun again to penetrate
>   into all the crevices
>   of my world.

At the end of his life, in a tone and circumstance reminding
me occasionally of de Tabley's *Churchyard on the Sands* and
in terms largely of European myth and experience, and not
of America, Williams celebrated as the justifier and illumin-
ator of life that imagination he had so infrequently displayed
in his own earlier poems; which is ironic and moving.

I am afraid, too, that this late, tender, delightful poem is a
warning – which came just in time for Williams – never to
dismiss a poet until the life and last lines are out of him.
But that is not to say that one should fail to dismiss his bad
poems meanwhile.

1963

Our Grandest Lollipop Man

Literature is the long sequence of the fatalities – or the victories, perhaps better say the victories – of human incompleteness, some authors bring more woefully or less victoriously incomplete than others. Tennyson, for example. Having Tennyson, almost all of him at last in one thick volume which I would hesitate to describe as a swollen box of marshmallows and lollipops,[1] we are now enabled to see better than we could before, the nature, whether negatively or positively, of this man's magisterial incompleteness.

His temptation was mood, always mood; leaving to one side a temptation – not entirely social or adventitious – to be declaiming morality in metre. His danger – and success – lay in repeating 'Alfred, Alfred, Alfred' to himself out in the dark, in forever asking why – why was he Alfred Tennyson, why was he one of the twelve children of the maddish rector of Somersby, why wasn't he a son of the rich manor-house, why was he marked out for sorrow, why must he go blind (but he didn't), why, like all parson's sons, must he be shut out of the house (and the garden, and the parish) of his childhood, why couldn't he marry Emily Selwood, why must he be a virgin still – though perhaps that question wasn't exactly formulated – at forty? His danger lay as well in answering his multiple why with little more than those three words he had liked so much as a child in the Lincolnshire hills, the words 'far, far away'.

When he was an old poet of eighty, ennobled and the rest of it, in public honour and celebrity, he reverted to 'far, far away' in a poem written after an illness which might have killed him – the poem celebrated for its line 'The mellow lin-lan-lone of evening bells' resurrected from a phrase of some fifty years before:

[1] *The Poems of Tennyson*, edited by Christopher Ricks (1969).

What vague world-whisper, mystic pain or joy,
Through these three words would haunt him when a boy,
    Far-far-away?

A whisper from the dawn of life? A breath
From some fair dawn beyond the doors of death
    Far-far-away?

I think one has only to recall those stanzas to rediscover
Tennyson's basic kinship – only he was better educated, less
isolated, and situated in real Europe, not abstract America –
to Edgar Allen Poe. This collected Tennyson is chock-full of
discarded ululation, of girl non-girls named Adeline,
Cadrilla, Eleänore. Full of the Ossianic, the Byronic, the
Shelleyan, the exotic, hundreds of pages ululate, before an
occasional firmness of poetry is reached.

    The callow throstle lispeth,
    The slumbrous wave outwelleth,
    The babbling runnel crispeth –

thousands of lines, from infancy onwards, had to be written
before Tennyson began to manage at all frequently an
accord between himself and his experience, or objectivity,
and the positions of his tongue; and one discovers that he
was at all times liable to fall out of that accord, at all times
liable to relapse into rubbish –

    I, Titania, bid you flit
    And you dare to call me Tit

– shrewd as he generally was, apart from his pulpit verse, in
discarding the rubbish afterwards.

When I was young in the late Twenties, in the dawn of
'Prufrock' and I. A. Richards, some caustic person, some
victim in a sixth form perhaps, invented the trick of reciting
Tennyson's 'Ballad of Oriana' (sanctified then by nearly a
hundred years of acceptance) with its refrain 'Oriana'
altered to the two less mystic words 'arse upwards'.

    At midnight the cock was crowing,
        Arse upwards. . .

> She stood upon the castle wall,
>   Arse upwards. . .

> The false, false arrow went aside,
>   Arse upwards. . .

> But I was down upon my face
>   Arse upwards.

The effect is irresistible, and critical, and deserved, illustrat-
ing the way in which the word-and-measure faculty, the
essential thing Tennyson had, requires educating. Yet the
educative environment, part of the necessary education,
begins to be assertive even inside that poem. A word or two
does get in. The Lincolnshire wolds appear, Somersby
appears – 'When the long dun wolds are ribbed with snow' –
even if such concreteness as quickly disappears. Tennyson
becomes, in fact, the poet we read and wish to read again,
the poet who is part of a part of ourselves we are not very
willing at the moment to acknowledge (unless we are iambic
members of the Victorian Society), when his 'far, far away'
is expressed palpably; when he asks, if he does not precisely
answer, the universal question of self-identity in terms of a
rather simplistic self-immanence. 'All souls are centres',
Tennyson wrote when he was twenty, in a short poem now
published for the first time,

> I am the earth, the stars, the sun,
> I am the clouds, the sea

– and a good many other things; God and the souls of other
men excepted. In spite of much self-argument in poems, he
hadn't so genuinely altered or 'advanced' at eighty.

With Tennyson, it is so much, one sees, a question of
biscuit and golden syrup. Biscuit, for example in the now
overestimated poems of Robert Frost, becomes too dry and
corny, golden syrup in the still rather underestimated poems
of Tennyson is all the time in need of biscuit or crumbs of
being, if it is not to be too warm and sickly.

'Far away', the soul, the bourne, the mystery, time, time

past – Tennyson's need, Tennyson's success, is to convey them, so that the poetry works, in snow, plovers, sand and waves at Mablethorpe, evening star, shooting star, Orion's belt, shot silk, varnished celandines, the gleam of a sliding river, or the thrilling echo of the Killarney bugle –

> O sweet and far from cliff and scar
> The horns of Elfland faintly blowing.

The best of Tennyson's lyrics build up closely around verbalized perceptions; and lyrics of the finest quality seem to me lost – or buried complete or incomplete – when perceptions of such quality are thrust into flattish lengths of Tennyson-on-the-run. Reading through this bulky edition it is worth looking for the footnotes marked (T) for Tennyson, often a quick guide to extraordinary felicities, since Tennyson knew very well when he had contrived a good thing, even if he did not always build it into a separate poem. 'Seen by me at Mürren in Switzerland', 'Seen as I lay in the New Forest', 'As I have heard and seen the sea on the shore of Mablethorpe' – and one looks up the page to

> the crest of some slow-arching wave,
> Heard in dead night along that table-shore,
> Drops flat, and after the great waters break
> Whitening for half a league, and thin themselves
> Far over sands marbled with moon and cloud,
> From less and less to nothing.

If I was making a volume of the essential best in Tennyson, I should disregard the contempt of superior members of the Society for the Protection of Ancient (and Tedious) Poems and give every such separate passage – down to the single lines such as 'A land of hops and poppy-mingled corn' – which may excuse a whole poem stretching inertly away on either side. A choice of Tennyson which lacked, for example,

> There twice a day the Severn fills;
> The salt sea-water passes by,
> And hushes half the babbling Wye,
> And makes a silence in the hills

I should think no more than a travesty, since whether one

likes it or not, lines or stanzas or 'fragments' are often poems unfakedly more 'complete' than poems.

Tennyson to Virgil may come at this point into disapproving minds – 'All the charm of all the Muses/ Often flowering in a lonely word'; one may derive disapproving conclusions, I mean, about the quality of the perceptions, inserted and otherwise, from recalling that when asked to write for Virgil's nineteenth centenary Tennyson produced a fine poem of ten stanzas, compared to seven lines, which say nothing but the briefly obvious and properly humble, when the Florentines had asked him for something to mark six hundred years of Dante; Tennyson's perceptions are certainly, some of them, self-indulgent, would certainly have been less pleasing to Dante. Tennyson's perceptions are certainly, some of them, poets inclined, by short-cut, to substitute the effects of poetry for the real thing. Yet enough of his perceptions, in between Claribels and lily maids of Astolat, surely embody the conditions of man.

About this edition itself, I admire the grand laborious persistence, years and years of it, expended on variants, annotation, and introduction, often invaluable when Tennyson is brought on the page to illuminate Tennyson; and I am as amazed that so much of this apparatus should be so trivial, so much of it attached to poems of no distinction at all. Do university students, teachers, and the general reader (who can handle a dictionary) require to be told that an ammonite is a 'whorled fossil-stone', or that sandal is a 'scented wood'? Possibly they ought to be told – and they are not, in more instances than one – of echoes in Tennyson essentially relevant to his interests and constitution, for instance, that 'Now sleeps the crimson petal, now the white' echoes a song stanza in the *Britannia's Pastorals* of (the not dissimilarly indulgent poet) William Browne – 'Soe shuts the marigold her leaves', etc. But then it is seldom, I am afraid, that editors feel the substance of their poet's peculiarity or sensuousness; they prefer – the old species never dies – to write in, above a poem, that 'The beautiful but ineffective consolations of Nature form a recurrent theme of *In Memoriam*' (which *is* slightly off the mark); or to add, bless them, 'For his relationship to the thought of his day, see: G. R. Potter, "Tennyson and the biological theory of immutability in species", *PQ* xvi (1937), 321–43'.

Still how valuable to have the grand poetic incompleteness of this master in a single volume more or less, as I say, complete, at last.

1969

Public Honours, or a Peerage for Tennyson

Why did Alfred Tennyson accept a peerage in 1883? Or why has Miss Muriel Sparke (a novelist) accepted this year an Officership of the Order of the British Empire?

Let's see if we can answer, for Tennyson. He was old, and vain. He was a parson's son from an unstable family. He felt an outsider, his father having been outrageously excluded from inheriting estates. Always indulgent of himself, he could (he did – see his letter to Gladstone) decide that a peerage for Tennyson was a peerage for literature. He took a day to say yes, said it, and was Inside.

Then we had Lord Leighton in 1896, to illustrate the dispersal of honour more among pretension than genius. The legislature could not be stuffed in this way with poets and painters. In 1902 the Order of Merit was thought up, for two dozen eminences, in 1917 the Order of the Companions of Honour for sixty-five eminences, also the now multitudinous Order of the British Empire, composed of Knights, Dames, Commanders, Officers, Members; its motto – of considerable unappeal, one would suppose, to some authors and artists (what about you, Officer Sparke, or you, Dame Rebecca West?) – 'For God and the Empire'.

Explore such politico-cultural honours backwards to Tennyson, imagine them conferred upon earlier authors, and one sees the pointlessness of accepting them. Should we care more (he *was* an author of merit) for a Southey O.M., less for a Coleridge O.B.E.? Find a Prime Minister to have created Oscar Wilde C.H. (why not? He wrote well), George Eliot O.B.E. (George Lewes dead, and Miss Evans safely Mrs Cross), or Percy Shelley O.M. (supposing the boat hadn't blown over, and that the atheistical rumpus had blown over, and girls, wives and court proceedings had been forgotten)? Never.

Do modern acceptors consider such modern nevers – honours withheld because private life is judged to outweigh public achievement? What do they think, as they write their reluctantly grateful letters of acceptance, of equivalent honour never extended to others whom they should, in decency, regard as worthier than themselves? How do they answer the objection that political choice in the arts has so more often than not been ludicrous? Wrong for others, right for me?

I suppose that in many modern instances we are back at Alfred Tennyson, at some 'inferiority', some gap or insecurity, pasted over by the honour. We are back at vanity, finding its excuse (one literary knight of my acquaintance[1] explained to me that he didn't feel 'important enough' to refuse). Shouldn't every writer, artist, composer – but musicians live in a foreign milieu – be aware that his ego and its yearnings are best extinguished in his work? Does vanity have to be delighted to wriggle on back or belly into the dog show of celebrities invited to the Palace or the residence of the Prime Minister? Shouldn't vanity – or pride – rest in the not easily measurable approbation of what one supposes to be one's public? (Instruction: before drafting your reply, read *Paradise Lost*, Book 7, first thirty-one lines. Also read, literary chestnut as it may be, that letter of a tough old republican author to a snooty political careerist and diplomat: 'Do not imagine I am unobservant of distinctions. You, by the favour of a Minister, are Marquis of Normanby; I by the grace of God am/ Walter Savage Landor'.) And anyhow what about that traditional public-in-posterity? To believe in it is at least to believe in one's work.

First Conclusion (for my no doubt, or often, unquestionable superiors): Accept honours and you harm society. To have writers, etc., labelled O.M., C.H., K.B.E., D.B.E., O.B.E., tells lazy people of shaky self-confidence who can be admired. It tells English newspaper men (the least sophisticated, least educated journalists of Europe, least respectful of the devising intellect) who needn't be admired – when he dies especially (*The Times* rid itself of D. H. Lawrence in a few inches of obit).

Second Conclusion (for the same): Accept honours and you hinder the establishment inside our slothful community

[1] The late Sir Herbert Read.

of a nucleus of the cultivated too fly to be fuddled by the fashions of art.

Third Conclusion: Accept honours and you don't help the community of makers (nucleus within nucleus within the commonalty) to decide on its own values and hierarchs.

Conclusion embracing other Conclusions: If as poets, novelists, dramatists, painters, sculptors, composers (I don't talk of actors and other performers, academics or art officials) you accept political honours, you degrade your calling.

So, O.M., C.H., Dame, Knight, Commander, and Officer, and Officer Sparke, however distinguished you are, or seem, or believe yourself to be, remember Alfred Tennyson. Repent (you might even send it back). Or if such degrading honour is in prospect, think of Alfred when the letter comes – rather than of Housman who refused the O.M. because it had been given to Galsworthy). Say no.

Better than yourselves have said no.

1967

A Sectary of Backness

Faced perhaps wrongly or wilfully with these letters by the late C. S. Lewis,[1] I shall postulate a very outside position, imagining a reader (not so far from myself) who is naturally aware of Lewis's reputation as a scholar, a teacher, a critic, a Christian apologist, and a writer of stories for children, but is not attracted either by the fame or by the little of him he has read. At last he is faced by this selection of the letters Lewis wrote between adolescence and old age: Query, after reading them through, after the plunge, is my outsider going to be hooked?

Will his prejudice be overcome, will he be enticed to a full exploration of *Perelandra, The Lion, the Witch and the Wardrobe, Screwtape, Allegory of Love*, and all (including the poems Lewis attempted)?

He will discover that Lewis came from Belfast, where he had been shut away from the Irish rain inside a nursery view of unattainable hills. From Belfast he was transported to Malvern College, under the blue crest of the hills of Piers Plowman. In 1916 he became a scholar of an Oxford college, in sight (when his war was over) of the perhaps unattainable blue flower of the inside life of inner Oxford; which he longed for (what a romantic goal!) – and attained.

When he was nineteen, Lewis had remarked in a letter that he made 'every effort to cling to the old life of books'. For years and years, my outside reader will now observe, a bookishness continues to envelop him, together with a sense, not a very amiable one, of being superior to those less gifted, less fortunate, and less snugly situated. His vocabulary, through the decade in which, if ever, the worn words begin to peel from the senses, remains obstinately stale. He

[1] *Letters of C. S. Lewis*, edited with a Memoir by W. H. Lewis (1966).

ejaculates *Forsooth!*, *Ye Gods!*, or *Ye Gods!!*. He is 'up be-
times', he reads 'friend Trollope', breathlessly one expects a
letter to end 'And so to bed'. He adds a coy adjectival *y* to
nouns (enjoying Oxford's 'cool brown oaky rooms'), he trades
in sentimental inversions ('my first passion for things Norse').
He *lies* and does not *sleep* at a place – 'We lay this night at
Tintagel, storied name' – and a place is likely to be characterized, not by means of itself, by its peculiarities, but by a
quotation: 'a pleasant land of drowsihead it was' (Forest of
Dean). He is fixed in an excluding talk of 'our set', 'our little
set' (also in a tweedy and donnish anti-womanism). If it is
windless, he writes – at twenty-six – 'not a breath of wind
stirring'. At twenty-nine, reading *The Woman in White*, he
is induced to exclaim: 'What spacious days those were!' At
forty-two he writes of someone who cared (Charles Williams),
that he 'really cared with every fibre of his being'.

Swaddled in his 'old life of books', Lewis in these letters
seldom enters into a new life of books; and when he does,
recoils with a kind of soft disdain or conceit, happier with
Jane Austen or Scott, with the familiar and the accepted, and
expressing judgements which are scarcely to be excused by
his dislike of the times he lived in; which is usually, I would
say, a dislike of living. When in rhetorical assent he asks (in
a letter to Ruth Pitter, a writer of poems much admired by
belletrists of one university and another) what point there is
'in keeping in touch with the contemporary scene', or why
'one should read authors one doesn't like because they happen to be alive at the same time as oneself', my reader from
outside the cult may decently sympathize. On *that* score it
will be all the same in two centuries.

But he is still ridiculous when he declares, in his backward
vein, that the early Yeats is 'worth twenty of the secondhand
1920 model', or when he says (to a writer of children's stories):
'I have just finished Vol. I of Henry James' letters. An interesting man, tho' a dreadful prig; but he did appreciate Steven-
son. A *phantasmal* man, who had never known God' – as if
that wasn't priggishness – 'or earth, or war, never done a
day's compelled work, never had to earn a living, had no
home and no duties.'

His sentiments and judgements accord with his soft vocalism and with the effete rhythm of his sentences – up to a point. The point is conversion, followed by loss and pain and grief. These do not transform the style. But the implicit superiority declines, cosiness is mitigated, clichés are smoothed into the generalized cliché of run and rhythm: the narrowness and parochialism of the scholar, the hiding in the past (theistical and theological as well as aesthetic and literary), are faced, if not defeated, by an at last ineluctable present. The blue hills of yearning have come up, and stand round, and show their teeth.

All the same I think that my postulated and prejudiced reader will have found his prejudices confirmed, and will decide that in the later correspondence (often to women in perplexity and distress) Lewis has walked away from himself, however meritoriously, into preachment and exhortation. I doubt if my outsider is going to be enticed any more by end than beginning. More likely he will be repelled by the literary mediocrity of these letters, he will more likely suspect an extension of the same puttyish quality into his other writings, into the scholarship, into the fancifying; fearing (though the stories have some charm of invention and narrative, as of an adult child to children) that they all come from that soft choice of our century which another, more virile Lewis described as back-to-the-engine travel; products of a timid, then defiant and conceited, then again humbled 'sectary of Backness':

> Are there not men convinced they are at rest
> Because their breasts are where their backs should be,
> Poor ostriches of Temporality!

1966

Housman

Would the following be a fair account of Housman on the evidence of his letters and the information with which they are linked, editorially?[1] A clever, physically unattractive boy (with quite hideous ears – see photo-portrait No. 2) of an educated and secure middle-class family grows up in Worcestershire able to see the blue hills of Salop on his western horizon – a blue distance easily and actually becoming symbolic to him as the desirable object, as the something which will reveal and satisfy.

At twelve this eldest child of seven children loses his mother (fanciers of the necessity of a Celtic element in all mere English imagination will grab at the mention in one letter that she was of Cornish descent). Conventional and somewhat authoritarian, like other eldest sons, the boy dutifully accepts the elderly cousin who now becomes his stepmother. 'My dear Mamma', his letters to her begin invariably as long as she lived; and they end as a rule 'I remain your loving son'. In between, these letters are as impersonal as can be imagined. A classic from his local school in Bromsgrove, Housman becomes an undergraduate and a scholar of his Oxford college. He works, taking a first in Moderations ('The impression he made on those around him was that of a well-behaved young man, studious and orderly, and anything but the common type of drinking, hunting and whoring rowdy').

In his last undergraduate year, 1880, Housman shares lodgings with his inamorato Moses Jackson, he discovers with distaste and dismay the extreme force of his sexual or homosexual nature inside his inherited impliable orthodoxy, himself 'short, shy and undistinguished', Moses Jackson 'tall, well-built, handsome and self-confident'.

Respectability is savaged, and turns savage, Housman collapses entirely in his finals, emerging at the close with no

[1] *The Letters of A. E. Housman*, edited by Henry Mass (1971).

more than a pass degree when he should have achieved a
first again.

This brings him to his twenty-third year: he has now
rejected the god of his upbringing. The respectable and the
secretly unrespectable cohabiting in him, orthodoxy and
shame, he works his way back out of double disaster and out
of a poorish job as a civil servant, into the academic; into his
trade – 'My trade is that of Professor of Latin'. In the dry
nit-picking of his trade (Moses Jackson lost now for years) he
experiences in 1895 the few weeks of sudden excitement, in
which the poems of *A Shropshire Lad* were written. It was,
more than incidentally the editor thinks, the April of the
verdict against Oscar Wilde, to whom he was to send a copy
of *A Shropshire Lad* when Wilde was released from Reading
Gaol.

The contradiction between his social orthodoxy and his
homosexuality, the discovered fraudulence both of God and
of the blue symbol – of all blue symbols – his Moses Jackson
gone, Oscar Wilde publicly in the state torturer's interroga-
tion centre – all these are in the poems; but something else,
we must suppose, some added frustration, raising hope and
destroying hope, was the immediate cause, whatever Housman had to say in a necessarily flippant cover-up about the
poems being triggered by sore throats and controversy over
manuscripts of Propertius.

> Nous n'irons plus au bois,
> Les lauriers sont coupés –

yes, but the ukase against

> Sautez, dansez,
> Embrassez qui vous voudrez

is absolute. At any rate he guards the poems of *A Shropshire
Lad*, that special collection of the enigmatically private made
public; he keeps them, now until the end, from anthologists
(and from broadcasting – 'I don't allow the wireless people
to recite my poems').

So begins, so continues, with *A Shropshire Lad* ascending
slowly into popularity, the long grey progress of that trade

of classical searching and sifting, of misanthropy, indifference, preferred loneliness, and (as a rule) sterility.

The short letters display considerable nastiness. He is still, for instance, the elder brother ready to sneer at the younger brother and bully him. To have had in the family such an inveterate scribbler as Laurence Housman must have been trying, but it is hard not to be dismayed by the P.P.S. of a letter of 1896 which says: 'I was just licking the envelope, when I thought of the following dart: I had far, far rather that people should attribute my verses to you than yours to me.' He becomes adeptly unpleasant – such particular unpleasantness is always tempting – to his admirers. To the American poet Wytter Binner: 'You seem to admire my poems even more than I admire them myself, which is very noble of you, but will most likely be difficult to keep up for any great length of time.' He chokes off editors who want poems, or young men who insist on sending him books by themselves:

Dear Mr Priestley,

I am much obliged by your kindness in sending me your *Brief Diversions.* Some of the parodies and other verses I had read with interest and pleasure in the *Cambridge Review.*

I am yours very truly
A. E. Housman

And so on in his brevities, until one sees, with some dejection, this greying Cambridge don, no great admirer of himself, in dark, dull rooms up a tall stairway in Trinity College, in Whewell's Court, lacing himself, but not very cheerfully, with sips of the pornographic and of the better vintages; one watches his progress to the uninspiriting repeated statement 'In philosophy I am a Cyrenaic or egoistic hedonist, and regard the pleasure of the moment as the only possible motive of action'.

Life is a sell. God – the god he finds, as well he may, an absurd delusion – is not mocked, he repeats to Gilbert Murray:

I rather doubt if man really has much to gain by substituting peace for strife, as you and Jesus Christ recommend.

Sic notus Ulixes? do you think you can outwit the resourceful malevolence of Nature? God is not mocked, as St Paul
long ago warned the Galatians. When man gets rid of a
great trouble he is easier for a little while, but not for long;
Nature instantly gets to work to weaken his power of
sustaining trouble, and very soon seven pounds is as heavy
as fourteen pounds used to be

– which may perhaps be read as a gloss on the immediate
rather than cumulative experiences which had generated
A Shropshire Lad?

Not only is life a sell, but A.E.H. is a fraud; he isn't
respectable, he only looks it, or only half of him is respectable, he doesn't deserve honours: offering honours to me, if
only you knew, is extra absurd, the basic absurdity of honours
apart. So no honorary degrees; so the letter refusing the offer
of the Order of Merit (an offering which usually induces
wavering or relenting in authors or sculptors or painters).
What on earth did the king's poor private secretary make of
Housman's second – and final – sentence of refusal: 'I hope
to escape the reproach of thanklessness or churlish behaviour
by borrowing words in which an equally loyal subject
Admiral Cornwallis declined a similar mark of the Royal
favour: I am unhappily, of a turn of mind that would make
my receiving that honour the most unpleasant thing imagin-
able.'

As for his poems, perhaps, you dolts who slobber over
them, they are a fraud, too: 'Certainly I have never regretted
the publication of my poems. The reputation which they
brought me, though it gives me no lively pleasure, is something like a mattress interposed between me and the hard
ground.' And as if it might have been one on the kisser of
that all too circumambient God who failed to exist, he tells
Grant Richards, his publisher, in one ironic letter (of 1916),
that doubling the price of *A Shropshire Letter* 'diminishes
my chances of the advertisement to which I am always looking forward: a soldier is to receive a bullet in the breast, and
it is to be turned aside from his heart by a copy of *A Shropshire Lad* which he is carrying there. Hitherto it is only the
Bible which has performed this trick.'

Housman's letters do not greatly illustrate or help with his poems, or with poetry. On the whole he is lessened by them. Without surprise we discover that Housman admired Leopardi, himself also wearing an irremovable if less palpable hump of sadness, we learn of the influence on his verse of Heine, Shakespeare's songs, and border ballads. His tastes are dicey, all the same; they educe both sympathy and recoil. He does discover an evident relationship with that altogether poetically more wealthy poet Thomas Hardy. (After they met he actually went to see Hardy in Dorset, though conversation does not appear to have abounded between them; and he was to be a pall-bearer at Hardy's funeral.) Always he was capable of curt, usually justified dismissal, for instance of that mean horrible poem by Frances Cornford about the fat white woman, which moved him to parody:

> O fat white woman nobody shoots,
> Why do you walk through the fields in boots
> When the grass is soft as the breast of coots

– as if Frances Cornford had been writing about herself. He will dismiss Meredith, of whom he remarked, in 1913, when he sent Laurence Housman two poems for an annual: 'I hope you won't succeed in getting anything from Meredith, as I am a respectable character, and do not care to be seen in the company of galvanized corpses. By this time he stinketh.' Alice Meynell, W. E. Henley, the Walter de la Mare of 1907, seem to him objectionable. Yet more and more I was impressed by the degree to which Housman is constricted, and by a literary fogeyism (which is not at all apparent, let's say, in Hardy's *Memoir* of Hardy). Verse by younger poets of 1922 (Eliot or merely the Georgians?) is 'new-fangled . . . but I have been admiring Blunden for some time'. He takes to poems by Edna St Vincent Millay, he thinks Conington's translations from Horace are 'among the best verse translations in English'. In an alarming way he reveals in himself the academic hardening of the arteries when faced, at the instance of Robert Bridges in 1918, with his edition of Gerard Manley Hopkins. He dismisses Hopkins, he compares his manner with that of Carlyle. Then Proust (to Grant

Richards, in 1919): 'I have read enough to form the opinion
that an English translation would not sell'. Lawrence is
mentioned, and James Joyce; but as if they were to be spoken
of with *Fanny Hill* (also mentioned), Housman having
perused *Lady Chatterley's Lover* and *Ulysses* for any pornographic titillation they might provide. Once he speaks of
Valéry – he is off to hear him lecture at Cambridge. A pity
we haven't another letter on the impression he received; but
it is possible to guess – and permissible to say that any page
of Valéry's *Analects* is certainly worth the total candle power
of all the four hundred and thirty-eight pages of Housman's
correspondence. After all, neither poetry nor living are
greatly illuminated when (embryo of *The Name and Nature
of Poetry*) Housman utters: 'I can no more define poetry
than a terrier can define a rat; but he knows a rat when he
comes across one; and I recognize poetry by definite physical
sentiments, either down the spine, or at the back of the
throat, or in the pit of the stomach'; which reminds me of the
present Lord Chancellor[2] once – in a Third Programme talk
– rebutting the philosophers A. J. Ayer and Gilbert Ryle on
the precedence of ethics to revelation by defining Christian
belief as what happens to a Christian on his knees in prayer,
of which *they* were no doubt ignorant. Houseman's aesthetics
were about as useful, in tune only with the requirements of a
very callow literary society or debating society in a suburb.
So too I can only shake my head in disheartenment when
*respect*able Housman rears up and pontificates – as if it
mattered – on Masefield as exactly the right choice for Poet
Laureate, 'as all the other good poets are too obviously un-
suited for the official duties'.

Startled as readers may be by such foolishness, and by
observing how this resolute small being was stunted, in his
not so long ago time, both by social repression and the narrow vulgarities of what could pass at Cambridge and elsewhere as a requisite level of response or inquiry either for
adolescents or for adults, there remain still – the poems;
which, when all such things are reviewed, appear a bleeding
miracle, no less. It will out. Turn to

[2] Lord Hailsham.

The mill-stream, now that noises cease,
Is all that does not hold its peace;
Under the bridge it murmurs by,
And here are night and hell and I.

There is flesh inside the exoskeleton of the spider-crab,
crawling sideways across Whewell's Court. Sadly we read at
last of his death in 1936 in the Cambridge nursing home,
Housman sinking into unconsciousness (after listening
delightedly to an improper story from his doctor), and 'holding the nurse's hand until the morning of 30 April, when his
life ended'.

There should have been more holding of hands.

1971

William Morris

1. Morris in Life and Design

Does it begin to be necessary to insist that William Morris was a great man? The English have long been evasive about him. This may be partly because the hitherto middle class or upper middle class of commentating Englishmen have been made uneasy by his frank and extreme socialism. But that is not all the truth: he is complex, he is hard to catch hold of, to isolate; and his person does emanate all the same a kind of healthiness, or an unmysterious quality, which is not attractive, superficially. It is a little as if Isaiah (but no doubt Isaiah was less complex) had been a good opening bat.

Bernard Shaw may have felt the slight tug of this peculiarity, when in 1949 he wrote a Sunday review of a new book on Morris. He dared anyone to denigrate him. And having himself known this squat and fiery energy bounding from one activity to another, having trudged with him in processions and stood with him on platforms to the jeers of the respectable, he insisted that Morris was great 'not only among little men, but among great ones'. Also he prophesied that scores of books would still be written about him.

Certainly the books multiply. In between the two which have just appeared[1] and the book Shaw reviewed there have been at least seven. Ray Watkinson's book introduces Designer Morris, who is the Morris in vogue. The other, by Philip Henderson, inclines, though it is a large biography, to the Morris of yesterday's vogue, Political Morris. The day before yesterday, and the day before that, the Morrises who counted were Beauty Morris, misinterpreted, Morris who damned the blind and bland eyes of architects and clergy in defence of ancient buildings, Utopia Morris, Middle Ages

[1] *William Morris as Designer*, by Ray Watkinson (1967); *William Morris*, by Philip Henderson (1967).

Morris, and Poet Morris (whose weaker poems, his com-
munism discreetly overlooked, were curtailed into school
books).

Mr Watkinson, I think, has had no very hard job – he has
done it well – with Designer Morris, where the thing is to
determine his degree of originality and his degree of influence, to reconcile his medievalism to his livingness, and to
tread out a progress of act and idea from the fabrics Morris
called Eyebright or Birds or Evenlode, from the wallpapers
he called Jasmine or Daisy, or from his Kelmscott *Chaucer*
and Kelmscott *News from Nowhere*, towards severer graces
of modern design.

But containing multitudes, like his contemporary Walt
Whitman, does this marvel of a man contradict himself? And
if not, where and what is the centre of him?

The answers should be found in a biography. They were
not given altogether by Mackail, son-in-law of his great
friends Georgiana and Edward Burne-Jones, in his remarkable more or less immediate version of Morris's life. Mackail,
wrote Bernard Shaw, considered that his hero had taken to
socialism as Edgar Allen Poe had taken to drink. In any case
Mackail wrote too soon, for an effect of finality. What about
that old admirer Philip Henderson?

Sixty-nine years later, it may also have been the wrong
moment for Mr Henderson, in a different way. For all the
facts, affection, stitching, and design, I would say regretfully
that he has given us pieces of the giant, or (it is not quite the
same) the giant in bits. Mackail, civil servant and friends'
son-in-law, was anyhow too smooth by nurture. Mr Henderson, in his writing, seems a shade too dismal for this contained
or renewed explosion of a man, a shade too apologetic, as if
love had cooled after a love affair to more criticism, more
reservation, than the grand case demands.

For one thing he is frequently off centre, or out of focus.
To give a telling, if small, example, May Morris relates that
when her father was worried and harassed by the burdens of
his work and the stresses of nourishing the political infant of
socialism, it was thought that a visit to a musical comedy
might ease him. Morris went – though it was hardly his kind
of exercise or outing – and he was heard to exclaim loudly

when the leading lady bounced in: 'Damned pink TOAD!'
Art, after all, should be served. Philip Henderson generalizes
this story: Morris seldom went to the theatre, 'though he
sometimes took his daughters, and when he did' – as if he
was always out to wound – 'he was liable to make audibly
insulting remarks about the actors and actresses. 'Damned
little pink TOAD!' he would growl at some leading lady.'

Out of focus, not quite in character.

I think there is no contradiction in the multaneity of
Morris. But then the need is to discover the centre, to detect
the unifying element, and hold it afterwards, devoutly,
through thick and thin, through politics, poetry, dyestuffs,
chintz, and wallpaper. Morris's now neglected poetry seems
to me one good way to the centre of him, where will be
found, in many lines and stanzas, a celebration of rest, of the
perfect environment – utopian, if you like impossible, news
from nowhere – which man at any rate deserves, though
again and again in the poems we see him deprived of it
through evil and greed.

This rest, happiness, equilibrium, calm in the centre of the
fire, is everywhere in Morris; and I would hope as well to see
it recognized as more than pattern or 'design', let me say in
the exquisite drawing, which Mr Watkinson reproduces in
colour, for a Vine and Willow wallpaper, or in various products which persist, despite all changes in fashion and vision,
in remaining lovable and imparting happiness. I often think
of Morris in one of them, also illustrated by Mr Watkinson in
colour, the Birds, the wool fabric I have mentioned, in which
pairs of birds front each other, with their heads and beaks
reversed and turned away from each other, among blue
foliage.

Or read the letter to a friend in some distress (perhaps
Georgiana Burne-Jones, who may have been the intellectual
love of his existence):

I wish I could say something that would serve you, beyond
what you know very well, that I love you and long to help
you: and indeed I entreat you (however trite the words
may be) to think that life is not empty nor made for nothing, and that the parts of it fit one into another in some

way; and that the world goes on, beautiful and strange and dreadful and worshipful.

It was the worshipfulness this great man wished to emphasize, the dreadfulness he wished to reduce, for everyone, so far as it is reducible. Mr Henderson's *William Morris* should be read, yes; but supplement it with those Morris letters Mr Henderson published in 1950, and with a visit to the now restored Kelmscott Manor; where you may still see, I think, a portion of those Birds among blue leaves, and realize, as you look at it, the meaning of a phrase by Pasternak, that we are the 'guests of existence'. It is a phrase Morris would have appreciated and dwelt upon, in the poignancy of its strength.

1967

2. *The Happiness of His Poems*

Landing at Le Havre from a late car ferry an Englishman of today could do worse than think of William Morris, aged twenty-two, walking the quays there at night in the August of 1855. Waiting with him for a boat back to England was Ned Jones, and after a last term together at Oxford, and an exhilarating tour of French cathedrals, it was there, so we are told in Mackail's biography of Morris, that they came to the decision by which one of them was to be transformed into the now more or less disregarded, if not forgotten painter Sir Edward Burne-Jones, and the other – without title or double-barrelled name – into one of the seminal idealists of the nineteenth century: they decided on the quay to forgo the idea of becoming clergymen and to become instead devotees of the practice of art.

Art was at once the root and the leaf of Morris's idealism and of all that career of enormous activity which so helped to sweeten the English mind and make the English readier to accept and promote a society of greater happiness and justice; and Morris's primal art was the one we are inclined to dismiss or push out to the margin nowadays when we celebrate the energizer, the designer, the craftsman, the aesthete, and the communist.

That night at Le Havre, it is true, the young Morris had

the making of buildings, not the writing of poems, in mind.
Thinking of the cathedrals he had just seen, the height of
Beauvais, the opulence of Rouen, the purity of Coutances, it
was to architecture that he decided to give himself, and
architecture which he was trying before long under G. E.
Street, only to abandon it for painting under the influence of
his friend Rossetti. But he was already aware that he could
write poems. After his trial excursions into architecture and
painting, his first book – and his best if we except *News from
Nowhere* and his *Icelandic Journals* – was poetry, published
in 1858, when Morris was twenty-four; and poems he was to
continue to write, enshrining, if not always obviously, those
hopes for mankind which he elaborated and expressed in so
many other ways, poems short, medium, long or immoder-
ately long, until his death in 1896.

That first book of his, *The Defence of Guenevere*, already
displays in poem after poem the *leitmotiv* of Morris's thought
and action, though it is too easily, and too frequently, dismissed as a backward ramble into day-dreams and mock-
medievalism.

> There were four of us about that bed;
>   The mass-priest knelt at the side,
> I and his mother stood at the head,
>   Over his feet lay the bride;
> We were quite sure that he was dead,
>   Though his eyes were open wide.

Such is the opening, direct and immediate under the influence of Browning, of one of these early poems, 'Shameful
Death'. A young lord is murdered, the circumstances are
described, the narrator is glad to recall, at seventy, how the
two murderers, Sir John the knight of the Fen and Sir Guy of
the Dolorous Blast, were caught up with and killed in their
turn.

If it is read too casually, enjoyed too casually, 'Shameful
Death' may be taken as no more than a poem of revenge or a
story of rough justice. Yet it is an embryo of Morris's concern. In a shameful way men who are evil and cowardly
come up behind the young Lord Hugh and catch him and
hang him:

He did not die in the night,
  He did not die in the day,
But in the morning twilight
  His spirit pass'd away,
When neither sun nor moon was bright,
  And the trees were merely grey.

He was not slain with the sword,
  Knight's axe, or the knightly spear,
Yet spoke he never a word
  After he came in here;
I cut away the cord
  From the neck of my brother dear.

This shameful death has been inflicted (and in Morris there
is no 'sick' aetheticism, no indulgence in death or its details,
no sado-masochism as there is so frequently in Rossetti or
Swinburne) on a man young and brave and good, newly
married and happy and in love.

They lighted a great torch then,
  When his arms were pinion'd fast,
Sir John the knight of the Fen,
  Sir Guy of the Dolorous Blast,
With knights threescore and ten,
  Hung brave Lord Hugh at last.

Happiness has been wilfully destroyed. For Morris, in love
with the hills of earth, and no believer in a heavenly paradise,
that was the cardinal sin, the cardinal pathos. His concern –
in his poems and in all of his roles – was happiness, his regret
that so many had so little chance to be happy, and that love
and happiness, those twins, so much to be desired –

To what a heaven the earth might grow
If fear beneath the earth were laid,
If hope failed not, nor love decayed

– are yet so vulnerable. His hatred – and Morris was explosive
as well as placid – was for those who fight evilly against the
actual and possible happiness of mankind.

I am threescore and ten,
  And my hair is all turn'd grey,

But I met Sir John of the Fen
   Long ago on a summer day,
And am glad to think of the moment when
   I took his life away.

I am threescore and ten,
   And my strength is mostly pass'd,
But long ago I and my men,
   When the sky was overcast,
And the smoke roll'd over the reeds of the fen,
   Slew Guy of the Dolorous Blast.

Critics have understood that Morris's concern for happiness
was not a contemptible motivation. Yeats, for example; who
knew him face to face, and wrote of him with perfect lack of
superiority in his paper 'The Happiest of Poets'. Yeats was
well aware of the limitation of his verse and his vision, yet
declared with approval that he made his poetry 'out of un-
ending pictures of a happiness that is often what a child
might imagine, and always a happiness that sets mind and
body at ease'; in which he was 'unlike all other modern
writers'. Readers had been taught 'to sympathize with the
unhappy until they had grown morbid', Morris's work was to
make them sympathize 'with men and women who turned
everything into happiness' because they contained some of
the fullness of natural life. Yeats's elaboration and celebration of the happiness which was Morris's concern, could not
be more generous. Yet it is curious that he leaves one to think
of Morris – others have done the same with less sympathy –
as a poet without the complementary words of sadness or
regret. He had just quoted the exquisite opening of 'Golden
Wings' (also in Morris's first book of 1858):

Midways of a walled garden,
   In the happy poplar land,
   Did an ancient castle stand,
With an old knight for a warden.

Many scarlet bricks there were
   In its walls, and old grey stone;

Over which red apples shone
At the right time of the year.

On the bricks the green moss grew,
   Yellow lichen on the stone,
   Over which red apples shone;
Little war that castle knew.

'The verses', Yeats said, 'ran in my head for years and became
to me the best description of happiness in the world, and I
am not certain that I know a better even now.' The poem
changes.

     The water slips,
The red-bill'd moorhen dips.
Sweet kisses on red lips;
Alas! the red rust grips.
And the blood-red dagger rips . . .

White swans on the green moat,
Small feathers left afloat
By the blue-painted boat;
Swift running of the stoat.

And with the stoat of shameful death coming to men and
women who deserve better, I wonder why Yeats made no
mention of apples now 'green and sour' and the moat, which
had been transformed:

The draggled swans most eagerly eat
   The green weeds trailing in the moat;
   Inside the rotting leaky boat
You see a slain man's stiffened feet.

So it is, in poem after poem: Sir Peter Harpdon shows
reluctant mercy and lives to be hanged ('Sir Peter Harpdon's
End'). The knight and his lady were killed, and the girl's
white skull was found with her gold tresses inside the coif of
the helmet which he had taken off and made her wear for her
own safety ('Concerning Geffray Teste Noire'). In 'The Blue
Closet', in which one sees the strangest and most credible of
the Pre-raphaelite or post-pre-raphaelite lilies –

Through the floor shot up a lily red,
With a patch of earth from the land of the dead,
For he was strong in the land of the dead

– death extinguishes the last vestiges of happiness and love:

And ever the great bell overhead,
And the tumbling seas mourned for the dead;
For their song ceased, and they were dead.

In 'The Haystack in the Floods'

Had she come all the way for this,
To part at last without a kiss?
Yea, had she borne the dirt and rain
That her own eyes might see him slain
Beside the haystack in the floods?

In 'Helen Arming Paris', one of the *Scenes from the Fall of Troy*, which Morris was writing between 1861 and 1866, when he began *The Earthly Paradise* (they were never finished, and never published in his lifetime), Helen wildly imagines his death and her return to Greece, happiness over; and when Morris (but less surely) emerges from that distancing which so often helps in rounding off and establishing a poem, and writes in *The Pilgrims of Hope*, twenty years later, about the Commune and the fighting in Paris –

So at last from a grey stone building we saw a great flag fly,
One colour, red and solemn 'gainst the blue of the spring-
      tide sky

– the 'new proletarian' of the poem loses his wife's love, and then his wife and his friend, whom she loved, on the barricades.

Reverting to 'Shameful Death', it is a poem which exemplifies other things creditable to Morris. One is Morris's power to actualize his dream-world or its defeat. Projecting that world into the past or into the future of *News from Nowhere*, Morris was able to feel it and to present it in the here and now of preferred environments; and when he does so, his language avoids archaism or verbal costume or the artificial silk common in too much of the mid or late nineteenth-century manner (compare the poetry language, unattached to earth or Earthly Paradise, of Morris's friend Rossetti, or the poetry language of those elongate figures so infinitely repeated by his friend Burne-Jones). Environmentally one thinks of Morris in his poems, or most of them, and in his calm and cool designs, as the socialist lord of Kelmscott along the Thames; but it was not until 1871 that he acquired Kelmscott as a country resort; in his earlier poems, so clear-cut, so economical, so direct in language, the young Morris is still only the proprietor, so to say, of the landscapes and properties of childhood. When he was six the wealthy Morris family had moved from Walthamstow (his birthplace – he had narrowly escaped birth in Lombard Street, in the heart of profit and capital) to Woodford Hall, which was his home until his father's death in 1847. There was a private park attached to the hall; and beyond the fence of these fifty acres of a first happiness there stretched, *ad infinitum*, as it must have seemed, the pollarded hornbeams and the bracken of Epping Forest, the gnarled growth and undergrowth of murder – and of 'A Shameful Death':

> He did not strike one blow,
>   For the recreants came behind,
> In a place where the hornbeams grow,
>   A path right hard to find,
> For the hornbeam boughs swing so,
>   That the twilight makes it blind.

I would see the fringes of Epping Forest too – hazels for hornbeams – in the Verville wood entered in the poem about Geffray Teste Noire, the Gascon knight and thief:

> And so we enter'd Verville wood next day
>
> In the afternoon; through it the highway runs,
>   'Twixt copses of green hazel, very thick,
> And underneath, with glimmering of suns,
>   The primroses are happy; the dews lick
>
> The soft green moss. . . .

The third home the Morrises came to occupy when his father

died, gave him the happy and less happy moated actuality of
'Golden Wings'.

Morris's socialism demanded more than the private park
or grounds; so it was around Kelmscott Manor, which became
the symbol of his dream, his career, and his personality, that
Morris envisioned his *News from Nowhere*, his 'Epoch of
Rest', his account of England in ideal content after revolution. He walked out of the garden wicket of Kelmscott
Manor, and the ideal state of the future, or the medieval
ideal of the folk-mote, was the practical actual hay meadow,
was the long unhedged open fields by the summer flow of
the Thames, was the enjoyed flow, placidity, purity, and
mirror-surface of the Thames, broken only by oars, or bleak,
or chubb, that upper Thames which is also William Morris,
under willows and past its tall water flowers of yellow or
rose-pink or reverberating purple. The river landscape makes
the language and cadence of the happy prose in *News from
Nowhere*, which has a quality of the light of five a.m., and of
many happy if regretful stanzas which were to be collected
in *Poems by the Way* (1891). The elements – as a mild wind
turns the willow leaves – which make the measured human-
ized external environment so pleasant, whatever the blemishes
of the day such as the pinched faces of ill-fed haymakers
under their flapping sun-bonnets, should extend again,
Morris pleads, into the nature of man, and into his ecological
circumstance. So, among the various elements of the
medieval, should that craftsman's state of mind which without question had raised the church spires and bell-turrets
above the horizons of that happy river-land ('The chancel . . .
was so new that the dust of the stone still lay white on the
midsummer grass beneath the carvings of the windows.' *The
Dream of John Ball*, chap. 1.)

If men went out to a war of arrows and axes in defence of
their dignity as men, it was the shorn hayfields and stubbles
of contentment they crossed in such poems as 'The Burgher's
Battle' or 'The Folk-mote by the River'. And it was the
Thames, twisting through Morris's thought and emotion,
which eventually widened past 'the high tower of the Parliament House, or Dung Market' (which it had become by the
time of *News from Nowhere*) into all the rest of the filth of

the civilization he repudiated, below the burrows of the deprived whom *The Times* spoke of so contemptuously, between inverted commas, as the 'unemployed'.

Contentment finds an autumnal apogee (Morris is a good hand at the stillness of autumn) in a poem of slow movement which comes in the middle of *The Story of the Glittering Plain*, one of the prose romances Morris wrote in his last years (and printed in his Golden Type at his Kelmscott Press):

> Dumb is the hedge where the crabs hang yellow,
> Bright as the blossoms of the spring;
> Dumb is the close where the pears grow mellow,
> And none but the dauntless redbreasts sing . . .
>
> Come then, love, for peace is upon us,
> Far off is failing, and far is fear,
> Here where the rest in the end hath won us,
> In the garnering tide of the happy year.
>
> Come from the grey old house by the water,
> Where, far from the lips of the hungry sea,
> Green groweth the grass o'er the field of the slaughter,
> And all is a tale for thee and me.

Certainly it conveys Kelmscott by the Thames, the ideal within the worldly, and the lapse of existence. But do such cadences and such a predilection convict Morris, in a fatal sense, of superficiality?

Superficial belongs to Class One of pejorative words, though surface matters are not *ipso facto* denied either a human relevance or fine qualities which give pleasure; and poetry is of many kinds; and we should avoid superiority when faced with a kind which no one could or would write in our own day, when we have found it so difficult to share Morris's 'reverence for the life of Man upon the Earth'. It is true that in his thirties Morris began to lose the passion and so the directness of his verse. The reasons seem partly in the pressure of his relentless activities as designer and manufacturer, partly in Morris's own nature, and partly in the discovery of the nature of his wife, who may or may not have transferred her affections – if she had affections at all? –

to Rossetti,[2] coupled with a possible realization that the
quality of love which *might* have come from a wife of such
matchless stupidity as well as such matchless beauty could
not in any case have been very satisfying. Certainly with and
after *The Life and Death of Jason* (1867) and the unpressur-
ized tales of *The Earthly Paradise* (1868–70) Morris takes
language and makes it flow and flow. Certainly he gave way
to an increasing archaism, certainly his lines elongate across
the page into a tom-tom rhythm which deadens the reader's
attention (true notably of the epic *Story of Sigurd the
Volsung*, in spite of its intermittent power). And then in the
Eighties Morris separated his idea from its expression in
poetry, fabrics, wallpapers, and the rest, brandished it naked,
and became an active propagator of revolutionary socialism.
He can be wearisome, as Yeats remarked so equably – 'His
poetry often wearies us as the unbroken green of July wearies
us.' What has so often been called his tapestry verse, even at
its happiest in *The Earthly Paradise*, hardly bears reprinting
('They are all too long and flabby, damn it!' – Morris to
Swinburne on the tales in *The Earthly Paradise*). His socialist
hymnology is mostly water off the boil, useful, but not poetry.
I shall speak up, all the same, for the long unfinished poem
The Pilgrims of Hope, which Morris contributed with so
much urgent political writing to *The Commonweal*, the
journal he edited for the Socialist League. Also for 'A Death
Song', one of those poems with a refrain which Morris
managed so well. With thirty-two years between them,
thirty-two years of a life of astonishing creativity, it recalls a
scene which may be set alongside that midnight pacing on
the quay at Le Havre. Morris wrote it in 1887 for the funeral
of Alfred Linnell who died of a broken hip some weeks after
the trouble between police and demonstrators over the right
to meet and speak in Trafalgar Square. Rightly or wrongly
the police were blamed for his death. 'Killed in Trafalgar
Square' was emblazoned above the hearse which took Linnell

---

[2] Read the tortured confessional poems of the late Sixties,
'Thunder in the Garden', 'Sad-eyed and Soft and Grey', 'Rhyme
Slayeth Shame', 'May Grown A-cold', 'Song', 'Why Dost Thou
Struggle', 'Fair Weather and Foul', and the September lines from
The Earthly Paradise.

in a long ragged procession from Soho to Bow Cemetery. It was then the dark of a December evening, and in a cold rain which had driven away most of the crowd, Morris and a few others chanted the Death Song above Linnell's grave.[3]

Omitting most of the tapestry (and most of Morris's explicitly socialist versifying) amounts to a drastic reduction. Nevertheless it leaves a body of poems now undervalued which would still be this man's title to a just remembrance, even if nothing else of him were known.

Yeats, who had watched Morris holding a glass of claret to the light and exclaiming that wine was no prosaic source of inspiration since the grapes which made the wine were themselves made by sap and sunlight, declared that we are a little happier when we look at his vision. So we are. It is as if Morris had wished, and then worked, to share the happiness of his own childhood with all of the deprived, as if he had hoped that the happiness of childhood could be prolonged, and extended into the rest of life, into everyone's life, untarnished by the disappointments of love and refreshed by that excellence of the earth which Morris loved with such poignancy. If he has been slighted lately as a poet, isn't it – for one thing – because we have been slighting the earth he celebrated, the only earth, the only life, we have, more than our disasters and discontents have warranted?

Towards the end he too believed that the arts had become unreal in his time. 'The arts have got to die, what is left of them, before they can be born again.' 'Nothing can take serious hold of people, or should do so, but that which is rooted deepest in reality and is quite at first hand: there is no room for anything which is not forced out of a man of deep feeling, because of its innate strength and vision.' So he was severe on his own verse as on his own life; more severe than we need be, who can look back, and compare, and see the realities and honesties of either one.

1969

[3] A peculiarly vigorous and moving, if prejudiced, account of the procession, of Morris and other organizers following the hearse, and of the chanting in the cemetery will be found in *The Times* for 19 December 1887.

3. *Iceland and William Morris*

When, if ever, should one go to Iceland? Answer, in one's early time, when one is able to endure miles upon miles of jogging on the broad back of an Icelandic pony picking its way along paths or trails between lava; when one is still attuned to camping; when one remembers Grettir the Outlaw; when one is inclined still to rebel against recollections of the classics – the Mediterranean and Aegean classics – badly taught; and before tasting the South and lying in the shadow of olive trees and watching the Lago di Garda rippling on to the hard ledges of Sirmio.

Thirty-seven is still young enough for Iceland, if you have the northern disease, which is perhaps no longer so catching as it used to be. Our great William Morris was thirty-seven when he visited Iceland for the first time, having his first sight of the new land at 3 a.m. on the morning of 12 July 1871. They were off Papey, the monks' island, once occupied by Irish hermits. And beyond this 'dark brown ragged rocky island', with its small skerries, Morris saw the mainland – 'a terrible shore indeed: a great mass of dark grey mountains worked into pyramids and shelves, looking as if they had been built and half-ruined; they were striped with snow high up, and wreaths of cloud dragged across them here and there, and above them two peaks and a jagged ridge of pure white snow'.

The sun rose above the heights, the pyramid mountain of Búlandstindr grew red, low clouds cleared away and Morris saw his first regular Icelandic hillside: 'a great slip of black shale and sand, striped with the green of the pastures, that gradually sloped into a wide grass-grown flat between hill and sea'. On the flat he could see the bright green of the home-meadow around farmstead after farmstead. So he described the beginning of his real acquaintance with Iceland, in one of the best of his books, his *Icelandic Journals*,[4] which have been printed before only in the great and not very accessible collected edition of Morris's work.

Morris was a special case of the northern disease, going as

[4] *Icelandic Journals*, by William Morris (1969).

well at a moment of pain and crisis in his life; leaving a wife who cared little for him behind at Kelmscott, and certain perhaps that another profounder love could have no return. He admired the sagas, he idealized the Middle Ages – for some qualities at least. He admired the resoluteness of the saga men of Iceland cornered by the inescapable, alive still in a great literature. In this way he came to discover their milieu beyond that terrible shore, to examine with his own eyes the saga-steads where such men as Gunnar, Njal, and Grettir had acted their tragedies: it was not so very long before he and the friends who had come with him, two English, one Icelandic, were jogging eastward towards the scenes of the *Saga of Burnt Njal*, or northward again to Reykjaholt, the home of that great medieval historian and chronicler Snorri Sturluson, author of the *Heimskringla*.

24 August, at Reykjaholt: 'A cold raw morning when I went out to bathe in Snorri's Bath, so that I felt grateful for the hot water up to my middle. The said bath is a round one sunk in the earth some 12 ft in diameter, lined and paved with smooth cut stones cemented with bitumen; there is a groove cut from it to the hot spring, Skrifla, which is some hundred yards off.'

I have a mental picture, and I value it, of the great rather squat William Morris up to his wide middle in the steaming Snorralaug, with the cold raw wind in his red beard and the red hair on his wide chest (though nowadays, I have been told by Icelandic friends, the Snorralaug, dry and shabby, is apt to be a receptacle for French letters dropped into it by American airmen). But do not think that these journals describe simply a kind of associational saga journey, as another traveller might be going in adoring piety to Bernard Shaw's suburban bathroom or Coleridge's *Kubla Khan* farmhouse.

Read the journals and you find yourself totally enveloped in one of the most formidable of the world's landscapes.

'I note here our riding over a huge waste of black sand all powdered over with tufts of sea-pink and bladder-campion at regular intervals, like a Persian carpet.' It is a transporting book, in prose tougher and more vivid than Morris usually achieved, at any rate in his romances. 'Just opposite me is a

long range of cliff down the face of which tumbles fifty feet
of grey glacier stream right into the sea.' 'Nothing lies between us and the great plain but a short space of utterly
barren shaly slopes populous with ravens.'

They come to black openings in sheer cliffs 'like hell mouths
in thirteenth-century illuminations'. They ford milky rivers
like rivers nowhere else (I suppose?) in the world, since the
glacial milkiness is apt to have its own special impurity:
'Then on we clatter over the loose stones till we come to the
river-side and ride up it: such an ugly looking water, quite
turbid and yellowish white, smelling strongly of sulphur, and
running at a prodigious rate, all tossed up into waves by its
rocky bottom.'

The landscapes of this universe of 'broken down mountain
walls black as ink under a dull cloudy sky' rise in actuality
from the pages. Here is all Iceland, swans, redwings singing
in birch scrub, the smell of low birches in flower, mist rainbows, volcanic pyramid-hills which are indigo, or deep
Indian red or purple according to the light and the time of
day. Here are pillars of basalt, rivers sliding along and then
slipping over the perpendicular of a gorge, clumps of wild
angelica, looking shiny and succulent, Arctic terns (sea
swallows Morris always calls them) as well as ravens nowadays bereft of corpses. Here are clumps of the red-purple,
red-stemmed Mountain Willowherb, which the Icelanders
call Shingle Rose, growing out of the bed of streams. Here
are those green home-meadows in the grey: roofs made of
turf (Morris was in Iceland before the era of galvanized iron)
vivid with heartsease, on houses half dug into the ground.

Here are Morris and his three friends playing whist at
some idyllic camping site (how wrong 'camping site' – version
1969 – sounds for Morris on the lonely Icelandic trail), or
parboiling a quarter of lamb in Blesi, the spring and pool of
boiling sulphur water in the Great Geysir group.

Morris makes the whole landscape a protagonist: they ride,
they camp, make their grog and fry their trout or cook their
golden plover, in a geology that disdains life, especially the
life of man, or which at the most tolerates it.

He pictures it almost like a Cézanne of the North, in
planes and shapes and cinder-colours; every now and then

adding a drawing in sharp detail – as when he looks into Blesi, the Sigher, that still and deep parboiler – 'The water of it is boiling an inch or two below the surface, and so clear that in the twilight I couldn't see that there was any water there' – the water being flush almost with the lip of the pool. 'As dim as the light is, I can see looking through the stream, its horrible blue and green depths and the white sulphur sides of it sticking out.' Or here – allowing myself the luxury of this extra quotation – Morris has to take a narrow pass between cliff and sea: 'Magnússon called out to us to look down below, where was a seal eating a salmon; and sure enough we saw the black head down in the green sea, dubbing away at a big fish.'

A capital book, a capital resuscitation of travel writings which are superior to most in our language.

1969

4. *After Morris, W. H. Auden*

All Scandinavia is not inhospitable Iceland, yet in many ways, many features such as those whose quality Morris caught so well, Iceland seems the properest habitat for that *outré* family of the divine who have their voice in the poems of the *Elder Edda*. Among these the eleventh-century 'Voluspá' is Icelandic – hot springs and all – rather than vaguely northern; which is a reminder, now that he has shared in translating the Eddaic poems,[5] that W. H. Auden found his in Icelandic matters in William Morris.

The translations seem very good to me, though I would warn the reader of the book as a whole not to be put off by too great a degree of take-it-or-leave-it in their presentation. Don't leave it simply because you find yourself at the outset insufficiently enticed – I mean by the introduction and the apparatus – into this territory of the unfamiliar.

Odin, Thor, Loki, Baldur and the mistletoe, Yggdrasil the tree of the world, we know them, in a shadowy way, from the potted myths and legends we encountered as children. Moderately curious, we may have acquired an extra tone of

[5] *The Elder Edda: A Selection*, translated by F. B. Taylor and W. H. Auden, introduced by F. B. Taylor and P. Salus (1969).

feeling from reading the Tolkien romances (this book is dedicated to Tolkien); we may just know of this or that link – in England – with a pantheon and a world-view which were so rapidly blotted out by Christianity. Odin or Woden is faintly present still, under his bye-name of Grimnir, the Masked One, in Grime's Graves in Norfolk, and Grim's Dykes, and Wansdyke; or he looks at us, or over us protectively, as God of the Spears, God of the Slope, in the Long Man of Wilmington. Tyr, god of battle, had his horse cut into the scarp of Edge Hill. Giants or demons, dwindled to hobs, have their holes in Yorkshire limestone. There are dwarf valleys – one not far from London – so named for their echo, echo (Germanically) having been the voice of dwarfs. Also we have the names of the days of the week. Yet on the whole the Norse, the Icelandic, the early Germanic pantheon *is* remote, more than in time; and is – perhaps – too full of sharp, hard names, characters, and properties, to seem all that attractive.

Such an abandoned past required, I think, subtler introductory pages than these about the Eddaic poetry, its circumstances, its forms, its prosody, and about the Nordic cosmology. They don't manage the trick. For a small example, why are these eleventh- or twelfth-century poems in Old Icelandic called the (Elder) Edda? The answer turns out to be confusing and not greatly relevant. But not being told, the reader remains puzzled by a peculiar name which should or might have a significance.

Those who have gone round Denmark looking at strangled bog-corpses, or those who have read that excellent book, Turville-Petre's *Myth and Religion of the North*, will have their own estimate of the attraction or the repellent quality of the ancient Scandinavian world, as it appears when unbowdlerized: a world of mind and action, in too many ways, haunted with black blood and beastliness, having its Aztec horrors. A barbarian world, anyhow. The Eddaic poems do redeem this image, a little. The gods, morally ramshackle as they are, have their points. The myth poems about them (or hero poems of the same time, a few of which are included from outside the Edda) have their virtue – the art being better than the time – rising in part from a cosmology which was not unsatisfying.

Take trouble, keep a thumb in the glossary of names, have
Turville-Petre at hand and so get the circumstances of each
of these strange poems right, and nearly all of them, gnomic,
didactic, mythological, narrative, *can* be read with an enjoyment which older English versions, full of obscurity and
verbiage, were incapable of giving. Read them, for instance,
if you like play with names of power, or if you like riddling,
or contests in knowledge between god and dwarf, god and
giant; of which we have relics, I suppose, in such folk-poems
as 'Riddles Wisely Expounded' or 'The Elfin Knight'.

With Morris, Auden is one of the few English poets
fascinated profitably by the ancient North. But a long concern with dwarf, giant, god, and rune, and howe, and dene, is
only one reason for his share in this translation. Another –
mentioned in the opening account of Eddaic poetry – is
surely the internal action of the poems, their exceptional
mixture of speech, event, and narrative. Each is a drama.
For that, god vis-à-vis the supernatural enemies of mankind
and so on, they must be read in *extenso*. Excerpts meanwhile
– whatever scholars in Icelandic may or may not have to
complain of in these translations – will take one back to an
earlier savour of the Audenesque, which I like, to Auden of
elf poems, of *Paid on Both Sides*, of the glowing blood of
Grendel, even if the particular poet doesn't push himself, on
this occasion, to what would. be an inappropriate idiosyn-
crasy.

> Dawn has broken, Dwarf,
>   Stiffen now to stone

are Thor's last words in the 'Alvíssmál', 'The Words of All-
Wise' (why do the translators call it 'The Words of *the*
All-Wise'?).

> He sent warriors forth: white their shield-bosses
> In the waning moon, and their mail glittered

comes from 'The Lay of Völund' – Wayland the dwarf, the
marvellously skilled smith of Wayland's Smithy on the Ridge-
way.

> Dew frozen, I am dead long,

are words of the complaining witch forced back from the

grave to prophesy Baldur's death. Or from that wonderful
poem the *Voluspá*, 'the Sibyl's Prophecy' (again, for this
spae-wife's poem, 'Song of the Sibyl' is hardly the right
title?), that Tree we're all acquainted with:

> I know an ash-tree, named Yggdrasil;
> > Sparkling showers are shed on its leaves
> That drip dew into the dales below.

And, from the same, death:

> Now death is the portion of doomed men,
> Red with blood the buildings of gods,
> The sun turns black in the summer after,
> Winds whine. *Well, would you know more?*

The Icelandic scene, or a Jutland heath, or a West Riding
dale, a lump of the Faroes battered by swell in the fog or
Sweden in November or December when the after-lunch
shadows lengthen – each may give a territory for dwarfs and
gods. We have a share in them, whether we like it or not.
So I think it lucky – Dawn has broken, Dwarf – to have had
two northern books of such related quality, such strength,
one after the other, as Morris's *Icelandic Journals* and these
Eddaic selections. And how is it I most remember from this
book, from the 'Hávamál', the words of Odin:

> To be blind is better than to burn on a pyre:
> > There is nothing the dead can do.
> It is always better to be alive,
> > The living can keep a cow:
> Fire, I saw, warming a wealthy man,
> > With a cold corpse at his door?

Are these poems so remote after all? And do we remember
how the North contributed to the good, earthly, unnorthern
vision of William Morris? We should.

1969

The Book of Quotations:
Hypocrisy, Vice, Virtue

What are 'quotations'? I shall just avoid pontificating that
they are spots of a disease. But certainly they all have two
elements in common: they incline to be corny, or to be
capable of corny application, and they resist, though without
entire success, our irritating liability to forget. Which is to
say they are various forms of a bloody nuisance, less succinct
than proverbs. It would be nonsense to dislike quotation
dictionaries either because St Polonius (who isn't one of the
holy helpers demoted by the Pope) must always be their
patron, or because you won't find in them the good but unfamiliar lines of essential poetry which you half remember
and which will not be there because they belong to the
fringes of your own individual exploration. Still, there do
exist better and worse quotation dictionaries. I think I am
right in believing that *Bartlett* was once, in some earlier
editions, marked by fairly good sense, if a little narrow, and
a little too American for our perhaps more Athenian appetite.
A note on its history, in this new 14th edition,[1] tells us that it
was first published in 1855, and that John Bartlett, as one
might expect, was a 'bookman', without much education.
However, he was daily among undergraduates and professors,
since he kept the University Book Store at Cambridge,
Massachusetts. He compiled his dictionary from his own
commonplace book of literary wisdom.

His day was the day of Emerson (who is given 17 columns
of quotation, though in fact he didn't make a way into
Bartlett until the third edition of 1858) and of such as the
first William Ellery Channing, whose address on 'Self-
Culture', delivered at Boston in September 1838, provides

[1] *Bartlett's Familiar Quotations*, edited by Emily Morison Beck
(1969).

the editor of the new *Bartlett* with her appropriate phrase of introductory uplift. Quotations (she has substituted quotations for books) 'are true levellers. They give to all who will faithfully use them' – by a short-cut – 'the society, the spiritual presence, of the best and greatest of our race.' And she is pleased to draw in Winston Churchill writing – of *Bartlett* – that 'it is a good thing for an uneducated man to read books of quotations'.

Mutton, American or English, cohabits with lion. Column juxta column, we have, let's say, Eliza Cook and Marx. 'Religion is the opium of the people' adjoins (now who could want this couplet in 1969?):

I love it, I love it; and who shall dare
To chide me for loving that old armchair?

The risky temptation – let's risk it – is to judge America, or one America, though not presumably the one to which so many English critics and dons now take their begging bowl, by the tone of *Bartlett 14*, 'revised and updated by a team of outstanding scholars'. Vice paying its homage of hypocrisy to virtue (La Rochefoucauld, *Reflections* 218) – but is that fair? – certain priorities are little changed or challenged. Shakespeare leads the parade (172 columns). Next comes the Bible, Authorized Version (108 columns), followed by Pope (24 columns), Tennyson (21½ columns), Wordsworth and Byron dead level (18 columns), and Emerson with his 17 columns; and just here comes the top modern, our own American-Anglo T.S.E., in 15½ columns (which must have cost a mint in copyright fees). Our times in fact creep in, down to Robert Lowell, in 4½ columns – rather improved, I consider, by excerption – a little jet of four lines from Philip Larkin, and another little jet of three lines from the 'Howl' of Allen Ginsberg.

So (some) Americans still are likely to want to quote 'Play up! play up! and play the game' (Newbolt, in case you do not remember). Some of them still cannot do without the boy standing on the burning deck or – invented also by our Mrs Hemans – 'The stately homes of England'. Some require their 12 or 13 columns of quotable Kipling. Bearing that guilt by the Bomb, they are held to require gestures from, or to,

the culture of once occupied Japan. So – *familiar* quotations?
– here they are equipped with two not very memorable
snippets from Sei Shonagon's *Pillow Book*, one from the Lady
Murasaki, and three from the great Chikamatsu Monzaemon;
snippets also, among moderns, from Tanizaki the novelist
(but not from Kawabata).

And how extra splendid that an American editor and her
scholars should be able to buttress Andrew Carnegie ('Upon
the sacredness of property civilization itself depends – the
right of the labourer to his hundred dollars in the savings
bank, and equally the legal right of the millionaire to his
millions') and Edison (on genius being '1 per cent inspiration
and 99 per cent perspiration') with seventeenth-century wisdom from *The Japanese Family Storehouse, or, The Millionaire's Gospel* of Ihara Saikaku, viz. 'to steer through life on
an honest course to the splendors of success – this is a feat
reserved for paragons of our kind, a task beyond the nature
of normal man'.

In general, I should say, the most quotable foreign wisdom
is patchily admitted, and when admitted given the most
unmemorable and execrable English form – 'Here are tears
of things; mortality touches the heart.'

I was going to remark that the new *Bartlett* hasn't exactly
caught up with a contemporary openness: to remark that it is
no use coming here to check that effing 'is the lyricism of the
people' (Baudelaire) or to verify that nicely turned – American – translation from Jacques Prévert,

God the Father who art in Heaven
Stay there.

But I do have to admit that a nitric drop has now and then
been allowed to fall into the homey unction. At any rate two
such drops. E. E. Cumming's Olaf the conscript does declare
'there is some s— I will not eat', and that he 'will not kiss
your f.ing flag'. Perhaps this is just one little double gesture –
since they calculate such things editorially in America – to all
possible users and purchasers who are anti-draft and anti-
Vietnam?

Should I conclude that, by and large, this *Bartlett* is
tailored to a mores lingering on our side of the Atlantic, let's

say in mental corners of Belfast, Lampeter and St Andrews?
Or should I more correctly pronounce that it is attuned, with
an American accent, to the shattering vulgarity of a lower
mental class which exists, semi-literate, in every country,
though in our own it expresses itself less blatantly and often
– so far – and is less obsequiously flattered?

What I shan't forgo is making my own quotation, my own
special quotation, from that historical note contributed by
the editor: 'Donne's "No man is an island", famous as the
source of Hemingway's novel *For Whom the Bell Tolls*.'

True, of course. But – our poor John Donne undone again
– it does indicate the key.

1969

On Collecting One's Reviews

Mr Anthony Burgess has collected his reviews.[1] Of this I do not complain altogether, things being what they are. Yet dog proceeding to eat dog, I shall ask, How does one review reviews?

Perhaps, to begin with, by abstracting sentences, to get at the mind of the reviewing writer, at his mental style; which I shall do, with one or two comments.

Page 11. Writing books 'engenders tobacco-addiction, an over-reliance on caffeine and dexedrine, piles, dyspepsia, chronic anxiety, sexual impotence'.

Not in everyone. And not all of them, I hope, in Mr Burgess.

Page 22. 'Mere authors will continue to despair of their ability to approach that prose perfection' – of the books of Evelyn Waugh.

Page 23. 'He is as welcome as is Apethorpe.' Style.

Page 31. 'It is right for the European novel to be interested in disease, since Europe itself is a disease – exquisitely but treacherously mined with fistulas.' – No comment.

Page 63. 'With the general acceptance of Yeats's greatness, a lot of life has gone out of Yeats criticism.' This is too bad.

Page 66. Taking Yeats's verse seriously 'means not poring over it in the study, but declaiming it to the waves and over pints of draught Guinness'. This is very masculine.

Page 89. 'Dylan was the greatest lyric poet of the twentieth century.'

Page 91. 'Look for a parallel to him' – Dylan Thomas again – 'in the literature of the past, and you won't go far wrong if you adduce Virgil.' A contradiction?

[1] *Urgent Copy: Literary Studies*, by Anthony Burgess (1968).

Page 99. 'Lament for a Maker'. Novel title for an obituary piece on T. S. Eliot.

These fair samples bring one about a third of the way through. I have quoted them less because they are silly (but some of them are surely a trifle bizarre?) than because the words do exhibit a quality – unlike the blue in Cézanne – which no one will find other than coarse and unattractive, I should think, or hope.

I find a desire to please, in rather an ignoble or sneaking way (the style that slaps its own back, and ours: 'One goes back to them' – the Pre-raphaelites – 'with love whenever one of our art students starts whining that nobody will buy the canvases he's ridden over with a wet bicycle.'). I suspect this reviewer's anxiety to convince himself (perhaps more than others?) that an insatiable liking for words amounts to an ability to use them well and to distinct purpose. Only some such literary anxiousness coupled with energy could explain writing and writing on with a badness at once so surprisingly defiant and so exceedingly obvious, or could explain the way Mr Burgess throws about in such a mode references to the obscurities of his own scholarship – 'Diffidently, since my Persian is rusty' – or the way he will drop suddenly into the argot of the academic: 'Mr Murray's survey of Milton's comparatively recent rehabilitation appears at the same time as the revised edition of E. M. W. Tillyard's indispensable long study, *Milton*.' It's no knockabout clown you're reading after all, literary editors.

Another trick – an allied trick – is to be where the rest of us usually are not. 'I was in Russia when Ernest Hemingway died.' Well, if he was, the fact doesn't in any real way affect what little Mr Burgess goes on to tell us about the art of Hemingway. He might as well have begun that he was paying his rates at the council offices or catching crayfish at Piddletrenthide or declaiming Yeats over pints of Guinness above the waves of the Bournemouth sewage outfall, when Hemingway died. In short I can never quite believe Mr Burgess, in this book (I know nothing of his novels). 'Old yokels in Adderbury, my former Oxfordshire home, talk of the Earl of Rochester as though he only died yesterday.' Really? And as they talk of him in their smock-frocks do they quote with an Oxfordshire – not Oxford – accent 'Drudging in fair Aurelia's womb' or 'Ancient Person of my Heart'?

Of course, like other readers (or reviewers) Mr Burgess is often sensible. He does promote one or two notions – for example, art offers unity instead of conflict; which really is no more than one of many puffs of wind from some familiar quarter filling out Mr Burgess's jeans and shorts to a masculine or muscular semblance on the clothes line of this rather small back garden. When I was younger 'collecting one's reviews' was a familiar sneer – I have used it myself in writing of others than Mr Burgess. But this is a parsimonious society which can spare little money to authors and little space for periodical criticism. So the sneer is perhaps antiquarian; and it *is* – it has to be – possible to say something in little. Even so I like the reviews I read – if this is not being too idiosyncratic for our day – less shaggy and loud, and less in the public bar.

1968

Emily Dickinson Reconsidered

There are some collected poems it is necessary to disconnect – if poetry is still to be considered an art – from the possibly affecting quality or tragedy, as it may be, of the poet's life. That is so with Emily Dickinson.[1] Americans, divorced from Europe, incline even now to exaggerate the merits of an American product. We flatter them, too. Our publishers, our encyclopedia promoters, our critics quite often, ingratiate themselves, like dogs on their backs hoping for more dog biscuit from the full American cupboard if they carefully fail to estimate an American painter or poet or novelist with the strictness they would apply to the home-born.

If the American product can be shown, also, to have come out of an interesting, pathetic, or enigmatic life, the trick is done. So Emily Dickinson is observed, spinster of Amherst, renunciant victim of forbidden love, dressed in white in her garden, a family recluse given to death, God, eternity, remembered love; writing, if her editor's projected count is to be relied upon, no fewer than 357 poems in the one year of 1862.

How wonderful! How moving! How mysteriously (outside ambition and all the other vulgarities of life from celebrity to profit or Allen Ginsberg) does Art, in the most unlikely places, follow its trail of destiny and fulfilment!

Among such exclamations only the poems fail to be inspected closely or with enough scepticism. Here the sacred myth of the 'nun of Amherst' has the support of 1,775 poems, short, in short lines, tripping (which is the *mot juste*, metrically) through a great many years of Miss Dickinson's self-isolation.

Before we make an estimate either of the best poems – O that weariness, to add one more exclamation, of going

[1] *The Complete Poems of Emily Dickinson*, edited by Thomas H. Johnson (1970).

through all the seventeen hundred and seventy-five of them!
– or of the corpus as now assembled and finalized, a few
things need to be said.

Raising his hands in worship, the editor preserves the
sacred idiosyncrasies of Miss Dickinson's often daily jotting.
She wasn't one for commas, colons, etc., only for dashes. She
was one (like other mid-nineteenth-century ladies, un-
delivered from the habits of the previous century) for
capitalization. Keep every hallowed dash, every hallowed
cap. So a poem, good or bad, has to combine jerk with trip,
to its damage:

> Are we that wait – sufficient worth –
> That such Enormous Pearl
> As life – dissolved be – for Us –
> In Battle's – horrid Bowl.

She could also at times, or often, be the whimsically sententious writer of album verses for her more or less private eye;
which means that she wrote on subjects; which can be easily
catalogued, unlike the subtler properties of verse, be the
writer Dickinson, Stitch, or Strong; which introduces, yes, a
Subject Index – Trees, Trial, Tribulation, victory over,
Triumph, Trust, Truth, Tulip.

Returning myself to Miss Dickinson, after years in which
I had been little tempted into her desolate garden, I would
calculate that she wrote (with a plus and minus like a radio-
carbon date) some thirty-five poems of remarkable success;
many as well in which there are surprising lines (though
what surprises us first in a Dickinson poem can resolve itself
quickly into nothing much). The best of the remarkable
poems catch us (when translated into sensible orthography)
in a cold grip, are pitiless to the self, to the reader, to life
(and to God, some of them, in her still theistical age). They
are fresh, colloquial, vividly untainted by fashion; death and
love poems without benefit of intervention of hope, despair,
or peace. Such are 'I feel a funeral, in my brain', 'I reason,
Earth is short', 'The Soul selects her own society', 'It might
be lonelier/Without the loneliness', 'After great pain, a for-

mal feeling comes'. Others, including 'It was a quiet way', or
'I died for Beauty', or

> Least rivers, docile to some sea,
> My Caspian, thee,

are total love poems.

Most of the remainder we could do without. They are
characterized, *ad nauseam*, by rhythmical monotony, and
similarity of form and mode, by an amateurism which is
exactly that of a Sunday painter, miss more than hit, who
could afford – in her case – to go Sunday painting seven days
a week. But then Emily Dickinson's exemplar in verse seems
to have been Emerson almost alone. Hardly a more feeble
one could be thought of.

Driving through her vast collection, what I remembered
was Yeats, in his *Trembling of the Veil*, warning us – a very
necessary warning now – of that 'chief temptation of the
artist, creation without toil'.

To say that most of Emily Dickinson's verse is worthless,
that she is usually a poet of meaning, not of words, substance,
or style, does not slight her desolation or bravery. It does
affirm that poetry amounts only to itself; that, however it
relates to such things, it is a substance other than autobiography, crucifixion, terror, despair, relief, enjoyment, or
information.

Not that thirty-five plus or minus is a poor total.

1970

Poems in Early Plain English: Edwin Arlington Robinson

Poetry nationalism is a game newly exaggerated. I see English poets – poets, that is, who write in English, even poets who have lived most of their lives or all their lives inside an English circumference of the place or the mind – claimed in various anthologies as Irish, Scotch or Welsh. Robert Graves in this way is at times 'Welsh', at times 'Irish' (he was in Wales as a child, his father was from Ireland). In Scotch anthologies I have seen kilts or some national vestment of the Lowlands draped around John Davidson, Harold Monro of the Poetry Bookshop, and my friend Norman Cameron, who was Scotch certainly, but never inclined to think of himself in the clothes of nationality. Also there is a Welsh anthology making Hopkins (because he liked Wales, lived awhile in sight of the mountains, and made some study of Welsh metrics) and Edward Thomas of London, Wiltshire, and the South, into Welsh poets, not to forget an Irish anthology rooting for the essential Irishness of Swift, Emily Brontë, Edward Fitzgerald, Oscar Wilde, and again Robert Graves.

Anthologists should stop being so ridiculous, particularly at this time when Americans, users of English in a big way, are taking over the language (and taking over some poets of English birth and nurture), and are so very exercised about *American* arts – especially if they are professors teaching the young.

What are *American* poems and *American* pictures? It is true they are now less copied – or revived – from European originals. Even so, to the European an italicized emphasis of that kind may seem to be a concentration on the wrong word, when he comes at least to read such a book as *The Continuity of American Poetry* by Professor Roy Harvey Pearce. As

Europeans – if we are not Welsh, Scotch, or Irish – we have not had to indulge in questions of that kind to any extent for a long while. As Europeans, whether English, Russian, Italian, German, French, or Finnish, we may feel it better to ask about poetry; which involves poems, whereas asking about American poetry involves history, a process which poems try to defeat.

Beginning in the seventeenth century Professor Pearce sees poetry in America as 'a series of songs of oneself', poets in America as a series of Adams, a series of first men, who have to look via their poems for a self-justification: each poet, each 'first man', is a guardian of the idea of man, necessarily a guardian of his (and so of all) human dignity, in a long, special, unremitting, ocean-to-ocean case of indignity and indifference. Now and again a non-Adam occurs, a poet – an Eliot, a John Crowe Ransom – relying not on a song of himself, but on an appeal to myth or culture (non-American).

This seems both interesting and true. But since Professor Pearce has been concerned, as he says, 'with the history which poems have made', it does mean that poems, *per se*, manage to be left out, or to evaporate; and long before he has read to the four hundredth page the reader will have concluded that in this procession from the overrated Puritan poet Edward Taylor to the overrated Adam (or half Adam, half mythologist) of our time, Wallace Stevens, the quality or effectivity of their writing hardly counts: to be an Adam is all, i.e. to be an *American* poet is all.

Even now the words which American poems are made of are still English words, mostly common to Englishmen and to Americans. So it is still possible for English readers to estimate American poems without inaccuracy. There are two conclusions they may come to: that modern fight-talk for *American* art causes too much writing which sniffs all round the stockade of poetry, but never enters – writing like that of Professor Pearce; that it also produces too much national-istic confusion of the feeble (which may fit a thesis) with the energetic and living (which is quite indifferent to any thesis).

Also if literary nationalism now does such a bad thing when it so absolutely divides verse in English into English and American verse (what are we going to do with Eliot, and

Auden? where are they to go?), I must also think that both
the English and the Americans do another bad thing, in
unison: publishers, poets, and their executors treat poems too
much as property: they charge too much for the reproduction
of poems, they reduce in this way the number of a poet's
poems in those anthologies which, like it or not, are the
means of introducing poets to those who become their firm
readers.

The case which makes me think of this at the moment is
that of Edwin Arlington Robinson. Here is one good
(American) poet who has suffered, certainly in England, from
this pair of unblest causes. Not many English readers – there
being literary chauvinism or intellectual laziness on both
sides – know much more of Robinson than his excellent yet
not so characteristic 'Miniver Cheevy', the poem of the
nostalgic New Englander who was born too late and kept on
thinking – who

> . . . coughed, and called it fate,
> And kept on drinking.

Now there is a selection of him, and a good one, published
on our side of the dividing curtain.[1] But I don't think many
people are going to buy it; I don't think it will be widely or
at all enthusiastically reviewed.

In hopes of a reader or two let me add the briefest note of
introduction. This poet of the ironic generation of Edgar Lee
Masters of the *Spoon River Anthology*, of Stephen Crane and
– to mix the nationalities for a moment – of Belloc and
Kipling, died in 1935. Early on he had his English favourites,
and two of them – he reminds me of both at times – were
Thomas Hood, 'who spat more blood and made more puns
than any other man' (according to his own epitaph), and
Crabbe, of 'Peter Grimes', of the sad nightmares in which he
was chased and beaten by leather lads.

Life in his poems is something like Hood's 'Haunted
House', it is haunted by nothingness, by no explanation, and
there is no consolation. For the men and women, in their
separate poems, who inhabit his Tilbury Town (as you might

[1] *Selected Poems of Edwin Arlington Robinson*, edited by
M. D. Zabel (1965).

say, his Dorking or Berkhamsted), living is a cage, even in comfort, under the rule of uncertainty or illusion, or might have been, or disillusion.

Sometimes he makes a poem toll with a repetition of such lines as 'They are all gone away', or

> Go to the western gate, Luke Havergal,
> Luke Havergal.

More often, as if the wind of actuality cut out the tolling, there is not even the ritual comfort of a bell as he spins a poem from the wavering, the doubts, the loneliness of his Seneca Sprague, at last talking out to the woman who never marries him, never lets him go, or of his old Eben Flood, having a party with himself, and talking to himself, and drinking with himself, under the harvest moon; the wavering, the doubts, the loneliness of all the rest of his Tilbury people, who are seldom far from the cemetery –

> He raised again the jug regretfully
> And shook his head, and was again alone.
> There was not much that was ahead of him.

A poetry dismal in effect? No, one which pricks the reader out of his complacency, disturbs him, and then lays a rhythmical benediction, if not absolution, on his disturbance.

Do I find this Adam of a nothingness specifically American, or sufficiently English? Both. And that way things should remain, remembering, as I say, that poetry is poems, and not flags or intonations.

Also – a point of sympathy – doesn't the specific nothingness in which Edwin Arlington Robinson deals, doesn't the consciousness of it, the feeling of it, seem now to be spreading across England, especially of the South and the Midlands?

1965

Lawrence Twice Over

1. D. H. Lawrence and the Foxgloves

I think it was Graham Greene who remarked that (author's) fame was a powerful aphrodisiac. It became both a stimulant and a powerful inhibitor of taste or judgement in another sense. A wave of increasing fame buoys an author – and few have the nerve or the coolness to examine the work, the nerve to disagree with the increasing overestimate, an entire process which also works in reverse, in cases of disparagement or neglect. Lawrence: could there be a better case of this inhibition of judgement? Or a better example of the subordination of the work to the hero? The academics are at him, swarmingly in America and in England. They are over him, they are in him, like maggots. They inch-worm the house in which he was born, the farm where he visited the Miriam of *Sons and Lovers*. Texas reaches out to Notts, and ageing memories, and bits are swept together, with the dust; the validity of which depends upon how just and strict the estimate is, *au fond*.

Two results are the exhumation of the 'personal record' by E.T., i.e. Jessie Chambers, i.e. Miriam, i.e. the girl Lawrence knew in his adolescence,[1] and the publication of *The Croydon Years*,[2] scraped together from the readings of a schoolteacher who knew Jessie Chambers and was close to Lawrence for a while in his own schoolteaching time.

Biographically, for picking and indications, they have their value. Absolutely, both books are valueless. *The Croydon Years* does not require much notice. Miss Helen Corke is an elderly lady, a history teacher in retirement, whose amateur writings on the electric creature she once

---

[1] *D. H. Lawrence: A Personal Record*, by E.T. (Jessie Chambers), new edition (1965).

[2] *The Croydon Years*, by Helen Corke (Austin, Texas, 1965).

knew have been assembled by the University of Texas.
Lawrence was remarkable, the two women were not; the
way in which Lawrence is recalled by Miss Corke and the
effrontery of the 'deferred conversation' between herself and
Lawrence on *Apocalypse* are likely to make the uncantharid-
ized reader mildly impatient.

> Our minds are extraordinarily intimate, and their percep-
> tions reciprocal. Our physical relationship has been that of
> brother and sister, but since early summer I have become
> increasingly aware of the demand that he, as instinctive
> man, makes upon me as woman. I cannot indefinitely
> ignore it; but there is no instinctive response of my body.
> My desire is not towards him.

Bother her desire, bother this excerpt, as it seems from an
unpublished novel by a retired schoolmistress which she is
reading at a local literary society (in fact it is 'autobiography').

Both women speak of the wonder of Lawrence, in his
twenties: but they don't establish it, in their words, in their
reporting. Miss Corke appears to have written of Lawrence
in the early Sixties, nearly fifty years after her association
with him. Jessie Chamber's *Record* first published in 1935,
five years after Lawrence's death, was nearer the bright man,
she did not have to go fishing and wishing in her memory:
she met Lawrance when she was fourteen, and lost him
when she was twenty-five: Lawrence had been the man and
the marvel of her youth – to whom, as her writing shows, she
was entirely inadequate.

She provides information, she is siftable for his life, if the
sieve is used with care, at that time of vivid early being in a
writer's career which to our loss is so very seldom observed
and recorded by others. But she is not Dorothy Wordsworth
writing of her brother, or Helen Thomas writing of Edward
Thomas, or even Mrs Hardy writing of her architect. He was
'a man apart', 'we were in a world apart', 'shining eyes',
'spontaneous gaiety', the 'mellow chimes', the 'soft radiance
of the moonlight', 'drinking in the beauty of the scene',
'I felt that I was in the presence of greatness'.

Her writing is of that order; and this girl of a suffocating

intensity, a pupil teacher like Lawrence, was for all her
recognition of him as unusual, too concerned with her own
self to be a recorder of another self's exceptionality: it is
Lawrence as person, as individual, which she hadn't the
skill, or the senses perhaps, to capture and hold, anywhere,
in any sentence. In the end she feels betrayed *in toto* by
Lawrence, not because he gave her up inch after inch, but
because the Miriam based on herself was defeated in the
novel by the Mrs Morel based on Lawrence's powerful
fiend of a mother: Mrs Lawrence had rejected her, in the
portrait of Miriam Mrs Lawrence's valuation was victori-
ous again. Lawrence had for always taken his mother's
side.

An understandable but narrow confusion, such an un-
truth, or such a truth only to herself. One sympathizes, closes
the door on her privacy, and re-enters the fiction.

Lawrence, however much one may feel that as writer (or
prophet or hero) he needs trimming to the actual, was as
bound to escape the cling of such a personality as he was
bound to escape from Bert into D.H. (rather than the snobbish 'David' of Miss Corke's recollections), or from values of
the Congregational Sunday School in his miners' village or
from the assumptions of those who taught him in Notting-
ham University College.

Yet Lawrence himself. The bright being. Isn't there also a
Lawrentian air of fake, of attitude, of truth twisted too often
to himself, or his thinking? And doesn't this go into the flabby
muscle, as it frequently is, of the way he writes?

I wouldn't make much of contradictions in these recorded
enthusiasms of a boy feeling his way into literary existence,
strange and self-cancelling as one may find, for example, a
passion for *Walden* coupled with a passion for the vapidities
of George Borrow. But in this personal record which is so
much too personal with the wrong person, there is a passage
which I thought unpleasantly true of Lawrence. Jessie and
Bert, pupil teachers both, go to the wood by Jessie's farm,
the Haggs, where she wishes to show him a colony of tall
foxgloves. She discusses Lawrence and flowers:

There seemed no flower nor even weed whose name and

qualities Lawrence did not know. At first I was sceptical of his knowledge.

'How do you know what it is?' I asked him.

'I *do* know,' he replied.

'But *how* do you know? You may be wrong,' I persisted.

'I know *because* I know. How dare you ask me how I know,' he answered with heat.

Of course he often didn't know about objects, about what was external to him – from flowers to men or women; in spite of popular opinion, he is an astonishingly, not unobservant but malobservant writer, who also twists objects from their realness, often lies about them, and prefers exclamation to objectivity. But – I know because I know. How dare you ask me how I know. And the daring isn't done, very often; though it is this readiness to pander to his own falsities, which, as I say, underlies so much unconvincingness in his writing, in his prose more than in his verse, where he has less room to strike attitudes, to cheat, and to use his sugar castor of *hot, blood, dark, soul, deep, strange, naked,* etc. There are similar weaknesses of the lie behind, and then in, the writing of Carlyle and Ruskin – a weakness of apocalypsy no doubt, all three, Carlyle, Ruskin and Lawrence, reminding me at times of a dowser sending thought out to various objects.

If I am correct, if to a wide degree Lawrence was a fabricator, a *flâneur* in relation to language, a liar of a kind whose lies prompt him to his weak exclamatory prose, then there advances the puzzle of the new acceptance of Lawrence, the lack of criticism of him as an artist, as a writer so extensively without style. There is some element in this puzzle other than Message, a word I do not capitalize with a sneer. One likes a Message, one likes Messages; which are criticized nevertheless, or tested, by their vehicle. I do not know the character of the American acceptance or eulogy of Lawrence; but I think the English acceptance has to do with class and with the fairly new emergence and liberation, as yet incomplete, into literacy and into the professions, especially teaching, of many more thousands of such people as Lawrence himself or the family at the Haggs. American readers may not recognize the role, vis-à-vis each other, of English

nonconformity (e.g. in religion, in chapel-going, in being
Baptist, Methodist, Congregationalist – or Jewish) and the
conformity of the Accepted. I suspect there is a strong degree
of this defiant rejection of conformity and 'inferiority' in the
defiance and the tortured English of the criticism (and the
habitually polemic correspondence) of F. R. Leavis, certainly
in the attitudes of those who have been trained in his influence. The emergence of Lawrence (nowadays I think he
would have remained Bert Lawrence), his defiance, his disdain of the bourgeoisie, blind them to the lie in Lawrence
and to his hollow bravura; perhaps to the truth in him as
well. Too often we need liberating from a liberator, so that
we can see again the reality of his virtue.

Perhaps the requirement in this case might be a stiff cool
dose of *The Prelude*? Or of some big brute of an unflawed
masterpiece, loud and prolonged?

1966

2. *Praeputium Laurentii*

It was inevitable that someone, some day, in the hagiographical pursuit of D. H. Lawrence, would assemble and
reproduce his pictures. I saw these celebrated pictures in
Dorothy Warren's gallery in London in 1929, before the
exhibition was closed by the police; there wasn't much
obscene or repellent about them except pretentiousness. But
then Lawrence had the modesty at times of a brass trombone.
He liked painting, he came to good, unoriginal conclusions
about it, he considered art was delight or nothing; and then
acted, by allowing that exhibition in Maddox Street, as if his
private delight in efforts to paint, Lawrence being Lawrence,
produced 'art', and not something very much else.

Still the police were interested in members, not pretensions
– in extensions; which occur ('I . . . put a phallus . . . in each
of my pictures somewhere'), but appear as rather poor
dangling little creatures, scared at being out, and not at all
answering to his 'positive belief that the phallus is a great
sacred image'. 'And I paint no picture that won't shock
people's castrated social spirituality.' O what a shocker I am!

But he's not. Lawrence hadn't the skill to shock, with paints and a brush. His pretention in believing that he had goes unrecognized in the entranced essays accompanying these wriggly jobs of lard male and lard female reproduced in Mervyn Levy's album.[3]

The essays breathe uphill all the way to a piece by Herbert Read. But first an editorial alleges that Lawrence '"saw" as a painter, and could always create in his writing, when he wished, an arresting sense of the pictorial'. Professor Harry T. Moore (to every great man his professor, in the end) bungles an effort to establish this by quoting a peculiarly unpictorial piece about Mount Etna which shows Lawrence as an unpictorial writer to the pitch of falsity who as a rule tried too hectically to see from the inside ever to notice outsides (is this to be called intuition or extuition?).

'I saw a girl with handsome bare legs', 'the lake is not beautiful', 'he was very handsome, beautiful rather' – such are typical Lawrentian views of the outside. 'Staring kills my vision.'

With Herbert Read's piece the reader and viewer comes, I am afraid, to the hilltop and prospect-tower of the nugatory. He intimates, to begin with, that the paintings are not, in fact, worth very much: we shouldn't bother if they had not been painted by a writer of genius. Pages elapse. These paintings, for Mr Read, have now become 'an integral part of his genius'; 'every picture lives'.

By the end the pictures, poor daubs, have been whisked up in the elevator above the biographical and the artistic floors to the Moral or the Moral Imperative: faced by the visual evidence of a great spirit's self-liberating struggles, we are challenged 'to cast off our own inhibitions'.

But the challenging power in art is artness, not – this is San Lorenzo's Day – not relics, to be worshipped and fingered, and perhaps bitten off, by the devout; and Herbert Read's argument (derived from the hagiographical application of history to art and letters?) is clerk's treason, of the kind, qualify it though he does, which confuses the willing self-educator, and harms what is good or excellent in Lawrence.

[3] *Paintings of D. H. Lawrence*, edited by Mervyn Levy (1964).

Lawrence said: 'The profound sensual experience of truth: Yes, this *is*! alone satisfies us, in the end.' Of course. But we can't say that of his pictures, in which concept is uninvolved in execution.

It is a question, not of forgiving or excusing Lawrence, since one accepts the absurdities of any considerable writer, but of recognizing the sottishness of those who become too soaked in emotion about art.

All the same, a sheepish epitomizing item ought not to be passed by. Lawrence admired Etruscan tomb painting and talked of the 'wonderfully suggestive *edge* of the figures'. Good. And then (it is here again, among the plates) he worked a copy of such an edged Etruscan figure – in wool.

1964

Walter the Rhymer

Years ago, in 1940, Walter de la Mare was persuaded to leave the Huntlie banks for a studio in Broadcasting House, where he discussed poetry with a poet of the Thirties (himself, on reckoning of the same kind, having been a poet of the Nineties or of the first decade of our century). 'Well', True Walter led off, *seniores priores*, 'before we begin our discussion, and even perhaps to disagree, I am confident of one thing, our love of poetry. We shouldn't be here now if we didn't share this consuming interest' – on which a different poet of the Thirties commented some weeks later that 'such a love of poetry is a slow poison poured around the roots of poetry and life.'

In that declaration of his, in which Walter de la Mare was neither entirely true nor entirely false to himself, and in that counter-comment which wasn't entirely misconceived, the virtues of a most remarkable poet lie too much obscured. There may be, I am sure there are, poems by de la Mare (that poetical name!) in the head of everyone at this moment who makes a habit of reading poetry, or writing poetry. But these current poems by de la Mare are few; and as if they had pushed long ago into heads which do not want them, are embarrassed by them, yet cannot get rid of them, a pontificator about the verse of our time never says 'de la Mare!' as he would shout Wallace Stevens, or Pound, or Heaven knows what other name at this moment, in a reflex action of intellectuality. He doesn't even whisper 'de la Mare' as an afterthought.

Why should he? The period style, which lapped around the personal style, is dead. But of course that is not a necessary invalidation; and now that we have all of de la Mare as a poet, more than a thousand poems, written over a space of sixty-two years, from 1894 or thereabouts, when de la Mare was twenty-one, to 1956 when he died,[1] we can ask, and have the full means of answering, the necessary questions.

Have we failed to do our sifting properly? Has de la Mare's present lack of high or urgent reputation been his own fault, the consequence of a too consuming 'love of poetry'? A fault of the kind of talent he possessed and developed, a fault of acquiescence as well as period? When enough time separates us from the alien quality of a literary style, and a life style as well, which we despise, shall we be able to accept again what we now so easily, or too easily, reject? And how much of it?

The second part of this complete de la Mare assembles nearly four hundred poems from scattered sources, as well as forty-nine poems which were never published. Most of these are bad or middling, only one or two will be found equal to his best. For answers, then, one must go still to the canonical collections, starting at the start with the emergence of 'Walter Ramal' in *Songs of Childhood*, in 1902. Then, as afterwards, de la Mare (who was by origin plain Walter John Delamare) gave way to a velvet-jacketed insipidity of innocence much *à la mode* in the first decades of the century. Fairies were about, ideal nannies presided over ideal nurseries inhabited by children of exactly the right degree of naughtiness, elders indulged in the wrought iron gate, and the denizens, of the Herb Garden.

Not long before these beginnings of de la Mare, Lady Alicia Gomme, in the popular pursuit of drawing-room folklore, had published her *Traditional Games of England, Scotland, and Ireland*, in two volumes, Volume I Accroshag to Nuts in May, Volume II Oats and Beans to Would You Know, a work which was to contribute much to *Come Hither*, and contributed meanwhile to the charms and versicles of this child poet of twenty-nine. De la Mare's early titles, or many of them, read like the game titles given by Lady Gomme, not a few of his early poems read like the snatches of game song excerpted and sentimentalized (in *Traditional Games*, runs a note in *Come Hither*, 'more than seven hundred games are described, including Rakes and Roans, Rockety Row, Sally Go Round the Moon, Shuttlefeather, Spannims,

[1] *The Complete Poems of Walter de la Mare* (1970).

Tods and Lambs, Whigmaleerie, Allicomgreenzie, Bob-Cherry, Oranges and Lemons, Cherry Pit, Thimble-bones, Lady on Yandor Hill, Hechefragy, and Snail Creep').

From such sources, from nursery rhyme, from the fairyism of Jacobean poetry, from border ballads, from herbals, de la Mare elaborated that word usage one encounters with discomfiting effect, and almost with incredulity. His adjectives were *dim* and *wan* and *thin* and *faint* and *wee*, his substances were such as foam and ivory; moon attached itself to shoon, ghosties, gnomies kept company to sounds of lute and jargoning, with beautiful ladies in cramosie, in a mist of glamourie, among fields of rosemary, tansy, pimpernel, asphodel and eglantine; though witches at hand might be infusing dwale.

Looking back from the talks studio of 1940, was this the substance of a love of poetry? The proper object of a consuming interest? De la Mare knew that poetry was more than such words, that there was more to his own poems than the beauty-words he was employing. But one may suppose it to have been the associational keepings of his vocabulary, of his properties, which won him so quick a celebrity. His third book, *Poems* (1906) – the second had been his prose romance *Henry Brocken*, in 1904 – was scarcely out two years before this young man in business, in the City, was awarded a pension on the Civil List; and if in 1912 *The Listeners and Other Poems* was less elfin, but not less haunted, he proffered full acceptable measure again, within a year, in *Peacock Pie*: many poems in which made it one of the most minikin finicking books ever published by a writer of ability.

Certainly one can pick ten or twelve virtuous poems out of the original eighty-two in *Peacock Pie*. These would include 'Five Eyes', 'All but Blind', 'Grim', 'Tit for Tat', 'Old Shell-over' (suggested by Snail Creep in Lady Gomme's *Traditional Games?*), 'The Song of Shadows', 'The Song of the Mad Prince', 'The Song of Finis'. Yet as edition followed edition, did de la Mare wryly regard, let us say, that extraordinary offering 'Peak and Puke' –

From his cradle in the glamourie
They have stolen my wee brother,
Housed a changeling in his swaddlings

For to fret my own poor mother.
Pules it in the candle light
Wi' a cheek so lean and white,
Chinkling up its eyne so wee,

– and so on? He never removed it, at any rate (it remains in
the *Collected Rhymes and Verses* of 1944).

In no future collection was Walter de la Mare ever to sink
so low, or so much to succumb – frequent though his lapses –
to the perils of being of the family of Herrick (with whom he
shared an epicene nature) or Browne of Tavistock, or Edgar
Allen Poe or Christina Rossetti.

There is a late poem, 'The Outcasts', one of the few by
de la Mare one may take to be autobiographical, other than
in the wide sense, in which he seems to turn against his early
celebrity, accusing Fame of having sucked his life-blood and
killed his youth:

And on her hated body I begat
Twenty abortions, but not one called truth.

A 'Vile conviction' had crept into him that he had lived like
a spider living on a fly. Certainly in this poet coeval, more or
less with Yeats, with Hofmannsthal, with Rilke (or with
Gorki and Gide), there had been no climactic realization of
the objective, no spare Yeatsian renewal; which is to be
explained by a shortcoming of intellect? But then one poet
cannot have all the gifts.

It was something, all the same, it was the self – if no more?
– that Walter de la Mare had exhibited in the poems of 1906
and 1912 and thereabouts; the line, the movement, the disturbance, in the best of them (which should include 'The
Comb', as well as those quickly familiar, unstaling pieces
'Napoleon', the 'Winter' which ends 'snow, snow, more
snow', 'All That's Past', and 'The Listeners'). What of course
many people at various levels accepted and enjoyed fifty
years ago, if few or none of them analysed it in any deep or
sophisticated degree (since it seemed to call for nothing of
the kind), was the unique subtlety of rhythmical and formal
invention, the 'deceptive cadences', 'the inexplicable mystery
of sound'.

For example, how early does de la Mare begin to work out
the possibilities of that simple inversion, enabling him so
often to dispense with the sound cliché of compounded
verbs, and providing him with a new, dramatic, strangely
resonant line? As far back as 'All That's Past' in *The
Listeners* –

> Through what wild centuries
> Roves back the rose

– or farther back, in the 'Characters from Shakespeare' which
began his *Poems* of 1906; de la Mare having found the clue
to this special device perhaps in the blue and gold Muses
Library edition of William Browne, published when he was
twenty-one.

His best cadences might not run often through the best
words, the words of the most direct and fresh connotation –

> Sad winds where your voice was;
> Tears, tears, where my heart was;
> And even with me,
> Child, even with me,
> Silence where hope was

– yet the effects can only have come from ceaseless self-
audition, from a ceaseless about-and-about with the line,
then with lines in combination, stanzas in combination. First
a cadence, then that cadence in words? It could have been
understood, perhaps, that the witch, the witchery, the
glamourie, the falsity of the words, was after all being
threaded on to life.

Circe, or whatever witch there is, exacts her reality, nevertheless: and looks for more. Sleep with her – read 'The
Journey' – and be brought again inevitably

> To the beauty of earth that fades in ashes,
> The lips of welcome, and the eyes
> More beauteous than the feeble shine of Hesper
> Lone in the lightening skies,

or choose 'the dark night's inhospitality'? A shivering prospect, however decorous de la Mare's expression of it.

Anthologists followed him that far, and about as far as

Motley and Other Poems, his collection of 1918. But then they faltered for various reasons. Yeats was one example, in that peculiar *Oxford Book of English Verse*. He included 'The Scribe', out of *Motley*: from *The Listeners*, the name poem, 'Winter' ('Clouded with snow') and 'All That's Past'; and from the earliest collections 'Echo' and 'The Silver Penny'. Out of *Motley* he balked at such poems as 'The Ghost' ('the sweet cheat gone'), 'The Revenant' ('Men all are shades, O Women'), 'Alone', 'Farewell', 'The Unchanging', and 'Life' (we must each be 'Of all things lovely the cold mortuary'). No mortuary for Yeats: the earthy, the passionate, however old he was; not abandonment, disillusion, or even the most exquisite resonance, on strings, of desolation or defeat. He would have found this content running through all of de la Mare in the end – as we may find it, and be depressed by it, in the spectrum of his work.

Yeats's introduction to the *Oxford Book* is less read than it should be. He confines de la Mare in a corner, with those descended not from Homer but from Virgil – with Binyon, Sturge Moore, and Edith Cooper, the younger of the two constituents of 'Michael Field'. He spoke of the 'facile charm', the 'too soft simplicity', which had been forced on post-Victorian writers, himself included, by reaction from Victorian rhetoric; adding that, in England, the necessary correction had been made by Thomas Hardy, 'through his mastery of the impersonal objective scene'.

That was in 1936. Seven years ago W. H. Auden made a selection from de la Mare. It is not altogether to be recommended, it gives status to rather much of the slightly whimsical, for one thing, it includes too much of the rather slow and heavy. But by the time Mr Auden reached the poems of *Motley* and *The Veil* (1921), he was not a quarter of the way through de la Mare. Endeavouring to right matters, he drew freely, within his limits, on de la Mare down to *The Inward Companion* of 1950, and *O Lovely England* of 1953. This at least was good, fixing in view many, though not all, the most moving poems of de la Mare's doubt or disillusion. But he stated a conviction, impossible to accept, in all its implication, at any rate – that de la Mare 'continued to mature, both in technique and wisdom, till the day of his death'. In wis-

dom certainly; in technique possibly – in knowing what to do
with the words and music he could still find; but in poems,
in the words and music he actually found, and in their im-
pact, no.

After *The Veil*, that disconcerting, sinister volume, a
change does take possession. It spreads, developing into an
uneasy resignation. The glittering lights, spectral lights, have
ceased to play as a rule, the short and long strings do not
sound. A well cooked, even subtly cooked stodginess super-
venes. De la Mare has turned elsewhere. He ends a poem in
Memory and Other Poems (1938):

> O Master, I cried in my heart, lorn thy tidings,
>   grievous thy song,
> Yet thine, too, this solacing music, as we earthfolk
>   stumble along.

The Master is Thomas Hardy, now influential, too, in the
shape, movement, and language of many of de la Mare's
poems.

Back (on furlough) from his seven times seven years inside
the howe of the fairies, Walter de la Mare in his late forties
has more than once visited old Hardy at Max Gate. They
contemplated tombstones together. But de la Mare told
Hardy that he liked to see them green. Hardy put it on record
that he liked to see them legible, and that he habitually took
with him a small wooden spadelet of his own making to
remove the green moss when he went to see the family graves
at Stinsford.

The best idiosyncratic features of each of them differed
too much (and it was too late, and in spite of Hardy, de la
Mare was still to ask himself – in 'A Portrait' – if the imagined
after all wasn't the breath of life?). Which is only to say that
de la Mare wearing Hardy isn't that de la Mare who flared
up, a phosphorous flame, a bright corpse candle, in certain
poems in *The Veil* – among these 'The Owl', 'The Last
Coachload', 'The Old Angler', 'In the Dock' ('When howls
man's soul, it howls inaudibly'), 'The Unfinished Dream',
'Maerchen', 'Goodbye' ('The last thin rumour of a feeble bell
for ringing, / The last blind rat to spurn the mildewed rye'),
and then died down to the astonishing, again dismaying

flicker of 'A Robin', in *The Fleeting and Other Poems* of 1933, brief victory of the old inversion:

Ghost-grey the fall of night,
  Ice-bound the lane,
Lone in the dying light
  Flits he again.

By the time he had written that, or had made it available, de la Mare was almost sixty. (Another unstodgy poem of his late years to remark, and to love, by the way, is 'The Old Summerhouse'.)

In truth, the best in de la Mare, as in other poets of his kind, did not have to wait on maturity. In such poets a maturity, at least a condition, is quickly established, intermittent, precarious, vulnerable, always tempted to counterfeit the 'something' if it fails to return, often liable to inject an inflationary high significance, beyond the self, into this 'something', the consciousness of which may arise only from one's biochemistry, and often compelled to face emptiness, after all, in shapes of obscenity or terror; out of which may arise many poems in *Motley* and *The Veil* (read also 'A Portrait' and 'Ariel', neighbouring symptoms of self-understanding in *The Burning Glass* of 1945).

So in this poet the best flashes up when it has the chance – for the most part early, in poems published between 1906 and 1921, when he was between thirty-three and forty-eight. The best hangs like a comet in a black sky, the last wisp of whose tail won't be there over the page, or perhaps for many pages, in this complete edition. Or crystals form, and then once more there is only viscous or amorphous stuff; counterfeit even, this last not outnumbered, if for sure outweighed, by poems of the order of 'Napoleon', 'Winter', 'Echo', 'The Bindweed', 'The Listeners' (not always will the Traveller be able to ride away safely from the hollow and empty house), 'The Three Strangers', 'Maerchen', 'The Comb', and 'The Scribe', as well as other poems whose magic (or that personal biochemistry?) is less white altogether.

His verse does find a primary language rather more often than the common characterization of de la Mare allows (the inward eye seeing outward at times with surprising and rewarding clarity – 'lean-stalked purple lavender', a mind 'Whose bindweed can redeem a heap of stones', 'A sappy, dew-bright, flowering hedge of dahlias greened the air').

Also his poems good or bad are all struck from the one substance: they emerge from the always recognizable consciousness which holds in itself a few subjects – the changeling, the revenant, the echoing sound in the empty house – *Who?*, snail life, bindweed flowers, the thin-voiced robin late in the year, the mouse in the wall, silence of snow, the word FINIS, the milk-white of mistletoe berries, the panorama of constellations – and again and again makes poems out of them, no matter whether the poems succeed or fail.

Yet one discovers his best poems by playing them. By means of sound, of cadence – little as common criticism helps with poems which exist in that way, little as it bothers with the scarcely biographical poems of the poet whose *Je est un autre* – these best things by de la Mare are going to prove as durable, in any case, as 'Steer, hither steer your wingèd pines', or 'The White Island', or 'Leonore', or 'In the bleak mid-winter', or 'Into my heart an air that kills'; which will not recommend Walter the Rhymer to some.

1970

That Very Fiery Particle

'Little Keats', wrote Sara Hutchinson (Coleridge's Asra), after seeing him; and perhaps there was something of the particular, something of the small person of the dead man, in Byron's memory when he wrote of the mind of Keats, 'that very fiery particle', having allowed itself (though it did nothing of the kind) to be 'snuff'd out by an article'. Relevant or irrelevant as it may be, we do forget how small a particle of a man Keats was – small, yet beautiful (on the evidence of that mask of his features taken by the assiduous life-masker Benjamin Robert Haydon). 'A small Greek god.' One virtue of the new biography of Keats[1] is that it livens up for us our image of the man who moved about on this earth and that it does emphasize and project his fieriness, his sparkling, crackling electricity, which fought with his death and which is to be seen in the full account of Keats dying slowly, decaying rapidly, in his rooms above the Spanish Steps – hating to die, a very fiery particle, loathing, resenting, screaming against the inevitability of its extinction.

Another virtue – not to speak of mere assiduity in the unclear backwoods of his family life in Moorgate and Enfield – is to leave readers sure of his achievement in fighting for the freedom of his uneasy and contorted nature. Keats looked into Keats with the acuity of a great man, he faced what he found, he was well advanced in sorting it out, in settling his relationship with a mother who had been what – a nymphomaniac? a soak? At any rate, bad (from the child's point of view and need), a traitor, a deserter, a loved and longed-for rejecter of the child's love, responsible for his own unpleasant relationship with women: which must also be investigated by him, straightened out, allowed for, until the imagination was free.

'I am certain of nothing but of the holiness of the Heart's

[1] *John Keats*, by Robert Gittings (1968).

affections and the truth of the Imagination': behind that see the unholiness of the lack of affection in a mother who had married another man less than three months after his father had been killed. That fiery particle was not snuffed out by criticism, only by the disease to which his family was prone, and which he caught by the most faithful nursing – in the holiness of the Heart's affections – of his brother Tom.

A wonderful man, in many ways; and we need to thank Mr Gittings for making this plainer than before. Also on the surface his biography is for no nonsense, no poetry-fawning stuff, about this man of wonder. Yes, he did have a dose of venereal disease, of clap probably, and it wasn't the curate's kind caught by peeing against the wind (for previous wrigglings on that matter, refer to Professor Bates's biography of 1963). Yes, connected with his own specific mother-relationship, with his Enfield upbringing, with his medical student company. Keats did have rather an embarrassing line of jocular sub-talk about male parts into female parts (Appendix Four – rather solemn – 'Keats's Use of Bawdy'). Yes, others have tidied him up in the interest of immortal bardolatry (Mr Gittings gives a nice example, Keats wrote from raining Teignmouth of being 'peedisposed' by Devonshire's 'urinal qualifications': this is edited in the *Letters* to 'predisposed').

So far, fair enough. But then biographies of poets do have to come sooner or later to poems: ultimately aren't they for or about the poems? Here in my opinion Mr Gittings falls into claptrap. The Keatsian problem – see Matthew Arnold, see the correspondence between Hopkins and Coventry Patmore – pivots on the man who might have been, even the actual man, and the actual poems. The poet, the style. The style, though it has been coating our tongues for more than a century, mightn't worry an elderly mistress teaching the Nightingale ode, or an elderly leader-writer on the *Daily Telegraph* (or should I say the *New York Times*?). But I wish it had worried Mr Gittings a little more.

Yes, Keats died at twenty-five. Yes, it is, it seems at least, inconceivable that a man of such fire and intelligence should not in the end have cleaned and changed his style (which is still meretricious, by the way, in *Hyperion*, and in *Lamia*, and in the Autumn ode). But there the style is, the style we have, in the only poems by Keats which we have – saccharine, preferring *cates* to *cakes* and *'tis* to *it's*, falsified with inversions, and adjectives wiggling into *-y*, and adjective-adverbs, and past-participle adjectives trailing into a weakly, poetically pronounced *-èd*, to say nothing of modes of rhythmical ingratiation; a style of, yes, *oozy* neo-classicism whose entablatures are upheld by columns of butterscotch.

I might have had my suspicions, in Mr Gittings's case, when I glanced at the frontispiece: his own copy of the life-mask photographed – I could almost accept it, but it was just a shade too poetic – among grass and daisies, large white garden daisies; and need I explain why this conjunction seems to go rather too well with that Appendix Four: '*Piece*, prostitute. *Ass*, arse... *Vallis Lucis*, valley, sluices, the female pudendum'?

How is it that so much in Keats is not observed? 'Syllabling thus', 'then Lamia breathed death-breath', 'far sunken from *the healthy breath of* morn' – how is it that such impossibilities are not discerned between the tongue, the palate, and the teeth (where poetry is seldom tested academically)? How can Mr Gittings announce with a poker face (but I suppose many others have done it before him) that the opening lines of *Hyperion* are 'one of the high points in all writing'? It does suggest to me a limited and amateur knowledge of English, let alone other, poetry. Also I notice that Mr Gittings is sure, along with two unseeing and indifferent artists, Benjamin Robert Haydon and Severn, of Keats's power 'to enter into the "identity" of everything he encountered, animate or inanimate'. He exaggerates. It was an uncertain power, at any rate in verse; and in that respect was well caught by John Clare, a finer-fibred if less forcible mind, in remarks never quoted, I think, by biographers of Keats, allowing him vision, yet justifying the charge of Cockneyism because he described nature by the light of his fancies and not of the facts: 'behind every rose bush he looks for a Venus and under every laurel a thrumming Apollo'. (Example: Autumn being discovered – uncomfortable it would have been – on 'a half-reap'd furrow' of corn, as if the furrows of the plough had never been closed up.)

I myself would accuse Mr Gittings of a similar Cockneyism in regard to words (a part of nature) and of style. Certainly I notice, as if Keats were mesmerizing him, in a way out of date or good keeping, that he himself prefers a magical far-foamed, often meaningless kind of pseudo-criticism. Meanwhile touch piously the Delphic harp in vulgarest 1968; or to change the metaphor, I notice on every page the fat pearly maggots of poeticism tumbling out – *mood, birdsong, strive, threshold, sped, lingered, task, oblivion, soul.* O female pudendum and ass equalling arse. Really in these matters the revolution of the last sixty years should go for something, should penetrate somewhere, should keep off the shoulders of poetry – harsh as this may sound after so much devotion, so much slogging – talents one would think better suited to harping the flower-fresh, lightly-lingering fragrance of a new body-lotion. (But isn't advertising, in women's magazines, a last niche of the Keatsian style?)

1968

Lytton Strachey at Last

I

Few readers are likely to reach the 460th and final page of this first volume of a life of Lytton Strachey[1] with much more liking for the subject, who appears – up to his thirty-first year – clever, entertaining, spiteful, snooty, pitiable, and odious; on the edge of fashioning a style in accord with his homosexuality.

I write 'homosexuality' with some trepidation, since anti-homosexualism is a prejudice as discreditable as anti-semitism; and I am not the late Roy Campbell. Recent legislation, though, makes a difference, lightening matters for critics, and biographers, as well as homosexuals. If a heterosexual subject went markedly after women, his biographer will usually say so. It may be relevant; and it may be no less relevant if a subject of different constitution went markedly after men. Strachey's biographer thinks it to the point, the reader will find it so, on the evidence, and this open biography of a notable queer (or is that too prejudicial a word to use?) does happen to be the first to be published since the criminality of homosexual activities was lessened. The Cambridge or Bloomsbury pederasty here revealed will at any rate spread the burden which continues to be heaped so unfairly on the back of poor Oscar Wilde.

Strachey was the child of an elderly if 'advanced' Victorian many years older than his wife. Lady Strachey dominated her son, always with an eye to his promotion, the right company, the right college, the right entry into public service. Strachey's early life combines a restless acceptance and rejection of this mother's influence and the influence of his

[1] *Lytton Strachey: The Unknown Years,* by Michael Holroyd (1967).

family, in their lugubrious late Victorian homes in Lancaster
Gate and on Haverstock Hill. His situation was complicated
by his weakness, ill-health, and hypochondria, and by the
exceptionally unattractive image which looked back at him
from the long mirrors of the bedroom. He reached Cambridge – and Trinity College – in 1899 (four years after the
trial of Oscar Wilde). 'Prim anti-puritanism' was one characteristic of this young man, able enough to be admitted into
the select society of 'The Apostles', in which he had the
company of Maynard Keynes (homosexual) and G. E. Moore
(sex subsumed, one supposes, in philosophical speculation).
Bertrand Russell, an earlier Apostle, wrote in the first volume
of his autobiography of the way the society changed after his
time, of a long battle between George Macaulay Trevelyan
(walking tours) and Strachey (anything but walking tours), in
which Strachey was more or less the winner, so that 'homosexual relations among the members were for a time common'. Keynes is also quoted. The Apostles 'repudiated
entirely customary morals, conventions and traditional wisdom. We were, that is to say, in the strict sense of the term,
immoralists.'

There are homosexuals and homosexuals. Here, for instance, is hard, assured, attractive, and easily successful
Keynes, a graduate, by way of Eton, from the intellectual
moralism of Nonconformity, here also epicene, self-loving,
self-hating Strachey, with the shape and voice of a daddy-
long-legs (if that insect could speak, wouldn't its voice be
falsetto, between giggles?), unsuccessful at first (the Civil
Service had only to look at him to say no), a graduate only
from the stuffiness and worthiness, but not the superiority, of
his class.

Strachey's biographer asks readers to accept him as an
artist. Then how extraordinary to look back at such length to
the false starts and continuations, to the desire to win university prizes, to the peculiar desire to go on shining – in later
life – in the provincialism of Cambridge, even allowing for
the self-satisfied provincialism of the decade before the First
World War. How extraordinary as well to look at the poems
he wrote, within the latter years of this first volume. Strachey
read Donne, Pope, Henry James – yet wrote poems and

continued to write them in the style of drawing-room versi-
fiers, 'in a strain of sub-dolorous insipidity'. In love, like
Maynard Keynes, with Duncan Grant, he wrote:

> You kissed me, and you kissed me oft
> – Was it my ghost or was it me? –
> Your kisses were so sweet, so soft,
> The happy cherubim aloft
>   Wept that such things should be . . .

Other poems (including a sonnet sequence 'probably
addressed' to Sheppard, the Apostle he was also in love with
for two years, and the future provost of King's College)
contain 'a truly phenomenal amount of copulation', and
were born from Strachey's at this time 'compulsive pre-
occupation with the male reproductory and excretory organs'.
We are given none of these. After sixty years, they 'remain
largely unpublishable'. But from letters we are permitted to
know the derisive nastiness of the sting developed in his own
defence by this brilliant daddy-long-legs. When Trevelyan
the Apostle married the daughter of the formidable Mrs
Humphrey Ward in a Unitarian chapel at Oxford in 1904,
with Edward Carpenter officiating, Apostle Strachey attended
and described the occasion in a letter to Apostle Leonard
Woolf. A slightly risible ceremony it must have been.
Strachey recorded the *bon mot* of Henry James, who was
there, and said that the ordinary marriage service, binding
and making an impression, was 'like a seal; this was nothing
more than a wafer'. But Apostle Strachey also wrote: 'The
bride and bridegroom were almost completely hideous. But I
suppose one must let copulation thrive. The service was
practically all balls in both senses.' Later he wrote to the
same correspondent about the happiness his own sister and
her artist husband found in each other:

> I must say I am sometimes a little annoyed at their
> affectionateness. Wouldn't you be? Two people loving
> each other so much – there's something devilishly selfish
> about it. Couples in the road with their silly arms round
> their stupid waists irritate me in the same way. I want to
> shake them.

How nasty, how insolent the tone is! And to be plain, that is one kind of homosexual: spiteful and ungenerous, and against those who do not share his condition. From the situation, the condition, arise, I should think, both the substance and the essentially coarse style of *Eminent Victorians* and *Queen Victoria*.

Of course one sympathizes. Of course one is again and again – a little mistrustfully and uncomfortably – amused. But the artist? The writer not, admittedly, 'among the few very greatest figures in English literature'? It does seem to me that Strachey's often deep-working and often undeceived panegyrist isn't following the logic of his own comments about this peculiar man or his circle. He analyses the milieu of 'Bloomsbury', which expanded from the refinements of Apostolic homosexuality, and appears more in agreement than he states himself to be with the condemnation of Bloomsbury by its enemy Wyndham Lewis, who found it a promotional and social fabrication by its members.

From another view – and evidence for this is supplied as well – this 'advanced' Bloomsbury seems to have been a re-actionary enclave from which life was excluded by a sneering unease, in which we are asked to believe, in this century of Conrad, Valéry, Proust, Rilke, Eliot, Colette, Pasternak, Yeats, Mandelshtam, Joyce, Auden, Babel, etc., that he displayed, this local figure, 'all the sheer ability of the most consummate artist'. So far, up to the age of thirty, the evidence points to a never independent or liberated essayist, in a style scarcely removed from *belles-lettres*. But we shall see. There is another volume to come. Let us hope it proves, and does not merely state, the opposite.

II

Reading extracts from notices of *Lytton Strachey* Volume One on the jacket of *Lytton Strachey* Volume Two,[2] I find myself to have been alone more or less – among reviewers – in thinking it a rather dubious construction. I thought Volume One false: it contradicted its own evidence, it advanced

[2] *Lytton Strachey: The Years of Achievement, 1910–1932*, by Michael Holroyd (1968).

claims for its peculiar subject which were not established. But giving us Strachey still short of his published beginnings as an author, though already out of his youth (if he could be said ever to have been in such a state as youth), Volume One left a chance: the great things were to come, were to be revealed, in the twenty-two years of the sequel, from 1910 to Lytton Strachey's too early death in 1932.

I took this to mean, not just that Strachey would be revealed in the composition of his famous books – it would hardly be quite so obvious – but that we should be admitted to a grand metamorphosis, should discover – though I doubted it – a maturity, a goodness, a grandness on the inner face of the diptych, having been shown on the outer face hardly a good writer so far, though certainly a choice ichneumon fly.

Personally I can always dispense with the life in favour of the works. Of course if the works are appealing, it is pleasant, though perhaps supererogatory, and interfering, to have the appeal confirmed in the life. '*That* may be a pity, but *that* I should have expected', and so on. Tracing the relationship – there you have the literary biographer's difficulty and privilege; tracing it without bias or distortion. I judge that Mr Holroyd, in his grand way (720 pages in Volume Two), acts as if there were no such difficulty. Here is Strachey, there are the works. The chapters divide in that way, a chunk of life, a chunk of critical exposition; in the chunks of exposed life, it seems to me, nothing at all alters except that Strachey grows older and a little less extreme – as you would expect – in his jabs, a little 'mellower', but hardly less nauseating. Mr Holroyd does not conceal. 'His candour is exemplary', as Mr Raymond Mortimer remarked; and it remains so, not merely in the sense that this biography of Strachey comes after the law against homosexual practices has been relaxed. 'I am not an admirer of Strachey. I knew him' (Santayana). 'I always enjoyed his learning and his wit, but found his humanism rather too narrow for my taste' (Aldous Huxley).

Yes, the statements, the denunciations are all here. The nasty evidence is unshirkingly, industriously sprinkled, out of the now bearded mouth, adding up, wit or no wit, to an extensive and shallow vulgarity of the animating principle.

I detest remark after remark that Strachey makes about his friends and intimates, always, or so often, behind their backs, the snigger, the sting out and in, conveying poison into the wound from an inexhaustible sac. Even allowing for the times, one of the pieces I found appalling and revealing comes from a letter to Ottoline Morrell, written the evening after he had been examined by a medical tribunal and rejected for military service. 'It was queer finding oneself with four members of the lower classes – two of them simply roughs out of the streets – filthy dirty – crammed behind a screen in the corner of a room, and told to undress. For a few moments I realized what it was like to *be* one of the lower classes – the appalling indignity of it!' So far one might just acquit him, the things *they* have to stoop to, but no, he goes on: 'To come out after it was all over, and find myself being called 'sir' by policemen and ticket collectors was a distinct satisfaction.' Given his pretensions, this is a monster speaking, however intelligent, however coruscating – or flashy.

How are all such things added up by Mr Holroyd? What figure does he make of them? He seems to have an additive or connecting power, until you look closely. A risible sample comes from an occasion in Ottoline Morrell's house at Broughton, which is quoted without a smile. Strachey had taken refuge there after a misdirected, most unnerving holiday in Scotland and Ireland. 'At night Lytton would become gay and we would laugh and giggle and be foolish; sometimes he would put on a pair of my smart high-heeled shoes, which made him look like an Aubrey Beardsley drawing, very wicked. I love to see him in my memory tottering and pirouetting round the room.' Unsmiling Mr Holroyd takes over: 'The atmosphere at Broughton, lively, soothing, comfortable, supremely civilized. . . .'

Of course, what Mr Holroyd most fails to connect are those chunks of life and those chunks of writing. He does not see how in fact they agree, and define each other. Blandly enough, he divides the writing from the writer, admits – and disregards, or takes it back again. I cannot recognize anywhere that he has the qualifications of a critic: a fact most obvious when he insists on putting Strachey against Eliot, or Lawrence, or Wyndham Lewis, in other words against a

writer of sterling creativity. Eliot, for instance. Of course
Eliot saw that Strachey was talented, and extended his feelers
towards Strachey, to test the matter. They approached, and
Eliot withdrew, and Mr Holroyd with an outstanding naivety
puts this down – in awkward English – to Eliot's account:
'he was an awkward person with whom to get on terms of
intimacy'. Eliot was in fact – more than most writers and
editors – generously quick to answer to the sign of 'truth' in
another writer; and that I would suppose is what he did not
find in Strachey, who lacked a general goodness, except of
the thinnest kind. A few of Eliot's letters are quoted; and I
would recommend to anyone the incidental contrast they
offer to extracts *ad nauseam* from Strachey's letters: suddenly one comes for a while on a man and not a confectioner.
These approaches between Eliot and Strachey belong to
1919, *Eminent Victorians* having been published the year
before. Two years later *Queen Victoria* appeared, then *Books
and Characters* in 1922, and the Leslie Stephen Lecture on
Pope in 1925; and by that time Eliot had evidence enough
for hanging Strachey. In 1926 he reviewed Quiller-Couch's
Oxford Book of English Prose in the *Times Literary Supplement*, anonymously of course, analysing in the review Lytton
Strachey's prose, as exemplified in the last paragraph of
Queen Victoria.[3]

This he compared incidentally with a passage from Joyce's
Portrait of the Artist as a Young Man. 'Here in eighteen
lines', Eliot wrote of Q's choice from *Queen Victoria*,

> are eighteen images or analogies, not one of which is
> original, not one of which is freshly felt or sincerely evoked,
> and consequently not one of which evokes in the mind of
> the reader the definite image it actually portends. Now
> examine the second passage [from Joyce]: there is not a
> single phrase which does not evoke – which does not force
> the mind to evoke – the image it expresses. Art, after all, is
> a question of effect; and does anyone give a second thought

[3] This review was shown afterwards to have been not by Eliot,
but by his friend Herbert Read. Michael Holroyd's mistaken
attribution does not affect his argument about Strachey's style, so
I leave my own account as it was written.

to the death of Queen Victoria as our author has described it? But merely to read of Stephen Dedalus walking on the beach is to have come into contact with the vibrating reflex of an actual experience.

The analysis is crushing and unanswerable. Misled by, or encouraged by, Eliot's slightly ambiguous talk of 'visualizing' images and analogies, Mr Holroyd tries to answer it. Eliot, he says, 'makes no allowance for the authentic and valid use of the stereotype, colloquial phrase'; and it will occur to readers, by this time, by page 436 of this second volume, that Mr Holroyd's own vast painstaking biography is composed in orotund stereotype, whether of notion or language. This leads him, for example, to a curious sentence, its verb most unfortunately chosen: that *Eminent Victorians* was a genuine pioneer work (it was, of course) which 'forged for itself a permanent place in literary history'. Exactly; and the writer of such a sentence is one I do not care to trust. In fact I was reminded by this book of one of those vast marble monuments (filling a modest chancel) commemorating the unimportant or the wicked, the total design one of commonplaces ingeniously composed around an effigy of bland, local, and indeed amateur carving. Talking of art, this volume has for frontispiece a reproduction in colour of a portrait of Strachey (by Vanessa Bell) of which the features are all but a blank. It seems to fit the major incongruity in Mr Holroyd's monument.

1967–8

Jonah Barrington, and the Parish of Myddle

It is a good week for a reviewer (and, he hopes, for those who may look through his reviews) when he comes on two books eminently off beat. I knew about the *History of Myddle*[1] and its display of human nature three hundred years ago in Shropshire. I did not know about Sir Jonah Barrington and his display, I won't say of Irish nature in the eighteenth century, but of his own nature. Yeats knew of him, James Joyce knew of him, and planted scraps of Barrington's tall stories in the mid-stream of *Finnegan's Wake*. But that would be introducing him too pedantically. Jonah Barrington was a lawyer, from a demesne in the Queen's County. He fell from prosperity, and in an old age without money, in Paris, where he was safe from his creditors, he wrote *Personal Sketches of His Own Times*,[2] three volumes, fourteen hundred pages, occasionally, we are told, prolix, sententious, platitudinous.

In between – well, quotation from these three volumes, now edited into one, gives the answer. Barrington recalls his grandfather and grandmother, Mr and Mrs French, who maintained a feudal arrogance, which often 'set the neighbours and their adherents together by the *ears*'. Both disliked a certain 'sturdy half-mounted gentleman' named Dennis Bodkin: and the grandmother, an O'Brien, 'high and proud – steady and sensible', was yet 'disposed to be rather violent at times in her contempts and animosities':

> On some occasion or other, Mr Dennis had outdone his usual outdoings, and chagrined the squire and his lady

[1] *Human Nature Displayed in the History of Myddle*, by Richard Gough, introduced by W. G. Hoskins (1968).

[2] *The Ireland of Sir Jonah Barrington*, selected from his *Personal Sketches*, by Hugh Staples (1968).

most outrageously. A large company dined at my grandfather's, and my grandmother launched out in her abuse
of Dennis, concluding her exordium by an hyperbole of
hatred expressed, but not at all meant, in these words –
I wish the fellow's ears were cut off! that might quiet him.

It passed over as usual: the subject was changed, and all
went comfortably till supper; at which time, when everybody was in full glee, the old butler, Ned Regan (who had
drank enough) came in: – joy was in his eye; and whisper-
ing something to his mistress which she did not compre-
hend, he put a large snuff-box into her hand. Fancying it
was some whim of her old domestic, she opened the box
and shook out its contents: – when, lo! a considerable
portion of a pair of bloody ears dropped on the table!

The company were horrified, and the Frenches' butler exclaimed: 'Sure, my lady, you wished that Dennis Bodkin's
ears were cut off; so I told old Gahagan (the gamekeeper)
and he took a few boys with him, and brought back Dennis
Bodkin's ears – and there they are; and I hope you are plazed,
my lady!'

This story stuck in Yeats's mind, his wife having read to
him from the *Personal Sketches*, and it is curious to see how
Yeats transformed it in his poem 'The Tower':

Beyond that ridge lived Mrs French and once
When every silver candlestick or sconce
Lit up the dark mahogany and the wine,
A serving-man, that could divine
That most respected lady's every wish,
Ran and with garden shears
Clipped an insolent farmer's ears
And brought them in a little covered dish.

I prefer the snuff-box to the covered dish. But Yeats, and
Joyce too, recognized Barrington's style, the right pace, the
right tone, the right and frequently surprising words for the
tall drama of the gruesome and comic, which were found by
his startling verve.

Joyce, I would suppose, preferred Barrington's more
triumphant and sardonic knockabout, Barrington describing

immense orgies, for instance, in which words bounce out for food, wine, and consequences. They have to be read a second time and a third time to be believed – no, not believed – especially in the tale in which two of the guzzlers wake up for breakfast to find hair and head embedded in the new plaster of the wall, soft when they collapsed against it, hard now 'from the heat and light of an eighteen hours' carousal'.

There is evidence of Joyce's liking for the story – the whole chapter-story – of Dr Achmet Borumborad, turbanned, bearded, pseudo-Turk, proprietor of hot and cold sea-water baths in Dublin, into whose deep, cold salt-water bath nineteen noblemen and Members of the Irish Parliament fell one behind the other, when the wrong door opened after the dinner party he gave for them. Still to come there is the story of John Philpot Curran cornered in his bedroom, naked, as he was washing, by his host's savage Newfoundland, the story of the Enniscorthy pig, which ate a Protestant parson killed in the rebellion of 1798, the story of skinning the black child to make it white ('a very striking example of the mode in which we managed a *lusus Naturae* when we *caught* one in Ireland five and forty years ago'). Also the story – surely a folk-tale or at any rate a much older tale newly costumed and situated? – of the faction fights which involved Barrington's great-aunt Elizabeth Fitzgerald. Her castle was attacked by the O'Cahils, the attackers were beaten off by her 'warders' but managed to capture her meek husband while he was taking some tranquil air. They came back under a flag of truce and offered her Mr Fitzgerald in exchange for the castle. 'We'll render the squire and you'll render the keep; and if yees won't do that same, the squire will be throttled before your two eyes in half an hour.'

> 'Flag of truce!' said the heroine, with due dignity and without hesitation; 'mark the words of Elizabeth Fitzgerald, of Moret Castle: they may serve for your own wife upon some future occasion. Flag of truce! I *won't* render my keep, and I'll tell you why – Elizabeth Fitzgerald may get another husband, but Elizabeth Fitzgerald may never get another castle: so I'll keep what I have. . . .'

Barrington always manages a curtain:

The O'Cahils kept their word, and old Squire Stephen Fitzgerald, in a short time, was seen dangling and performing various evolutions in the air, to the great amusement of the Jacobites, the mortification of the warders, and chagrin (which however was not without a mixture of consolation) of my great-aunt, Elizabeth.

The reader is going to be left wondering how many good things may still be lurking in the rest of the original three volumes, how many more grotesques transmuted by Barrington's writing. For instance, what about the anecdote of Mr Knaggs, the doctor of Mount Meleck, who 'injured his character as a practitioner of judgement by attempting to cut off the head of Sam Doxy of the Derrys' – an anecdote which proved 'too sanguinary for the present editor's taste, and is therefore omitted'?

Getting my hand on a fuller and earlier reprint of the *Sketches* I found it also omitted Mr Knaggs. Could it be worse than another decapitation Barrington recorded and dramatized, the story of the mower carrying his scythe, who came to a river and attempted to hit a salmon with his scythe handle, cutting off his head, as he did so, with the blade – 'unfurnishing his shoulders'? 'His head came off splash into the Barrow', to the astonishment of his friend, who could not conceive 'how it could drop off so suddenly'. Then the curtain:

> But the next minute he had the consolation of seeing the head attended by one of his own ears, which had been most dexterously sliced off by the same blow which beheaded his comrade.
>
> The head and ear rolled down the river in company, and were picked up with extreme horror at the mill-dam . . . by one of the miller's men.
>
> 'Who the devil does this head belong to?' exclaimed the miller.
>
> 'Whoever owned it,' said the man, 'had three ears at least.'

It would be interesting to inquire into Irish literary inventions of the grotesque, not only in such as Barrington (or

James Joyce). In Barrington's *Sketches*, one of that not easily
categorized group, I would say, of imperfect classics which
get lost in the cracks of literature and libraries and then re-
appear, the humour is akin to that of such ballads, literary
rather than 'folk', as 'The Night before Larry was Stretched'
or 'Johnny, I Hardly Knew Ye', and others, for instance 'The
Cow Ate the Piper' or the 'Lay of Oliver Gogarty' in the
collections made by Colm O Lochlainn.

Grotesques of the kind are compacted around crystals of
the 'real' or pervaded by them; and they have come from
individuals in a society – perhaps this is, or conceals, the
explanation – in which education, oppression by foreigners,
poverty, and primitiveness have cohabited, with a certain
arrest of time.

The History of Myddle is another example, a rough early
or too early example, of the imperfect classic, a remarkable
idea realized imperfectly, before the literary means were
available. Myddle itself – but really, or from one view, this
is nothing to do with the matter – is a parish and village near
Baschurch and Shrewsbury. When he was sixty-seven –
rather older than Sir Jonah Barrington at the time when he
composed his *Personal Sketches* – Richard Gough began
writing a history, not so much of his parish as of its people.
This was in 1701, so that Gough's own memories went back
to the Civil War. There is no other such 'history'. He drew
out a plan of the pews in Myddle church; in which each
seating went with a tenement. Pew by pew he described
families and individuals. One is in the company less of the
good than of the liars, the lecherous, the mean, the lazy, the
shiftless, the boozers. 'This Peate was a slothful prating
fellow.' 'The worst of this Michael was, that his lewd con-
sorts were such ugly nasty bawds.'

Language has changed rather more than life, I found
myself thinking, or rather more than our nature; and I turned
a page to recognize the Wenlocks, father and two sons, all of
them bad lots, who 'never stole any considerable goods, but
were night walkers, and robbed orchards and gardens, and
stole hay out of meadows, and corne when it was cut in the
fields, and any small things that persons by carelessnesse had
left out of doors.'

Yet in many senses everything is different: this is a world
not solely of farmers and office and factory commuters, but
of woodmongers, cheesemongers, weavers, glovers, spinning-
wheel makers, smiths, coopers, cobblers, drovers, quarrymen,
shepherds, small gentry. It is a world rather more violent,
locally. Witness the story of the master who flicked water
into the maid's face as she held a basin, so that he could wash
his hands; and the mistress who thought her husband's action
too familiar and 'in a rage tooke up the cleaver, and gave
her' – not him – 'such a blow on the head that shee dyed'.
Or the story of Robert Morrall, 'a strong robusteouse person
of a rude bawling carriage', who met his 'utter enimy', old
William Tyler, at a stile. 'Discourseing friendly, they sate
downe on each side of the stile; but Tyler haveing an halter
in his hand, cast itt about Morrall's necke and drew him over
the stile, and was likely to have hanged him: but Morrall by
his strength and agility freed himselfe, and did not forebeare
to beate Tyler severely'. It is a world of ups and downs, the
downs – 'he that sits on the ground can fall no lower' – more
disastrous than would be the rule today. But one observes, in
the interwoven lives of these Shropshire people of the seventeenth century, charity and sense and a lack of extremism or
harsh judgement, not least in the justices of the peace.

The *History of Myddle* does have *longueurs*, and is without shape, living by phrases, by sentences, by single sum-
maries. Of course for historians it is a document miraculous
and unique. It is something too for the reader or explorer of
peculiarities, adding flesh and character and vital circumstances to names which as a rule are simply dry entries in a
register of the dead and done with. One reads – and thinks,
far ahead, across the Atlantic, of Sherwood Anderson's
Winesburg, Ohio, or Edgar Lee Masters's *Spoon River
Anthology*, or Peter Taylor's *Happy Families are All Alike*.

1968

The Freedom of Horace Walpole

At one time I should have rejected the idea of sitting down to read three big volumes of Horace Walpole's correspondence.[1] I could never have brought myself to work through so much of so notable an Establishmenter (as I would have thought of him, had the concept of Establishment then been established), so much of one of those amateur writers on the quiet who slip by a side door into a front box of posthumous literary reputation they do not always deserve; sensitive, of course, yet always able to fall back – or to be pushed back – on their comfortable status as gentlemen if they are by any chance exposed or found out in their role of writer or aesthete.

That at any rate was the mood – inappropriate very largely in this case – of a Thirties man, so called, towards a culture hero of the Twenties. During the Thirties it is certainly true that Twentyish sub-Walpoles abounded, on the make, occasionally but usually not Eton and King's (as Walpole had been), elegant, effeminate, catty without tenderness, inclined intellectually to weak chins and to the composition of thin verses in the early quatrain manner of T. S. Eliot's irony. They read Christopher Hussey on the picturesque. They admired Strawberry Hill Gothic (though in a different way from its amused indulgent creator); and they are now (I suppose) to be caught faintly and intermittently protesting, in someone else's wake – or at some one else's wake – against the demolition of some ecclesiological horror by G. E. Street.

Looking back, I would now see Walpole's friend Gray rather than Walpole as their prototype, at least of their snootiness and of their desire to be 'in'. That may also be unfair, although the record that Gray 'walked as if he had

[1] *Horace Walpole's Correspondence with Sir Horace Mann*, edited by W. S. Lewis (1967).

fouled his smallclothes, and looked as if he smelt it' does describe the snooty aesthete with the accurate exaggeration of satire. And if Gray (mother-fixated, and born into trade and not the Establishment) left good letters, he left also those concocted poems, some of the most spurious – the *Elegy* excepted – that have ever been accepted by a toadying posterity, and that have ever plagued the young.

Walpole was very different in any case. He was 'in', to start with, from birth. Towards the end of his correspondence with Sir Horace Mann he declared he had pride, but no ambition: 'I have shunned every advantage of fortune, when it would have laid me under obligation to any man who did not deserve my esteem.' These three volumes of a life's correspondence with one of his less sparkling friends are on Walpole's side largely 'gazetteering', 'politicizing', Walpole's aim having been, he said, to keep up the acquaintance between his friend (away in Florence, where he was British envoy) and his country. Even then his letters are warmed by his tender nature and humane responsibility, by his extraordinary zest, his amused and dancing eye. Kings are trivial, he has no liking for them, though he will relate their absurdities. Lords, ladies, generals, admirals, heroes – and patriotism – are frequently absurd. So are divines (such as the Bishop of London – 'whom Mr Chute and I have agreed not to believe till he has been three days in a whale's belly' – taking advantage in his pastoral letter of the harmless earthquake of 1750: 'You never read so impudent, so absurd a piece! This earthquake, which has done no hurt, in a country where no earthquake ever did any, is sent, according to the Bishop, to punish bawdy prints, bawdy books . . . gaming, drinking (no, I think drinking and avarice, those orthodox vices, are omitted) and all other sins, natural or not.').

Walpole is exceedingly proud of the Walpole motto *fari quae sentiat*, of speaking his mind; but he is worldly, and the wonder is that in a politely dictatorial society he remained so responsive, so open to the world, so undoped and unduped, so honestly and keenly Horace Walpole, bawdy in reasonable degree, fastidious, witty, not incapsulated but as independent as his own letter style of naturalness and good nature. Seeing through pretension did not twist him or dismay him: 'You must look on me for the future as a man who has totally done with the world but for my amusement. I know it, my dear sir, I know it. I laugh at it. I divert myself with it, it does not make me cross; I find all men are like all men; and how can one be angry with everybody?'

Whatever his faults, it is certain that Horace Walpole won himself a freedom few of us attain or maintain; so he doesn't lose his relevance in, shall I say, our own situation of a double Establishment or condominium, political, social, and literary, of which one half can be symbolized – still – in Eton and King's and the right clubs or the desire for them, and the other, equally bigoted and bigoting, in Coalpit Row and Redbrick.

There is one actual footnote worth mentioning, by the way, in this instalment of the superlative Yale Edition of the letters, since it shows how the maintained freedom of a Walpole can be smudged by his editors. Those words that couldn't be used! Those mild concepts that could not be envisaged politely! When Sir William Stanhope acquired Pope's house and garden at Twickenham and cut the trees and bushes, Walpole wrote to Mann that now alas 'there was not a muse could make a little maid's water, but she was spied by every country fellow that went by with a pipe in his mouth'. In 1833 Lord Dover printed this letter, for the first time, and changed that sentence to 'there was not a muse could walk there . . .'.

Every later edition did the same – until the present one.

1967

Edward Thomas among his Inferiors

These letters from Edward Thomas to Gordon Bottomley,[1] to a bookish poet of an entirely different nature, help us to see into a darkish personality, into an enigma of turbulence and control. One question is why Thomas never found himself as a poet – though other men's verse had been a major concern with him – until he was thirty-six, within two years of his death from a fragment of shell on the Western Front.

We know, of course, how the switch was turned on for him, how he met Robert Frost at East Grinstead in 1913, and how they communed in Gloucestershire in the twelve months that followed; and how Frost, himself fresh and direct, convinced him that writing poems was his *métier*. Those two moving, truth-telling, and all the same evasive books, *As it Was* and *World without End*, by his widow Helen Thomas, gave the shadow of an answer: they show Edward Thomas caught in the multiplicity of a trap, personal, marital, and historical, they show him poor, difficult, delicately balanced, they show him married too young, with too much early responsibility, honest, talented, yet not enormously so, caught in the more than usually dishonest, sticky artificiality of letters in late Victorian and Edwardian England. To Gordon Bottomley he wrote about himself with an unexpected openness, and it is my reading of these letters, which remind me in many ways of the worried, honest letters of John Constable, that gradually, gradually, Edward Thomas came to a full consciousness of the trap. When he was at last out of it, partly by luck, partly by his genuineness, which could not be put down, he recognized and celebrated his freedom. 'I am

[1] *Letters from Edward Thomas to Gordon Bottomley*, edited by R. G. Thomas (1969).

sending you a few more verses', he wrote to Gordon Bottomley, in the summer of 1915. 'If Marsh' – that is to say,
Edward Marsh, well-placed, self-elected busybody for poets,
occupied then with his anthologies of *Georgian Poetry* –
'likes any of them, well and good. But I should not be vastly
interested in his adverse opinion.' He had come to recognize
the soft places, the marshes of his world, and had reacted in
full.

To go back, marrying too soon, and not too sensibly, had
only capped a difficult situation. He had managed to become
an undergraduate at Oxford, in the least regarded, least
fashionable corner of the university. He was socially unsure
of himself, the son of a self-educated civil servant, a staff
clerk in the Board of Trade, who had no sympathy for his
inclinations. Solitary and unsociable, this boy who liked
words, but was not sure what to do with them, finds that his
middle-class girl is pregnant, he marries, in 1899, aged
twenty-one, and his first child is born. His wife's mother
breaks with his wife, his father and himself have no more to
do with each other.

For his own words he hadn't a form. In poverty he took to
the obvious, the market and climate being what they were –
to country essays and essay-books and *belles-lettres* and book
reviews, to hacking for mean publishers, and mean literary
editors (then as always inclined to cut the point out of reviews). He was not strong, he was too anxious in mental
constitution for that kind of earning.

Living was hell at times. Finding strength to presume, to
begin to overcome his convictions of social and intellectual
inferiority, he saw the nonsense of the kind of writing which
editors and publishers liked and which he churned out for
them. 'Must I fall back on gentle clergymen who are fond of
gardens and old books and of course possess sundials?' 'I get
sick' – he was writing of another ingratiating anthology
compiled by E. V. Lucas – 'of geniality and odd charming
characters all extracted from their context as if you should
spread jam over toffee and eat it with honey.' He hated
'Inkitas Inkitatum' and the 'pohetical' – in which he was
forced to deal; he signed himself 'ever your hurried and
harried prose man'.

Thomas looked at other marriages, and found them happy.
He looked at his own marriage, and saw what respectability
demanded of him. 'I use boot trees now – also plates with
Monograms. If I live twenty years longer I shall be well-
dressed. The pity of it is that I don't sincerely want to be.
I am buying a dinner-gong with my last sovereign.' 'The
pain', he wrote, 'of going on living and not being able to do
anything but eat and drink and earn a living' – so had his
family increased – 'for five people.'

He was out of love, and he felt on and off near insanity.
At best 'I slink down a side street and mess along'. 'The
damned blues are on me and will never go, I think.' 'An east
wind or a wind from underground has swept over everything . . . I crawl along the very edge of life.' 'Shall I ever
have the relief of true and thorough insanity?' 'How nice it
would be to be dead if only we could know that we were
dead.'

If he was out of love – 'I long for some hatred or indignation or even sharp despair, since love is impossible' – his
wife was his wife, his children were his children. 'I must
believe in myself or forget myself and I cannot.' 'I feel sure
my solution depends on a person and that person cannot be
Helen because she has come to resemble me too much or at
least to play unconsciously the part of being like me with a
skill that could make me weep. It is unlikely to be a woman
because a woman is but a human being with the additional
barricades of (1) sex and (2) antipathy to me – as a rule. As to
men – here I am surrounded by schoolmasters' (he was living
in some degree of association with Bedales, the very middle-
class co-educational school), 'while in town I can but pretend
to pick up the threads of ancient intercourse, a task as endless
as the counting of poppy seeds or plovers in the air.'

There seemed no way out, and no man. Yet both appeared
– the war; preceded by Robert Frost, and poetry. The sharp
reviewer of new poetry became the poet, the form and the
power were discovered: 'I have begun' – letter of 2 March
1915, Edward Thomas then thirty-seven – 'to write in verse
and am impatient of anything else.'

As for the army, I think I am right in saying, on the
evidence of these letters, that the army appeared to him the

one possible, less blameworthy way out of a situation in marriage which was a torture. He was intellectually free, he was writing poems, persuaded to do so, given confidence to do so, by Robert Frost: he might live (and write more poems) or he might die. Either way military service would be the quickest good for his family and himself. Not long before he crossed to France, he was asked by Gordon Bottomley why it was that he had looked for a commission in the artillery. He replied: 'To get a larger pension for Helen'; and perhaps at this point one should read two, in particular, of his new verse. One is that loving poem of not being in love, 'No One So Much As You'. 'My eyes scarce dare meet you', he writes,

> Lest they should prove
> I but respond to you
> And do not love.

He confesses that he had been unable to burn with the love she had

> Till sometimes it did seem
> Better it were
> Never to see you more
> Than linger here
>
> With only gratitude
> Instead of love –
> A pine in solitude
> Cradling a dove.

The other poem is 'The Owl', written, it seems, in Wiltshire, in 1916, when he was an artillery cadet, on the way back to his barracks at Trowbridge. He walks downhill to an inn, he has food, fire, and rest, he hears 'An owl's cry, a most melancholy cry', which salted and sobered his repose, the bird's voice

> Speaking for all who lay under the stars,
> Soldiers and poor, unable to rejoice.

It was one distinction of this new poet, writing from a past or from a substratum of misery, to commiserate and to bless.

William Cooke's biography of Edward Thomas[2] confirms all that we may learn or deduce from the letters, putting extra details into the outline of his creativity. I would say that he makes rather too much of Edward Thomas as a special or extreme case of melancholia and morbidity. Poets may have their oddities, but they are not so extra special as a rule, they do not have wings, they walk the common ground, they face the common problems, for instance, between bed – double bed – and board. Edward Thomas had been environed among the wrong people and he had married the wrong woman. Environed rightly, his blackness lifted, and light flooded in: with Frost he experienced a short, intense, liberating communion, and Frost says nothing of awkwardness and difficulty between them. It was towards the end of 1913, in October, that they first met, and Frost went home to America early in 1915. Frost's wife wrote that her husband and herself found Edward Thomas 'quite the most admirable and lovable man' they had ever known, as if with the Frosts, in the peculiar daffodil country below the Forest of Dean, his sense of guiltiness disappeared altogether. Frost wrote later on that Edward Thomas was the only brother he had ever had: 'I fail to see how we can have been so much to each other, he an Englishman and I an American and our first meeting put off till we were both in middle life. . . . We were together to the exclusion of every other person and interest all through 1914 – 1914 was our year. I never had, I never shall have another such year of friendship.' Frost also made the very pertinent remark – that Edward Thomas had been 'suffering from a life of subordination to his inferiors'. He was subordinated to inferior poets (not to mention the inferior publishers' men and the inferior journalists) who looked on him as the man who reviewed their books. And several of them – how riled they would be – are now remembered only because they knew Edward Thomas. Footnotes about them are his footstool.

In the American, Edward Thomas recognized a new poet delivered – at that time – from the common falsities. In the

[2] *Edward Thomas: A Critical Biography*, by William Cooke (1970).

Englishman, Robert Frost recognized someone who surely
was a poet failing, for whatever blend of causes, to write
poems.

I am fascinated – fascinated, but not surprised – to discover
two other things from this biography. One is that when
poems at last poured out of Edward Thomas in 1914, 1915
and 1916, they often grew from a verbal and emotional
percipience dating back to his adolescence or to early experiences before his marriage and before that long subordination
to the riff-raff of letters. The other is that Edward Thomas
had, after all, written poems, or a few poems, before Frost
walked into his life. They were not bad, judging from the two
which are printed, one of them written when he was nineteen. William Cooke agrees with Robert Frost in laying it
down that Frost no more than helped this poet into freedom
and self-acceptance, on his way to the final depth of the
wood:

> I have come to the borders of sleep,
> The unfathomable deep
> Forest where all must lose
> Their way, however straight,
> Or winding, soon or late;
> They cannot choose . . .

1970

Knots in the Timber of
Robert Frost

A writer of poems, having had a life of which his poems are
in some sense the children, must nowadays be subject to
biography, once he is dead. From what motive? A sheep's
head question, possibly. We assume, sciences of the psyche
having developed, that probing into an artist's life, once it is
over and complete, can explain his art – if he is a poet, can
explain his poems, his vocabulary, images, movement, pattern, ideas, his temperature, kinships, derivations, and the
swell and slack of his productivity or creativity. But then one
has to mention such obvious agents of the biography trade as
profit, and gossip or curiosity. There are universities, in them
and out of them there are writers with a living or a reputation to make, an advancement to procure, and little of themselves, of their own, to project; there are publishers,
booksellers, book reviewers, book pages to fill; there are
public libraries – and readers. Many are the causes of a
biography.

The properest motive, so far unmentioned, is hagiographical, performing an act of piety or homage, dedicating
an altar, painting a triptych. Of course Professor Lawrance
Thompson is a hagiographer in his huge biography of Robert
Frost, now two-thirds completed in more than 700 pages of
a second volume.[1] But then 'truth' intervenes, hooding the
inducements and demands of gossip: we mustn't be evasive,
we must have everything.

Elinor Frost dies, after her long life with the poet:

Lesley, almost overcome by her own grief immediately
after the cremation, unintentionally revealed a habit of

[1] *Robert Frost: The Years of Triumph, 1915–1938,* by Lawrance
Thompson (1971).

vindictiveness she had acquired from her father. When he asked if he could make his home with her during the remainder of his life, she bluntly said no. Then she burst into an almost hysterical accusation which further amazed him: she said she had seen him cause so much injury to the lives of his own children – particularly to Irma, Carol, and Marjorie – that she would not permit him to move into her home, where he might also injure the lives of her two daughters.

So gossip – gossip of course may be true – intervenes in compliance with the demand for unevasiveness and entire truth in biography.

Her rage increased as she went on to insist, through her tears, that she could not forgive him for having ruined her mother's life. It was his fault, she said, that her mother was dead, for it was his own selfishness which had forced her mother to climb those stairs to the upper quarters, repeatedly. Lesley had pleaded that she and her children should live up there, so that her mother wouldn't need to climb. But her father hadn't wanted to hear the children's feet over his head, and that was typical of his selfishness, Lesley cried. Then she hurt him most by concluding that he was the kind of artist who never should have married, or at least never should have had a family.

True, Robert Frost himself gave those details to his biographer in a letter (he gave appalling details of other things to other acquaintances in other letters); true, his daughter Lesley confirmed the account. But we may ask possibly another sheep's head question: do we know Frost, i.e. Frost's good or justifying poems, a scrap better by knowing of this nasty scene, and of other nastinesses? The answer is certainly that we don't. That Frost was in some ways insensitive, sentimental, selfish, brutish, brutal, may be discernible in several bad poems; we cannot help discovering that, in perusing him for the good. How much further, then, are we entitled to go? How much are we entitled to use or look into a Frost – or a Swift – as a case-history? Indulging our curiosity, our taste, our very salted and human taste, for gossip, don't we give way to prurience?

So much for questioning the basis and the value of all modern biography, which, after death, is compounded, with whatever else, of gossip organized, made permanent, and greatly disseminated. Thinking at random of poets, 'it was Matthew Arnold's express wish that he might not be made the subject of a Biography'; Hardy himself wrote as much of his own biography, in a shape unautobiographical, as he cared to reveal, and then destroyed as much of the material as he could; Auden remarks, introducing *A Certain World*, that this commonplace book is the nearest he will ever come to an autobiography, and that 'biographies of writers whether written by others or themselves, are always superfluous and usually in bad taste. . . . No knowledge of the raw ingredients will explain the peculiar flavour of the verbal dishes he invites the public to taste: his private life is, or should be, of no concern to anybody except himself, his family and his friends.'

Who bothers? The hyenas advance, led at times by the subject, who is being hyena to himself. If one may conclude, after finishing this second volume of a biography which is masterly in its genre, that such an organized and permanent revelation of his secrets, the mad and the bad and the good, is just what the Old Hickory Root himself would have approved, behind 'the rare twinkle of his grave blue eyes', then (consult the index: Fear, Gossip, Hate, Jealousy, Pretension, Puritan Rage, Revenge, Spoilt Child, Vindictive Gestures etc., etc.) so much the worse for Robert Lee Frost, but not necessarily for the poems of Robert Lee Frost. As an introduction to them we may prefer the Frost of the first volume of the biography, the Frost who matches, or seems to match, the verbal dishes we most enjoy, the younger, the once unknown poet.

Now, a quick flash from Abercrombie; now
A murmured dry half-heard aside from Thomas;
Now, a clear laughing word from Brooke; and then
Again, Frost's rich and ripe philosophy
That had the body and tang of good draught-cider,
And poured as clear a stream.

That (by Wilfrid Gibson) was the Frost of 1914, Frost with

poets of his own age in the daffodil fields of Dymock, and what Volume Two of the life displays is cider turning or turned into a sharp vinegar.

Certainly in considering his rather small output of fewer than 350 poems, all at hand now in a finalized edition,[2] we need to discard, or disregard, much that does not belong to them, but only surrounds them or accompanies them, in a circuit wider than that of Professor Thompson's research, so far. Over here the difficulty of doing so will be less extreme. It is in America, not England, that worship of the silliest kind put Frost into a public suit of a weave and a thickness we ourselves haven't seen since the days and death of Tennyson, or since the latter days of Wordsworth. Such a situation is complex. Usually when a huge public, not deeply or genuinely responsive to life and the arts, wraps a poet round in its notion of poetic holiness and – if the pun may be overlooked – poetic suitability, the poet himself is partly to blame; he provides some of the cloth, at any rate; he wears the damnèd suit; and it means that somewhere he has given way, parading along the cat-walk.

Both Wordsworth and Tennyson may be recalled, introductively or passingly, in this respect; and in particular relation to Frost. Wordsworth had written with a sublimity of – as we appreciate – justified egoism that, stand clear as he would of ill-advised ambition and pride, he felt 'an internal brightness' had been vouchsafed to him 'that must not die, that must not pass away', Wordsworth came to be ineffectual Wordsworth, came to write his Waterloo Ode, to accept the laureateship on Peel's insistence, to earn from Browning (and ironically, what was to become of Browning?)

> Just for a handful of silver he left us,
> Just for a riband to stick on his coat.

As for Tennyson, great poet even if he never stood on the midnight summit of Snowdon in Wordsworth's mental style, even if Arnold insisted rightly that he was no *grand et puissant esprit* – Tennyson as well advanced to his laureateship, to his lordship also, Tennyson wrote his poems of patriotic

[2] *The Poetry of Robert Frost*, edited by Edward Connery Lathem (1971).

thump and his 'Locksley Hall Sixty Years After', Tennyson, when it suited him, abandoned the slap and thunder of his verbal waves on the long beaches of Mablethorpe, and the stillness of his pools.

Faced by this very much smaller man of San Francisco and then Massachusetts and New Hampshire, one does have to admit that he advanced from his clear cool vision to liking the sound and ignoring the smell of Fame's posterior trumpet, which was, and is still, blown so loudly for him out of a *Dunciad*: he advanced to connive in the cut, the fit, the wearing of his public suit, inside of which his talents shrivelled.

Professor Thompson leaves that clear (one knew it well enough from Frost doing the old sage on television, on one of those Sunday occasions when Broadcasting House throws a penny to the arts); it will be clearer still in the volume of the biography which is still to come, *The Years of Glory*; and the poems also make it clear: the reader need only place 'The Death of the Hired Man' (which the *New Republic* was glad to print in 1915, in its radical, vigorous youth) against such a poem as his political pastoral 'Build Soil' –

> Don't join too many gangs. Join few if any.
> Join the United States and join the family –
> But not too much in between unless a college.

('As delivered at Columbia University, May 31, 1932, before the National Party conventions of that year'); or against the poem for President Kennedy's inauguration –

> A golden age of poetry and power
> Of which this noonday's the beginning hour

– or against (how much rhythms by themselves reveal) the movement of 'Accidentally on Purpose' (1960) –

> The Universe is but the Thing of things,
> The things but balls all going round in rings.
> Some of them mighty huge, some mighty tiny,
> All of them radiant and mighty shiny.

(The message of that poem might have been suggested to him by an episcopal F.R.S. writing a Bridgewater Treatise in the 1860s to uphold design and Paley's *Evidences* against Lyell or Darwin: in fact the poem is one of those decayed, 'comforting' or ingratiating ones by Frost – things aren't so bad or difficult, after all, are they now? – which make one think rather ill of his intelligence, arguable as it may be, for sure, that poems can manage well without the intrusion or support of intelligence, though they may not so easily survive too copious an infusion of stupidity.)

Connivance or no, of course the fair thing, the *sine qua non*, is to forget what Frost did to himself, and to refrain from making too much of Frost in a decline which in fact begins very soon in the run of his eleven books – at any rate after the *New Hampshire* of 1923. Readers will have to squeeze into the new collected edition through a curious entrance, the blame for which belongs half to Frost, half to his editor. On one side there is a photo of the old Robert Frost, horny hands, open shirt, snowy hair, wearing a look about his eyes and mouth of a now benign President Emeritus of General Motors, and sitting on what one supposes to be an old-style loose stone wall surviving in New Hampshire. It does not seem to announce a poet, this icon, but on the other side it is flanked by a poem, an early one, which it seems we are to have at the beginning of all editions of Frost, just as all editions of Tennyson now end, by Tennyson's wish, with 'Sunset and Evening Star'. It is 'The Pasture', the poem which introduced his second, and best, book, *North of Boston*, in 1914; in which 'book of people' it was perhaps an overflow from the brief and generally less certain poems of his first book, *A Boy's Will*. Birth for death, you may say, comparing it with Tennyson's poem of goodbye. But in its repetitions, its sentiment, it is assuredly Frost popular or popularizing – even if, at that time, to no more than an audience of one, the poet's wife – rather than Frost clear and crystalline:

> I'm going out to fetch the little calf
> That's standing by the mother. It's so young
> It totters when she licks it with her tongue.
> I shan't be long. – You come too.

Frost liked this two-stanza scrap of the *faux naïf* (with which

he opened the selected and collected editions of his lifetime)
as if it perhaps originated in some occasion profounder for
him than the expression of it can be for us. Reading it, we
realize that a note of his decline was also sounded in his
beginning. And we may expect that note to recur in between;
which it does.

Yet Frost quickly realized what his early associates in the
daffodil fields and daffodil copses of red Gloucestershire failed
to realize, Edward Thomas excepted. Read Wilfrid Gibson,
not a very talented 'naturist' certainly, yet one who half
understood the need of being versed in something other than
literature. If Gibson's verse tales, such as 'The Money' (in
Fires, 1914), inclined Frost to his new 'poems of people',
and ordinary people, one sees at once how he recognized as
well the weaknesses, the clinging poeticism, and the trickiness of Gibson's method, achieving a 'poetry', in place of the
thinness of Gibson, partly founded in a close, genuine
objectivity (the wife, for instance, in 'The Death of the Hired
Man', when the moonlight poured into her lap – 'She saw it/
And spread her apron to it'; and immediately after, though
it is involved in a frigidity or at least an image which doesn't
succeed, the way she puts out her hand

> Among the harplike morning-glory strings,
> Taut with the dew from garden bed to eaves).

Instructive it is to read of Frost's pleasure that he had gone
beyond Wordsworth into plain speech; and of his confidence
that Gibson, remaining where he inevitably was, amounted
to a bit of a sham. 'A realist I may be,' he wrote to Edward
Garnett in 1915, 'if by that they mean one who before all
else wants the story' – i.e. in the story poems of *North of
Boston* – 'to sound as if it were told the way it is because it
happened that way. Of course the story must release an idea,
but that is a matter of touch and emphasis, the almost in-
credible freedom of the soul enslaved in the hard facts of
experience.' He went on – and the reference unquestionably
is to Gibson's poem, just mentioned, out of *Fires* – to say how
much he hated the story 'that takes its rise idea-end foremost,
as it were in a formula such as It's little we know what the
poor think and feel'.

'All he insists on' (Edward Thomas to Gordon Bottomley
in answer to condemnations of Frost by Sturge Moore) 'is
what he believes he finds in all poets – absolute fidelity to
the postures which the voice assumes in the most expressive
intimate speech.'

So one recognizes the problem he proposed to himself:
honest illumination, by honest rendering of such things,
including such quirks of delight, as caught him and intrigued
him. And it was in his second book, in those terms, that he
arrived at the pitch of his conscious artistry and self-freedom,
in his forty-first year.

The means are simple, a personal line, a Frost-line or
movement conveying so much of the same mood that it need
not vary a great deal; in forms which are also not greatly
various; unrhymed narration, and inside the poem, not itself
many pages long, some drama of division or activity; simple
combination as well of rhyming couplets, or of once rhyming
or twice rhyming quatrains.

Poeticisms are shut out (but not disposed of, they hang
round, and, if much reduced, they wiggle back into his poems
again whenever Frost balances on his poetry pedestal).

Essentially 'good Frost' is to write, in 'After Apple-
Picking',

> My instep arch not only keeps the ache,
> It keeps the pressure of a ladder-round

– compared with which doubtfully good, or precarious, Frost
endangers his lyrics, for all their charm, by a too obvious
rhyming which leads him to poetic archness or simple-
simonism or to enunciation of archly proverbial dogmas of
life something in the folk-mode of *The New England Primer*,
which he liked so much (for some reason three lines from the
Primer which he used to prefix *A Witness Tree*, are printed,
listed, and indexed as if they had been written by Frost himself).

Much favoured lyrics demand scrutiny again and again.
For instance, shouldn't it be clear that the legitimacy of his
'Dust of Snow' fails beyond the first stanza?

> The way a crow
> Shook down on me

The dust of snow
From a hemlock tree

– that is the poem, the rest, heart's mood and rued, is kapok;
an elaboration, for the pattern to match, of 'cheered me
up'.

About thirty poems, from first to last of his less than a
dozen collections, amount to the canon of the virtue of this
poet – poems in which suggestive nature is marked for its
witlessness, without that recurrent personalization of the
inanimate which induces sentimentality. A warmth about
the human race – or the God in whom Frost doesn't disbelieve
– does not distinguish them; and when the self of this
Calvinistic poet becomes insistent, when the self refuses to be
lost in his response (and of course when he eventually does
the Old Kaspar in the sun answering – or provoking – little
Wilhelmine, and sticking a surreptitious pin into her now
and again), one can justly apply to him a remark by Valéry,
that 'A second-rate mind loses the power of retrieving the
path mapped out by its nature'.

One may regret in Frost that delight leads him so much
into bleak finalities, thumbs down, with only small tunes for
momentary touches of comfort. It has to be accepted, it is
him (or the way be became), it explains some of the attraction now so widely exerted by his poems. Not for Frost, let
us say, that melody beyond, above, himself, like rising air,
that inexplicability of verbal deliciousness and directness
which Wordsworth (another poet who lived on the touch-
line of melancholia) constructs in 'Among all lovely things
my love had been', or in the self-surrender of

Oh! might I kiss the mountain rains
That sparkle on her cheek.

It is a weakness, all the same ('Come with me', says Frost.
'I go to you', says Wordsworth). The white poem, unevasive,
defiant either of a *nox est perpetua* ahead or of torture now,
isn't in our world an impossibility, and is perhaps a duty – if
one can write it. It is the form of greatest sympathy. The
black poem or the poem which proceeds from white to black,
is at any rate a misfortune – even if it cannot be evaded.

Some poets make poems which are like unripe persimmons, bitter outside, with a true sweetness internally. Frost does the reverse. The outside of his poems is often sweet, the inside hell. 'The footpath down to the well is healed', Frost writes, in a poem of 1906, about living in a ghost house (his habitual dwelling) – as if there was nothing for this Calvinist self-torturer to do except relapse into being debarred from wells of life or healing.

> I dwell with a strangely aching heart
> In that vanished abode there far apart
>> On that disused and forgotten road
>> That has no dust-bath now for the toad.
> Night comes; the black bats tumble and dart.

Frost, a poet fascinated by the capturing, directive power of roads, paths, tracks, and by a predestination, and by the steady indifference of everything from hard rock to elegant birch, a poet whose delight leads to the repeated revelation of self-centred bleakness, a poet intermittently sure in the manipulation of limited means, is neither beast nor angel. Nor major poet – a claim which would be ridiculous.

Only now, when movement within form is neglected, could the teasing limited subtlety of Frost, strong as he may be in *North of Boston*, be supposed to match or surpass the teasing subtlety of the ranging humanity of his friend Edward Thomas (whose sentimentalities, too, give less offence).

A minor poet; to whom – such is his line – one is drawn back repeatedly, even reluctantly, but drawn back; and I think in Frost we should not overlook one, on a first reading, slightly sentimental poem, 'Never Again Would Birds' Song be the Same', in which Frost loses himself almost, yet recovers his ruefulness, his obstinacy, in a last line of the most revelatory oddness. The voice of Eve, according to the poem, had given an oversound to the voice of birds which they had kept ever since: he would declare it, he could believe it, Frost says. But – the fraud of life and love, the fraud of being one of the descendants of Eve, one of the race of men, one of the lovers of woman –

> To do that to birds was why she came.

She came only to feed the illusion. We are always defeated? That depends on what we reject and what we expect. And in any case read Wordsworth, undespondent Wordsworth, once more, on bringing the glow-worm to the orchard.

1971

Four Ways of Making Fudge

1. *Treading the Region Elenore*

Admirable poets abroad in the last thirty years – Pasternak for one – have opened their senses and their intellect to 'nature', not as a rose-hip syrup and not as a second-hand divinity; and they have made poems out of an exact and exacting scrutiny of existence. But less so in England; where nature, stickily understood, has been one of the dirty words of a too limited intellectualism.

J. C. Reid's book on Francis Thompson helps us to see how this came about.[1] One cause was reaction against simple and not at all passionate feelings about nature promulgated at one time by the *London Mercury* poets, themselves reacting against the Wilde case and *fin de siècle* decadence. The results were odd. Taste was not armoured as it could have been against returning flows of a romanticism become septic. Eliotism – an Eliot emery paper applied to language (which is only one element of a properly understood 'nature') – was not enough. Hopkins was taken wrongly, Wyndham Lewis was disregarded; and in the consequent – and continuing – infant school of appreciation, even, for example, Francis Thompson (to say nothing of more recent flushes of grandiloquence) has survived to some little extent.

It is now his centenary. Though I cannot think this will be a happy festival or that it will set Thompson's pastiche shoulder-high again, I do think that this centenary book is valuable and fascinating. It is an exposé. The pattern exposed – though with some inconsistency of judgement – is one of indolence and self-delusion.

Thompson was born into a Catholic doctor's family in the North on 18 December 1859. Out of the cotton-wool of home and sisters he was sent to Ushaw in hopes of making him a

[1] *Francis Thompson, Man and Poet*, by J. C. Reid (1959).

priest. His pastors reported that a 'natural indolence' unfitted him for ordination. His father tried to make him a doctor. He slouched around Manchester with his shoe-laces undone. He dreamt lazily; and, as at Ushaw, read poems, and more poems. He pictured himself a De Quincey, took a cradle refuge in laudanum, and feebly vanished into London on the De Quincey pattern (although vigour and not feebleness distinguishes De Quincey's mind), sinking like a white grub into abject destitution.

From destitution and mental sloth he was half pulled by the not-very-literate journalist Wilfrid Meynell, then editor of a Catholic paper named (a little sycophantically, I should say) *Merry England.*

Mr Reid has looked into the mechanism of opium in relation to personality, poetry, and dreams; and concludes that the Thompson poetic gusher gushed in hyper-aesthetic phases of sudden withdrawal from opium. The first of these withdrawals occurred when Wilfrid Meynell enticed his ragged genius into hospital and then into convalescence in a monastery. From the stored-up dreaming of the poetry-addict there now came the first wild half-digested gush which included the 'Hound of Heaven'.

The rest of the life divides itself into laudanum relapses and incomplete recoveries – pitiable, but little to do with the authenticities of literature. If the ironist smothers his pity for a while, he will relish a last scene of indolence in the lapsed period before Thompson's death in 1897. Katherine Tynan (a poet) expected Alice Meynell and Thompson to lunch at 1.30. Alice Meynell arrived – at 3.30 – (with or without Thompson? The account appears evasive) almost in tears. She had gone to collect the lapsed angel with one of her children. 'Francis Thompson', she explained, 'would not get up, although the gayest of little radiant girls had threatened him with the cold-water jug.'

Critically, Mr Reid is half in, half out of the Infant School of Poetic Appreciation. Thompson repels him. He recognizes the impotent Narcissus whose environment was limited not to poetry, but to the one section of it in which Shelley, Keats, and Poe had been ascendant. He quotes Martin Turnell saying of the 'Hound of Heaven' that soundness of theology or majesty of central idea are beside the point in a poem, the language of which is tired, effete, and stale – and then he veers, he cannot quite affirm that even Thompson's 'good' poems are quite remarkably bad ones. 'Pass the gate of Luthany, tread the region Elenore' – instead of saying 'Rubbish!' he still has to ask what Thompson meant by Luthany and Elenore.

It is the consequence of such uncertainty that in a case in the Carmarthen Museum they are now exhibiting the cuff-links of Dylan Thomas, *élève* of Francis Thompson. Yet for the sensible reader this book does fix the character of those poems which do not see reality, and of that process by which a poet of Thompson's kind is canonized – for a while – among the credulous who have only a poetic criterion of poetry. Thompson required an early death and a tale of opium and rags. Both were supplied, and the sales of his rubbish rocketed year by year – so we may guess what *we* are in for – for more than twenty years.

1959

2. *Being Bysshe Vanolis*

Miss Anne Ridler, editing the poems of another Thomson,[2] another fudger I think we must agree, says that the poetry of the earlier part of the *City of Dreadful Night* seems to her 'to look back to Dante and forward to Mr Eliot'.

I can't believe this is a very useful statement, though it does suggest a parlour game of making parallels (the Albert Memorial looks back to Ghiberti and forward to Robert Rauschenberg). Certainly the poet of the *City of Dreadful Night* read *The Inferno* (if rather in the sense of estimating it through the illustrations by Gustave Doré?), and Mr Eliot when young read the *City of Dreadful Night*, and we are all at some time or another affected by inferior influences. But that does not elevate the *City of Dreadful Night* into a poem it is at all necessary to read. Dismal–abysmal, fate–gate, frail–veil, tomb–gloom (or –doom), mighty fane–organ

[2] *Poems and Some Letters of James Thomson, B.V.*, edited by Anne Ridler (1963).

strain, it is a monument stickier than fudge to a confusion
between life and poetry which we should regret, and be
ashamed of, in as far as we ourselves encourage it.

Thomson was a Victorian pessimist; he was a cosmical
unbeliever, a friend of Bradlaugh – so far so good. He was a
melancholic, he drank, he was poor, he was alone, he was a
failure. He walked about London in frayed bedroom slippers
in the winter night by the gas flares, he collapsed, with internal bleeding, in the rooms of the blind poet Marston. The
Secularist Burial Service was read over him in Highgate
Cemetery. His poems paid for the coffin. But if you are a sad
and saddening creature of our race (mental hospitals are full
of them), and if you write poems, and if your poems are
related to a mood better voiced by others, it does not follow
that you yourself are a Leopardi, or anything else than a
fudger and rubbisher. Outside the sloppy hell of the *City of
Dreadful Night*, 'capital of teen and threne', there is not
much fun in discovering that Thomson wrote even more
weakly – most weakly of all when he leaves such haunts (the
mot juste) as the ravine, the blackest stormiest night, the
centre of the fire, the middle of Waterloo Bridge, or the
desert (the eager vultures hanging overhead):

> And in the spot most thrilling-sweet
>   Of all this Love-Realm rosy
> Our traunt pair had found retreat,
>   Unblushing, calm and cosy:
> Where seats too wide for one are placed,
>   And yet for two but narrow,
> It's 'Let my arm steal round your waist,
>   And be my winsome marrow!'

– which wouldn't need to be quoted if there were not some
idea around that James Thomson, rightly considered, is a
Waste Land poet, for ourselves, of existential courage.

In contrast or support Miss Ridler positions around him
Shelley, Clough, Browning, Melville, Leopardi, Baudelaire,
Novalis, Kipling, Housman, Hardy, Wilfred Owen, Edwin
Muir, Robert Graves, Mario Praz, and Paul Elmer More, as
well as Dante and Eliot. She does her best (but how did she
forget Charles Williams?); and I am grateful – mildly – to

have learned from her introduction why this sad creature she mothers, distinguished himself from that superior fellow-Scot, Thomson, the poet of *The Seasons*, as James Thomson (B.V.).

B.V. stood for Bysshe Vanolis, his pen name: Bysshe for Shelley, from whose faults – O World, O Life, O Time and Bird thou never wert (doesn't 'wert' stick in your throat like a sticky jack?) – he derived many of his own; Vanolis for the romantic Novalis of the blue flower and the *Hymnen an die Nacht*, a night of less lugubrious illumination. I could of course have discovered about B.V. from the nearest encyclopedia, but I mention that bracketed B.V. as an indication, in shorthand, of what may happen when a great surge in the arts is at last in its dotage or decay.

1963

3. *With Icing-Sugar and Lollipops – by the Damned Homunculus*

Wasn't the taste for Swinburne like one of those strange medieval epidemics – the Sweat, for example – which historically-minded doctors write about when they retire? In the 1904 edition of his verse, there are six volumes. Almost all one can bear to read, without embarrassment at the automatic flow and the foolishness and the self-aping of this eminent man, comes in the first volume, reprinting that first series of *Poems and Ballads* which startled a smug England in 1866. He was made king of the cats, in the Yeatsian phrase, by that rhythmical signature-tune which he flogged for forty years, on and on

> From the depth of the dreamy decline of the dawn
>   through a notable nimbus of nebulous noonshine.

Legend supported – still supports – the rest. Swinburne was ambivalence. He was the thrill under the surface. On top, the icing-sugar of the Muse, directed – *Vicisti, Galilæe* – at Victorians and Edwardians

> As they grope through the graveyard of creeds
>   under skies growing green at a groan for
>   the grimaces of God.

On the under side, an assortment of the lollipops of life's invisible *curiosa*, the laurel allowing a peep of the whip.

Introducing these 'miscellanea nova et curiosa',[3] Professor Lang warns us that the quantity of Swinburne's unpublished writing is enormous. The quality? If you have not tried the fairly recent public offering of *Lesbia Brandon*, in this volume try Scene iv of Act II of a now fragmentary burlesque, *La Sœur de la Reine*, treasured in the Library of Congress, about a twin sister of Queen Victoria, who grows up to be a tart in the Haymarket. The dear Queen holds an audience. The Archbishops are there and the Privy Councillors and members of both Houses. Girls are to be presented (including the tart-twin, now mistress of Lord John Russell). An usher makes the announcements in a loud voice:

> Milady duchesse de Fuckingstone – mistress Rodger Cox Tandy – milady comtesse de Bitch – miss Sarah Butterbottom – milady Quim – milady marquise de Mausprick – miss Polly Poke, presentée par milord duc de Shittinbags – milady Cunter, par milord marquis de Bumbelly.

Other pieces *nova* rather than *curiosa* are marked by an exactly corresponding tone in criticism (or what loudmouthed, nasty, bullying, enthusiastic little Swinburne believed to be criticism). Having it both ways, if there is another writer to be abused Swinburne, like others of his kind, will blandly employ the automatic prejudices of respectability, decency, patriotism, nationalism, and so on. Ibsen: Ibsen has a dirty view of life, 'a writer who has rivalled and exceeded Wycherley in obscenity of subject . . . the stupidly disgusting author of *Ghosts* . . . such gorillas of letters as the squalid Sardou and the fetid Ibsen'. Arnold: a ludicrous critic, 'the very hoarsest frog of the Oxonian frogconcert'. Whitman (in spite of his praise of Whitman and his poem 'To Walt Whitman in America'): 'I must be allowed to remark that the foremost place among American poets – I do not pretend or presume to judge whether it be or be not Whitman's – can hardly be higher than that of a little, a very little European.'

[3] *New Writings, or Miscellanea nova et curiosa, by Swinburne*, edited by Cecil Y. Lang (1964).

The editor drives his partiality for Swinburne rather hard, of which one example may do. In his ignorant, lazy, condescending, vulgar, exclamatory way Swinburne admired Blake. He naturally read the edition of Blake brought out in 1893 by Ellis and Yeats, noticing that they considered Blake to be of Irish descent, and himself to have been 'innocent of any knowledge of Blake's meaning.' He reacted in a typically insolent paragraph printed here as it was first written: 'Some Hibernian commentator on Blake, if I rightly remember, has somewhere said something to the effect that. . . .'
But he was glad to hear of Blake's Irish ancestry, since it explained

> how so admirable and adorable a genius could be flawed and vitiated by such unutterable and unimaginable defects. Now that we know him for a Celt by descent we understand whence he derived his amazing capacity for gabble and babble and drivel: his English capacity for occasionally exquisite and noble workmanship we may rationally attribute to his English birth and breeding.

Characteristic drivel of his own. But there was a sequel. Swinburne used the paragraph in prefacing the 1906 reprint of his *William Blake*. Yeats's father saw the reference to 'some Hibernian commentator', and was stung to reflect on Swinburne in his letters to his son. He expatiated on Swinburne's brand of aristocratic insolence, his self-complacency –'a sure mark of intellectual underbreeding', his malignancy, his starved personality – 'Swinburne is the poet of surely the thinnest humanity ever known'.

> To be a poet it needs more than that you be an aristocratic cad even tho' you have in addition Greek and Latin, an Oxford education and a gift of language that is like the sea for strength and copiousness.

Harsh, and true. But there is not a squeak of this reproving sequel in the notes, full of obsequious bonhomie, which have been appended copiously by Swinburne's editor. The one good thing among the poems, critical essays, hoaxes, and burlesques he has collected, is a translation, once privately printed, of Villon's *Ballade de la grosse Margot* – superior to his other, for his times publishable, turnings of Villon in the second series of *Poems and Ballads*:

> Then when we wake her womb begins to stir;
> To save her seed she gets me under her
>   Wheezing and wining, flat as planks are laid:
> And thus she spoils me for a whoremonger
>   Inside this brothel where we drive our trade.
>
> Blow, hail or freeze, I've bread here baked rent free!
> Whoring's my trade, and my whore pleases me;
>   Bad cat, bad rat; we're just the same if weighed.
> We that love filth, filth follows us, you see;
> Honour flies from us, as from her we flee
>   Inside this brothel where we drive our trade.

But that is nearer Villon than Swinburne in decay.

1964

4. *Guarding Ancient Springs*

It would be nice – well, for some – if something after all transcended our perceptions. Then we could go back and write the same poems over again, with Miss Kathleen Raine marching at our head under a stitched banner of a unitive mystical emblem, which might be a cube of that already mentioned sweetmeat, or, shall I say, the semi-colon of Edwin Muir as interpreted by Miss Raine. Muir dreamt of a semi-colon, he told Miss Raine. It was his whole dream, it was the point reached by poems, beyond which they go into transcendence or indicate the Something. Beyond that semi-colon, beyond that pause, beyond a poet's statement, 'is something more, that completes his meaning. We can never define it,' says Miss Raine, 'yet it is part of the poem, and part of what the poet communicates to the reader.'

In the essays so introduced[4] Miss Raine proclaims the

---

[4] *Defending Ancient Springs*, by Kathleen Raine (1967).

virtue, the virtue which transcends and excludes all others, of the poets of ancient wisdom, of Jung's Collective Unconscious, of Yeats's Anima Mundi, Blake's world of Imagination, or Plato's world of Ideas; it is 'the test of the authentic poet at all times that his work should draw its inspiration from this source', this collective of ancient springs – I nearly said bubbling out of the earth, but that would hardly do – which are one spring and the same.

The difficulty of defining the perennial wisdom Miss Raine evades by a movement decidedly, and unexpectedly, circular. What is Imagination? It is undoubtedly the Soul. What is the Soul? It is undoubtedly Imagination. And Miss Raine proceeds by a repetitive, rather cocksure confrontation of terms, given little or no gloss, which are either Praiseworthy or Disparaging, Divine or the Devil's. Praiseworthy terms are *prophetic, profound, primitive, the race, archetypal image, age-old traditions, mystery,* and *cosmic.* Disparaging terms, of insufferable weakness, if not wickedness, are *modern, realist, conscious, individual, Auden* (a forgotten term surviving from the Thirties), *positivism, Empson* (things have changed), and *scientific.*

Dogmatism can be smelt here; also a considerable, if less unpleasing, naïvety. Overlooking how ridiculous it is to posit a law for 'the authentic poet at all times', as if there were no other cultures than our own, one may concentrate on the naïve dogmatism; which is in part historical, or a refusal to take account of history. A medicine-man carries into a cave in Ayer's Rock a lump of crystal: it sparkles, it contains perhaps the 'meaning'. Yeats, for the crystal, contemplates – so far as it can be seen – the Anima Mundi. I would agree that ecstatic lyrical art, *some* of the art which seems to hold up its hand and pronounce a benediction, has come from such contemplation, such a sense that the 'meaning' – we have all longed for a meaning – has been touched, such a sparkling of the rock crystal. But for creditable rather than discreditable reasons (we know more, whether Miss Raine likes it or not, and we can explain our extra knowledge in terms far more precise and sufficient than Miss Raine can employ for the Anima Mundi), art of that once supposed 'inspiration' and perhaps of that power of benison must shorten in supply.

And I do not easily understand Miss Raine's abject (and self-satisfied) defeatism on the subject. Is it a form of masochism, or is it the defiant pleasure of belonging to a secret society? To each his Ku Klux Klan. In one of her better essays, on St John Perse, she quotes from Perse writing, in his *Winds*, 'Everything to recapture. Everything to reproclaim. And the scythe of our glance drawn against all our property.' If we have grown out of our past, out of our old supporting property, out of supernaturalism, out of intimations of a desired 'meaning', aren't we challenged to new vehicles of consolation, if not benediction, at any rate to a new nerve?

Pretending we are not out of supernaturalism can, and on Miss Raine's criticism and power of recognition does, have some tiresomely softening effects. She quotes Coleridge on 'the eternal *in and through the temporal*': she also says that 'those who look to a timeless world are least likely to fall into archaism of style'. Certainly Miss Raine in these essays suffers from weakness in the temporal, exemplifying that those who try short-cuts to the 'eternal' fall into the unreal. The reader needs to be patient with archaic approaches, no doubt, and hopeful, too. But is there a reward for such talk – still falls the drizzle – of 'the poet's task', 'the Celtic genius', 'the haunts of the heron', and this or that which is 'fraught with meanings and messages of the soul'?

Yes, when Miss Raine is informative, for instance about Yeats or St John Perse. No, when she praises Shelley for his short-cutting (or faked temporality). No, when she asks us to admire 'Little lawny islet, with anemones and violet like mosaic paven'. No, when she reads out to us a rather ludicrous (temporally ludicrous) passage from David Gascoyne, beginning 'At night I've often walked on the Embankment of the Thames/ And seen the Power Station's brick cliffs dominate the scene'. No, when she tells us that this passage is 'at once grander and more intimate than Eliot's depiction of *The Waste Land*', and that the poem it comes from asks to be compared with Blake or Dante. No, when she mistakes intention or inclination for performance. No, when she attempts to sandbag or mesmerize the reader, in a prose stubborn with self-righteousness and immodesty, uncertain in grammar, and rife in cliché. If he keeps his head, the reader may find himself recalling that the Semi-colon, in the under-shrubbery of the World Soul, degenerates often into the three dots of spurious significance . . .

1967

Dorian Gray: John Gray

Reasons for reading about John Gray are because one knew him (which I didn't) or knew of him in the legendary era of his Roman Catholic priesthood in Edinburgh, with his odd other half of the legend, André Raffalovich, living nearby in wealthy aesthetic pietism; because one admires some of his writings (which I do); and because he exemplifies a double problem, of life, and of 'modernism' in literature growing out of the equally queer stuff of 'decadence'.

To Gray, in the beginning, Raffalovich was tied rather as Rich Little Ugly to Unrich Aloof Beauty. Several essays in this book[1] are biographical, a little cautious in not denying things which they don't actually say, and which the reader will infer. Gray, then, was an aesthete from the working class, born in 1866, to a carpenter in Woolwich dockyard, himself first a metal-turner and draughtsman, then a Post Office clerk, then (how did that transfer come about?) a librarian in the Foreign Office, aged twenty-two, slim, exceedingly handsome. His friends were Dowson, Wilde, Symons, Beardsley, then Raffalovich, Parisian, Russian-Jewish banker's son, and youthful dilettante rejected by his beautiful mama, who had set him up in London where he was liked but laughed at (by Wilde, for example). Before he encountered Raffalovich, Gray – how, on his salary? – was already the poetical, aesthetical, social dandy, given to first nights and archery in white flannels. Also before long he was a Catholic convert.

Yeats told a tale that Gray and Raffalovich the Rich cruised in a yacht painted black and named *Iniquity*, that they put into an Italian harbour where religious festivities were going on, and were suddenly 'called'. In fact Raffalovich was converted later and Gray had seen his light in a dirty

[1] *Two Friends: John Gray and André Raffalovich*, edited by Father Brocard Sewell (1967).

wayside Breton chapel, where an unshaven priest was
gabbling mass to peasant women. 1892 – Gray twenty-six
years old – seems to have been a critical year: he sued *The
Star* for stating that Mr Gray, 'who has cultivated his manner
to the highest pitch of languor yet attained,' was 'the original
Dorian of the same name', he met Gide's friend the young
Pierre Louÿs, and he was near suicide. *Dorian Gray* had been
published the year before, and though *The Star* retracted,
essays in this book provide evidence that Gray did see himself, and that Wilde did see Gray, as the wonderful, awful
Dorian. In 1893 Wilde paid for the printing of Gray's first
poems, *Silverpoints*, widest margins, binding and typography
by Ricketts, period confections (including translations from
Verlaine, Rimbaud, etc.) not without rhythmic and verbal
intimations of a reality which would be long delayed.

After *Silverpoints*, he wrote affected religious poems; also
– with Raffalovich – an Ibsenish-ninetyish play about black-
mail in society. Then 1895, the Wilde Year, during which
'every suitcase in London was packed for instant flight'.
The trial made Raffalovich write a book on homosexuality,
and he, too, now became a Catholic. Gray also left the
Foreign Office, and became a candidate for orders, not long
before Pierre Louÿs married a different bride, the poet
Heredia's daughter. Louÿs to Gray: 'Oui, mon cher ami, je
me suis marié, on ne t'avait pas trompé. Nous sommes arrivés
toi et moi, presque le même année, à un tournant de notre
vie. Estu content de ta décision?'

Gray was soon – and for the rest of his life in the new
century – a priest, not in corrupt London but cold Edinburgh; living in a presbytery and serving a church, which
were both built at the expense of Raffalovich; who settled
nearby, maintaining with Gray a friendship at once close
and formalized, and with the élite of that provincial city an
irreproachable Sunday *salon*. Thereafter the story becomes
one of a controlled, cultured pietism, ending with the deaths
of little Raffalovich and the remote mask-wearing saintly
priest, one after the other, in 1934. Both had retreated out of
decadence, and their youth, renunciators, far from Wilde's
London or Louÿs's Paris. Their milieu, all the same, was
aesthetically religious. Gray's diamond-paned soft-carpeted

presbytery struck one contributor as 'filled with elusive twi-light', suggestive of Maeterlinck or Debussy. The sheets on Gray's bed were of black linen. In the church prayers were asked for the soul of Verlaine. In Raffalovich's house every Sunday evening the bell rang, the maid announced 'Canon Gray', Raffalovich jumped up, bowed, shook hands, and exclaimed: 'Dear Canon, how kind of you to call!' When Gray was off on one of his striding holidays (over hills in Scotland, the Cotswolds, etc.), every evening he would send Raffalovich a telegram.

In another way there was no retreat, but an advance out of soft into hard language. Small books came out rather privately, and two of them matter. About *Park* (250 copies, 1932), an admirably written story of cultured, philosophic (Catholic) Negroes who have conquered England and breed horses on Cotswold, while the English live a mass rodent life in Tube tunnels, contributors have something to say. About the poems in *The Long Road* (1926, another 250 copies, but both can be read in the British Museum) little is said, and in nineteen pages on Gray, Mr Iain Fletcher does not even mention Gray's long, hard, sharp, strange single masterpiece, 'The Flying Fish', one of the good 'modern' poems of our century. This is a critical feat like assessing Eliot without 'The Waste Land' or Coleridge without 'The Ancient Mariner'.

In this poem held tightly together in rhyming quatrains by its tone, which is quizzing, inconsequent and consequent, by its scenery and geography, mid-oriental without being specific and yet precise (reminding one of a story by Conrad placed where Chinese and Malaysian meet), by its mineral or consonantal collection of words, its slightly ironic, archaic 'modernism', one is without preamble put into the company of Hang the buccaneer:

Myself am Hang, the buccaneer,
whom children love and brave men fear,
master of courage, come what come,
master of craft and called Sea-scum.

Student of wisdom and waterways,
course of moons and the birth of days:

to him in whose heart all things be,
I bring my story from the sea.

Hang quickly introduces himself, his guise on the quay of
the merchants, Hang undisguised on his pirate junk and in
his palace and his gardens in the island sea.

So cotton rags lays Hang aside;
Lays bare the sailor's gristly hide;
he wraps his body in vests of silk,
ilk is as beautiful as ilk.

He enumerates, leaving the description of himself, the six
strange birds which fly in the farthest sea:

I mind the fifth, I forget the fourth,
save that it comes from east and north;
the fifth is an orange white-billed duck;
he diveth for fish like the god of Luck;

He hath never a foot on which to stand,
for water yields and he loves not land.
This is the end of many words,
save one, concerning marvellous birds.

Save one: Hang, having dealt with marvellous birds, now
enumerates marvellous fish, beginning with the dolphin and
the swordfish; and ending with that one he hasn't mentioned,
since 'The last strange fish is the last strange bird' – the
Flying Fish, whose bitter enemies are the other five fowl and
the other five fishes:

In sea and sky he hath no peace,
for the five strange fish are his enemies.
And the five strange fowls keep watch for him,
they know him well by his crystal gleam.

Oftwhiles, sir Sage, on my junk's white deck,
have I seen this fish-bird come to wreck;
oftwhiles (fair deck) 'twixt bow and poop,
have I seen that piteous sky fish stoop.

Scaled bird, how his snout and gills dilate,
all quivering and roseate!
He pants in crystal and mother-of-pearl,
while his body shrinks and his pinions furl.

His beauty passes like bubbles blown;
the white bright bird is a fish of stone.
The bird so fair, for its putrid sake,
is flung to the dogs in the junk's white wake.

The sage, in the second part, interprets the Flying Fish as
a symbol of aspiration born of fear; though the Fish remains
and does not lose its shining solidity in the abstract.
In the throbbing heart of this farthest sea the fish says, in
his own iridescent heart, how splendid are his eyes, how his
back 'has the secret of every shell': it is the ugly birds who
devise his ill.
Not wishing to be a son of air, he wishes nevertheless to be
rid of water:

All his hope is a fear-whipped whim,
all directions are one to him.
There are seekers of wisdom no less absurd,
Son Hang, than thy fish that would be a bird.

Texture, tone, movement – though one may see the poem
as a distanced image of Gray's own life, all lives of aspiration
– sufficiently mark 'The Flying Fish' and on this level make
it entirely acceptable and memorable. On the interior level,
or in its entirety, one sees how the poem relates to the image
of *Park*; but in that novel no dead-fish-and-bird is flung
contemptuously to the congers: a dream instead is realized,
the ugly have retreated into their holes, even if the vision in
the end is withdrawn.
Otherwise John Gray is a poet – so far as we have all his
poems? – of now and then sparkling oddments or images:

You see fleet and fair
gazelles by hippogriffins torn,
a wild curvetting unicorn
across a cherry-coloured morn.

But enough of him there is to establish an individuality of style and imagination.

'The Flying Fish' is most easily found in not always congenial company in the anthology which John Masefield published in 1906 and called *A Sailor's Garland*; and as if to show that its farthest junk-ridden sea was not so divorced from a less exotic reality of fish and sailors, Masefield included another poem by John Gray, 'Wings in the Dark':

. . . passing fishers through the darkness call,

Deep greeting, in the jargon of the sea.
Haul upon haul, flounders and soles and dabs,
And phosphorescent animalculae,
Sand, sea drift, weeds, thousands of worthless crabs.

Darkling upon the mud the fishes grope,
Cautious to stir, staring with jewel eyes;
Dog of the sea, the savage congers mope,
Winding their sulky march meander-wise.

Suddenly all is light and life and flight,
Upon the sandy bottom, agate strewn.
The fishers mumble, waiting till the night
Urge on the clouds, and cover up the moon.

But secrets of John Gray's existence are there too, on the mud of that more ordinary, yet also extraordinary sea. Like Ivor Gurney he is one of the half-hidden poets who cannot be left out of this century's account.

1967

The Poet Who Did Not Care for Life

Does everyone who writes about Thomas Hardy's poems begin by saying that to the end Hardy looked upon himself as a poet, and not as a writer of fiction; that Hardy wished to be remembered, expected to be remembered, by his poems?

Well, it was so. He began with poems, he ended with poems. In between, and in a way because he had to, so as to be independent and free, he wrote the novels that in spite of themselves, in spite of an often appalling periphrastic manner, do rise to their exasperating greatness. I do not know of any artist in fiction who has ever been happy about Hardy's fictional lapses and awkwardnesses, even allowing for the imperfections of the most perfect works of art. Imperfections are the not very exorbitant price we pay for what we are lucky to be given, but one does read Hardy's novels, if at all, with despair; one is inclined to compare his fictional in-artistry with the artistry, say, of Giovanni Verga in Italy. They are contemporaries, Verga and Hardy, both are more or less 'country' novelists, concerned with poverty, injustice, and fate, but Verga's ideas, Verga's conclusions are presented in the drama of happenings, persons, speech, and behaviour; whereas in Hardy's novels, from first to last, opinions and conclusions, and generalized or abstracted perceptions sprawl sententiously, in an extra presence, on the flow and surface of his fictional activity. If only Thomas Hardy, doomster, law-upsetter, lawgiver, pronouncer, would be kind enough to go out of the room, and let his novel get on with itself. D. H. Lawrence, his follower, himself lawgiver and law-upsetter and pronouncer, said that 'the tiresome part about Hardy is that, so often, he will neither write a morality play nor a novel'.

Often these colourings and inadequacies and awkwardnesses of his novels are put down to Hardy's provinciality.
Wrongly. 'Provinciality' – if that is the word for not standing
in the central crowd – is Hardy's strength; Hardy's weakness
in fiction arises arguably from his dislike of fiction; or from
preferring the poetry he would rather have written all the
while; and to which he did not return, in full strength, at any
rate, until his novels came to an end and a climax with *Jude
the Obscure*. If the novelist does not often write good poems
(try the poems of George Eliot, or Thackeray, or Dickens, or
Mr Kingsley Amis), the poet is seldom a good novelist. His
business is – decidedly – with moments of vision, with lyrics,
with powerful brevity, not with the huge complexity and
extension of the novel. Faced with contriving again and
again twoscore or threescore chapters and hundreds of pages,
it seems to me that in fiction Hardy often imitated fiction,
often filled in between, precisely, moments of vision. He
would circumlocute, which gives a stylistic appearance of
self-satisfaction or pomposity or facetiousness. In *Jude the
Obscure* Jude makes his first visit to Arabella's house. 'A
smell of piggeries came from the back, and the grunting of
the originators of that smell.'

The grunting of the pigs – that is about all there would be
room for in a poem – becomes 'the grunting of the originators
of that smell'.

It is interesting to see the poems and the fiction of Victor
Hugo, a very much greater writer than either Hardy or
Verga, contrasting in the same way. Hugo's poems, the best
of them, are concentrated visions of majesty, insight, and
always convincing actuality, whereas preachment does intervene and interrupt in his novels. Hardy is the poet whose
true *métier* has to come up again and again in his false or
adopted one. A familiar example is the first appearance, in
Jude the Obscure, of the child who carries the sinister nick-
name of 'Little Father Time', who will be the instrument of
horror, of the children hanging dead by the garment hooks,
and the note saying 'Done because we are too menny'. The
page, the description of Little Father Time, has the qualities,
suddenly, of a poem, a moment of vision in one of those
third-class carriages, those vehicles of common life in which

Hardy looked around and meditated so often on what he saw, a vision both momentary and everlasting, a concentration out of the normal keepings of fiction. This prose-poem of Little Father Time with the key around his neck is, in fact, worked up from a moment of vision which had its simpler or less annotated outcome in the actual poem 'Midnight on the Great Western':

> In the third-class carriage seat sat the journeying boy,
>   And the roof-lamp's oily flame
> Played down on his listless form and face.

In *Jude* the vision is expanded and glossed to the extent of turning the child into 'Age masquerading as Juvenility, and doing it so badly that his real self showed through crevices':

> A ground swell from ancient years of night seemed now and then to lift the child in this his morning-life, when his face took a back view over some great Atlantic of Time, and appeared not to care about what it saw.

In Hardy's work the debt is from poetry to fiction, not the other way round. What I insist on is the amateurism of Hardy as a novelist (though amateurism, like provincialism, may have its triumphs) and the professionalism of Hardy as one of the peculiar, if not one of the more splendid, poets in our language.

Even then it is true that the explicit rather than the implicit view of universal fate can be too obvious in the poems. I choose for an example Hardy's poem 'A Plaint to Man', from the great volume of 1914, *Satires of Circumstance*, in which he included several of the poems one would least be without, such as the Lyonesse poem, and 'A Thunderstorm in Town', and 'In Death Divided', 'The Voice', 'After a Journey', and 'The Phantom Horse-Woman'. The plaint is made by God, who never existed, and is about to die; and Hardy set the poem – this would not have been accidental – between his lines on the life, the poems, the death, and the grave of Swinburne who had given his kick to the complacent falsities of his time –

> It was as though a garland of red roses
> Had fallen about the hood of some smug nun –

between that poem to Swinburne and the poem in which mourners next attend the funeral of God, who has at last succumbed. God admits that he was created by man, a kind of projection of a lantern slide, for praying to, he says he is dwindling

And to-morrow the whole of me disappears,
The truth should be told, and the fact be faced
That had best been faced in earlier years:

The fact of life with dependence placed
On the human heart's resource alone,
In brotherhood bonded close and graced

With loving-kindness fully blown,
And visioned help unsought, unknown.

This poem – I shall say more of it later on – is of a kind, skilled and effective as it may be, that I regret and as a rule pass over or put in Hardy's second or third rank. It is a thought poem, a poem of personified abstraction of a kind he has a fondness for. He said more than once that we should not look for an harmonious philosophy in his poems, or throughout all the things he had written. He said, introducing his second book of poems in 1901, that 'unadjusted impressions have their value, and the road to a true philosophy of life seems to lie in humbly recording diverse readings of its phenomena as they are forced upon us by chance and change'. When theism was passing out, to survive only in formal institutions and backward provinces of the mind, well enough and proper enough to write on the death of God, and to insist upon our necessary resort to brotherhood and loving-kindness – 'on the human heart's resource alone'; yet here, in a poem as well, an opinion, a conclusion seems to sprawl on the surface, on the flow of the rhythm from one triplet to the next; whereas in the best poems by Hardy the felt phenomena *are* the poem, through and through; incorporated with the form, the movement, the thought, the emotion.

A less known poem, seldom excerpted and reprinted, amalgamates man, his anguish, all that is inflicted on him,

and the landscape which holds him, with more immediacy
and success. This is his poem 'In Front of the Landscape',
apparently one of those poems written out of that backward
and present survey stirred in him by his wife's death in 1912.
Two times, early and young, late and old, two landscapes,
familiar Dorset of

> the coomb and the upland
> Coppice-crowned,
> Ancient chalk-pit, milestone, rills in the grass-flat
> Stroked by the light

and unfamiliar North Cornwall of the headland 'gnawed by
the tide', are held together, the flush of love and the dead are
remembered, and Hardy supposes that people who go by,
say of him

> Ah – whose is this dull form that perambulates, seeing nought
> Round him that looms
> Whithersoever his footsteps turn in his farings,
> Save a few tombs?

That is better, Hardy in the world, Hardy among people,
Hardy in time, Hardy, who sees nothing around him but a
few tombs, establishing that communion with the past which
is one of the salutary and essential gifts of literary art,
abundant in Hardy, as in that also appropriately slow-moving
and rightly favourite poem by him

> William Dewy, Tranter Reuben, Farmer Ledlow late at
>> plough,
> Robert's kin, and John's, and Ned's,
> And the Squire, and Lady Susan, lie in Mellstock
> churchyard now!

(which must be taken as the necessary dignifying supplement
to *Under the Greenwood Tree*).

Of course, the right way to read, not a poet, who cannot
be read, but the poems of a poet, is to recognize them as
separate acts, as 'unadjusted impressions'. An image for this,
and for not doing it, for the wrong reading of poetry, would
be that of mushroom and mycelium. The poems are the

mushrooms, to go digging below them for the intricate
causative mycelium, the poet, the complex of threads
through the chemistry of the mould, is not perhaps imperti-
nent or foolish, but pointless – tempting but pointless; since
as much as can be recovered and established with any cer-
tainty or even likelihood amounts to no more than an
approximation of the total. Critics are inordinately tempted
– and in part this is Hardy's own fault – to this act of digging
up his mycelium while they neglect the actuality of his
poems.

More attention to the poems, to their rhythmic and
stanzaic variety, their resourceful rhetoric, their unstarveling
personal language contrived of common speech and pause,
and neologism, archaism, and inversion, would diminish these
complaints – which are still advanced in spite of the concur-
rently admitted effectiveness of the poems – that Hardy all
round, in verse as in fiction, was a clumsy, inept, and half-
educated writer.

The fact is that the willing devotion to verse and the
prudential self-assignment to fiction produced in Hardy's
poems and novels different peculiarities, which should not be
confused. It is an old confusion. Long ago, before Hardy was
at all thoroughly digested, Yeats talked of Hardy's verse
lacking 'technical accomplishment'. If that was yesterday,
from today, from the new holder of the Oxford chair of
poetry, I take the following, that Hardy had 'a peasant's
view of life', a 'peasant's realism'; that he displayed a
'clumping earnestness'; that his poems 'are very like the
work of a village craftsman', that in his poems 'there is
always a certain stiff deliberation, the unhurried gait of the
countryman going about his immemorial business'. Another
recent Hardy editor accuses him of the oddities of 'incompe-
tence', or 'a simple-minded determination to squash dialogue
into verse at the expense of sense, usage and common
decency', of there being 'something essentially home-made
about Hardy's style'. I do not know where else styles are
made than at home, but let everyone have his fancy, and for
a moment let me go rather a long way off for a different
comment to apply to Hardy.

It happened that before I began this piece on Hardy I was

reading a book on the early life, notions, and poems of the Chinese modernist Kuo Mo-jo;[1] and I was hit by this state-fent of Kuo Mo-jo's: that 'The language of poetry is not a human effort to express emotion, but emotion's expression of itself'. It seemed to this Chinese poet, student of Whitman, Goethe, Heine, Tolstoy (and of Hardy, for all I know), that 'real poetry, good poetry, can only come into existence when one has reached this state in which substance and form are completely undifferentiated'.

'Emotion's expression of itself' may seem, and may be, an ideal hyperbolic statement, artifice being inevitable in art, even perhaps in a sudden brief exclamation of pain or pleasure. But the language of poetic art, the work of poetic art, must be as nearly as possible emotion's expression of itself, and substance does not admit – without strain or disaster – of a form alien to itself. Or to say that both of Kuo Mo-jo's statements are well fitted to Hardy's poems is to say without trimmings, 'Hardy's are poems worth attending to.'

Let me recall three irreproachable poems – poems of love and pain, one written early, and two written late, in Hardy's life, in which I see, not a misfitting of substance and form, but a true appropriateness of language to emotion; in which phenomena are of the substance, and what is conveyed is implicit, not pulled out and framed. The early poem is 'Neutral Tones', written when Hardy was twenty-seven, in circumstances of which we are ignorant, except in the suffi-cient terms of the poem itself. Hardy and a girl meet in winter by a pond edged with greyish leaves:

We stood by a pond that winter day,
And the sun was white, as though chidden of God,
And a few leaves lay on the starving sod;
– They had fallen from an ash, and were gray.

The smile on the girl's mouth 'was the deadest thing/ Alive enough to have strength to die': and deception in love and the occasion shaped to Hardy, for keeping, the girl's face, the God-cursed sun, the ash tree, and the pond and the leaves.

[1] *Kuo Mo-jo: The Early Years*, by David Tod Roy (Harvard University Press, 1971).

The other two poems, the late ones, are similar expressions of related moments of retrospective vision and awareness, printed in a group in *Moments of Vision*, in 1917 (Hardy was then seventy-seven), about the first years of his marriage, in the villa at Sturminster Newton. In the first, 'Overlooking the River Stour', the tone changes with an inversion after stanzas describing the flight of the swallows and the way in which a moorhen rips over the water throwing up shavings of spray as a carpenter's plane throws up shavings of wood.

> Closed were the kingcups; and the mead
> Dripped in monotonous green.

Then, in conclusion,

> And never I turned my head, alack,
> While these things met my gaze
> Through the pane's drop-drenched glaze,
> To see the more behind my back. . . .
> O never I turned, but let, alack,
> These less things hold my gaze!

(The movement is one imitated, or echoed, later by Robert Frost.) The other poem, 'On Sturminster Footbridge', shifts to autumn. Hardy is outside, this time, and looks up at the window of the room which contains his young wife, the gleam in the darkness of the world, when the leaves are rotting and the swallows ready to go:

> Reticulations creep upon the slack stream's face
> When the wind skims irritably past,
> The current clucks smartly into each hollow place
> That years of flood have scrabbled in the pier's sodden base,
> The floating-lily leaves rot fast.

> On a roof stand the swallows ranged in wistful waiting
> rows,
> Till they arrow off and drop like stones
> Among the eyot-withies at whose foot the river flows:
> And beneath the roof is she who in the dark world shows
> As a lattice-gleam when midnight moans.

Each of these two Sturminster Newton poems says, but

through the visible, through the observed, through the record of each situation, that Hardy did not value, at the time, did not sufficiently value, that which he would look back to, in misery, in deprivation, as among the few genuinely felicitous moments of his life. A common experience, uncommonly, yet at once convincingly, put.

Hardy, the peasant of clumping earnestness and a peasant's view of life, etc., jotted down several remarks that fit in well with these particular poems and with his practice as a poet. One was a sentence quoted from his friend Leslie Stephen (the father of Virginia Woolf) – that 'The ultimate aim of the poet should be to touch our hearts by showing his own, and not to exhibit his learning, or his fine taste, or his skill, in mimicking the notes of his predecessors'. Another was 'My art is to intensify the expression of things, as is done by Crivelli, Bellini, etc., so that the heart and inner meaning is made vividly visible'.

In a third meditation, put down in 1887, when he was forty-seven, he declared his feeling that Nature was 'played out as a Beauty, but not as a Mystery', that the simply natural was no longer of interest, that 'exact truth as to material fact ceases to be of importance in art', and was only a student's style, 'the style of a period when the mind is serene' – as his own was not and never had been and never would be – 'and unawakened to the tragical mysteries of life': he wanted the artist's mind to bring something 'to the object that coalesces with and translates the qualities that are already there'.

The unfamiliar yet not opaque language of Hardy's poems, his compressions, his conveyance of something direct enough with the aid, for example, of knobbly and often polysyllabic rhyme – these belong to Hardy's special apparatus of intensification.

Objects coalescing with qualities and translating qualities, and a mind, the mind of the poet, bringing its own something to this objective, phenomenal mixture and translation – there you have more than a little of Hardy's verse. In above nine hundred poems the quantity of Hardy's just and peculiar recognition is enormous and is not easy to exhaust. That good poet the late Andrew Young, who was in various respects

one of the better children of Hardy, told me that he read
right through Hardy's *Collected Poems* once every year,
each time finding or becoming for the first time conscious of
things he had missed; and I believe that it is common for
some hitherto disregarded poem, or line, or image, in Hardy,
to come forward suddenly out of the crowd and establish
itself altogether *de novo* in the reader's or the devotee's
intrigued consciousness.

Reverting to that poem 'A Plaint to Man', may I recall
God's dismal closing complaint that the whole of him is disappearing, and his less dismal insistence that life must
depend 'on the human heart's resource alone/ In brotherhood bonded close and graced/ With loving-kindness fully
blown/ And visioned help unsought, unknown'.

With that in mind – and it is *not* a pessimistic statement –
I would push forward some other remarks by that culturally
different, ecstatic, exclamatory Kuo Mo-jo. Kuo Mo-jo said:
'It is our objective to destroy the lair of the demon with
bombs of life.' His demon was the economico-political demon,
distorting naked humanity. And such negating distorting
forces were hateful to Hardy (who began his fiction with a
novel unpublished because his publisher found it too social-
istic, and ended it – in *Jude* – with the most swingeing and
contemptuous assault on shibboleths of class, property, and
accepted religion).

'All sincere artists', Kuo Mo-jo declared, 'are pure revolu-
tionaries.' Hardy, for us, revolutionized the substance and
language of poems. Much could be left discarded, buried,
mummified in Sarcophagus College, in the un-universal
university of inaccessible and self-satisfied Christminster.
Nature, which nevertheless so delights him in its phenomena,
is played out as a beauty: 'An object or mark raised or made
by man on a scene', said Hardy to his notebook, 'is worth
ten times any such formed by unconscious Nature. Hence
clouds, mists, and mountains are unimportant beside the
wear on a threshold, or the print of a hand.'

And yet – and yet I do not, and cannot claim too much for
this revolutionary poet, this renovator of an art. I admit that
I read him less and less as I grow older. Why? Because he
has too much to question, to negate, to demolish. When

theism was a dry, universal, or all but universal scab, it was
admirable to have a poet – to have poems, regretful poems,
in which God was put forward to deny his own stifling
existence or to announce his demise. But coming to questions
of life, of living, of man and woman, of love, I accept the
proposition that Hardy was probably incapable of a full,
profound, physical relationship, with consequent drawbacks
or peculiarities for his art. (Parenthetically, that is why the
search for the other woman in Hardy's life is never going to
come to much, or to much that is significant.) I would accept,
and applaud, in him an androgynous nature, which can
speak for women as well as men, complaining, all the same,
of a deficiency which makes him celebrate satisfactions – if
celebrate is quite the word – only by pointing over and over
again to their absence. *If* – to what a degree that brief
diminishing limiting vocable is important in his poems – *if*
life was so and so, *if* I had dared, *if* you had loved me or
if love had continued, *if* you were here and not elsewhere
and hadn't broken the appointment, *if* you were not dead.
Think how that motif recurs – 'I should have kissed her if the
rain / Had lasted a minute more', or less familiar, 'Faintheart
in a Railway Train':

> At nine in the morning there passed a church,
> At ten there passed me by the sea,
> At twelve a town of smoke and smirch,
> At two a forest of oak and birch,
>   And then, on a platform, she –

But no, he didn't dare, he didn't get out to that radiant
stranger, he could not think of what to say, and he let the
train take him on.

>   O could it but be
> That I had alighted there.

Someone has wittily said that Hardy made love to women,
but at a distance of three and a half feet. Could that have
been the trouble, or part of the trouble, between him and
Emma Hardy? And isn't it a faint presence even in those
demonstrations of the heart, which touch our own hearts
so extremely, in the famous laments of Hardy's return to

Cornwall? What is missing is the celebration of body with body, or flesh with flesh, at the same time as spirit with spirit, the two together (was Hardy a reader of John Donne? I think not). So often *if* instead of *now*, the conditional instead of the performed, the enjoyed, extending widely into the valuation of all the experiences of life, not merely the sexual ones:

> There trudges one to a merry-making
> >   With a sturdy swing,
> On whom the rain comes down.
>
> To fetch the saving medicament
> >   Is another bent,
> On whom the rain comes down.
>
> One slowly drives his herd to the stall
> >   Ere ill befall,
> On whom the rain comes down –

And so on, until the rain comes down on to the dead and insentient. Grateful as I am to Hardy, for me the rain falls too incessantly. It is not that I ask for a fake salvationist, a false back-slapping comforter in the old style. We know what personally and collectively may become of us, what naturally and physiologically must become of us. But what do we receive from our human status and our human senses, what have we to be grateful for? More, I would say, than Hardy allows for in his 'epitaph':

> I never cared for Life: Life cared for me,
> And hence I owed it some fidelity.
> It now says, 'Cease; at length thou hast learnt to grind
> Sufficient toll for an unwilling mind,
> And I dismiss thee – not without regard
> That thou didst ask no ill-advised reward,
> Nor sought in me much more than thou couldst find.'

In other poems as well, such as 'Regret Not Me', and the famous 'Afterwards', Hardy almost acts the small boy who says to his parents: 'You'll be sorry when I'm dead.' Preferring fanatic indignation, declaimed in the bright sunshine, to

murmurs in the gloom, or more of such murmurs than the
patient's case allows, we have reason also to demand the
soaring rhythm in our arts. But we have to go elsewhere for
that. Rationing my Hardy, I admit I now turn more to 'The
Wild Swans at Coole' (and not, a kind of sequel to Hardy for
which Hardy cannot be blamed, either to Philip Larkin's
grey flux and reflux of the tide soup of Hull or to the Poet
Laureate's decaffeination of Hardy to an ingratiating sentimental pastiche); I turn to

> Unwearied still, lover by lover,
> They paddle in the cold
> Companionable streams or climb the air;
> Their hearts have not grown old,

or to George Herbert rising from black depression, not because I share his Heaven, but because I can share, and I
require, his relish:

> Grief melts away
> Like snow in May,
> As if there were no such cold thing. . . .

> And now in age I bud again,
> After so many deaths I live and write;
> I once more smell the dew and rain,
> And relish versing: . . .

If I am sorry to end negatively, perhaps treasonably some
Hardyists will think, it is relish of which Hardy has not
enough to offer, and without which we cannot live well in
the mind.

1973

Three Eastern Notes

1. *Sei Shonagon's* Pillow Book

When I was asked the other day to go out and get three bay leaves for the kitchen, I found myself bringing back three leaves covered, or rather lined down the midrib, with frozen snow. Very pretty they looked, and as the snow melted on the leaves in the heat of the kitchen, I realized that my choice of the leaves with snow had been a tribute either to Sei Shonagon's *Pillow Book*, or to having read, long ago, the Lady Murasaki's *Tale of Genji*, or to both.

Sei Shonagon was born about 965, some ten years before the Lady Murasaki. She was a lady-in-waiting to the Empress Sadoko in the Japanese capital, Heian Kyo, the City of Peace and Tranquillity, today's very different Kyoto. Her *Pillow Book* – so called because the notebook in which it was written from day to day would have been kept in the drawer of Sei Shonagon's wooden pillow – could be most nearly described, in our terms, as a commonplace book. I thought when I read it, in this first complete English translation,[1] of Dorothy Wordsworth writing up her journal in the Quantocks and the Lakes. 'Sometimes one's carriage will pass over a branch of sagebrush, which then gets caught in the wheel and is lifted up at each turn, letting the passengers breathe its delicious scent.' Miss Wordsworth's brother could have turned that into a poem. Or this: 'As it became sunnier, the dew gradually vanished from the clover and the other plants where it had lain so heavily; the branches began to stir, and then suddenly sprang up of their own accord.'

But then Sei Shonagon was a Heian lady, in a sophisticated court, and not a brown gypsy-like (if also in a different way sophisticated) poet's sister on the verges of Grasmere.

[1] *The Pillow Book of Sei Shonagon*, translated by Ivan Morris (1967).

Miss Wordsworth and William Wordsworth would not have appreciated Sei Shonagon on her love-affairs, in a time when gentlemen sent their ladies a 'morning-after letter':

> In the winter, when it is very cold and one lies buried under the bedclothes listening to one's lover's endearments, it is delightful to hear the booming of a temple gong, which seems to come from the bottom of a deep well. The first cry of the birds, whose beaks are still tucked under their wings, is also strange and muffled. Then one bird after another takes up the call. How pleasant it is to lie there listening as the sound becomes clearer and clearer.

No, Sei Shonagon is nearer Colette than Dorothy Wordsworth. Or imagine a cross (feminine instead of masculine) between *The Fruits of the Earth*, which André Gide wrote when he was young, and Cecil Torr's *Small Talk at Wreyland*. Sei Shonagon particularizes, she generalizes, she turns from nature to men (and women), from snow and moonlight to shrewd gossip.

Ivan Morris, her translator, has written an admirable book, *The World of the Shining Prince*, in which he describes the Heian culture of Japan, which overlaps at either end with the T'ang and Sung periods in China. Everyone – everyone who belonged to the court – was addicted to aestheticism and the arts. Every Heian gentleman and lady was given to viewing moonlight, cuckoos, fruit blossom, snow, waterfalls, lakes, springs, rivers, and mountains, was given – like Sei Shonagon – to love-making, to calligraphy, music, writing poems, and the art of blending incense. Mr Morris quoted one decidedly Calvinistic historian of Japan on this Heian aristocracy. 'In the ringing phrases of the kirk', this Scots professor called them 'An ever-pullulating brood of greedy, needy, frivolous dilettanti – as often as not foully licentious, utterly effeminate, incapable of any worthy achievement, but withal the polished exponents of high breeding and correct form'.

One gathers that there have been historians in Japan who would concur. But it won't do. The Heian sensibility differed

about as much from the thin spurious sensibility of the
Nineties or the Twenties in London, let us say, as from the
sensibility (if that is the word) of the kirk in Aberdeen.
The Pillow Book, for all its wit and elegance, is very much
more than a book of cold hedonism. It contains a vision of
life as well as things.

Sei Shonagon likes to put down her preferences and aver-
sions in the shorthand of lists. When she is not exclaiming
'How delightful!' – at the same time recreating the delight
by the way in which it is presented – she will enter in her
Pillow Book a list of 'Depressing Things', or 'Shameful
Things', or 'Squalid Things', or 'Things that People Despise',
in which some item or another goes to the heart. 'Things
that People Despise' include 'The north side of a house',
'Someone with an excessive reputation for goodness', and
'A mud wall that has started to crumble'. 'Depressing
Things' include various items out of time or season such as
'A dog howling in the daytime', and then continue 'A lying-
in room when the baby has died. A cold, empty brazier. An
ox-driver who hates his oxen.'

The senses of this excellent writer – all of them – are open
in every direction. Among 'Squalid Things' she will list 'The
back of a piece of embroidery. The inside of a cat's ear';
among 'Things That Have Lost Their Power', 'A large boat
which is high and dry in a creek at ebb-tide. A woman who
has taken off her false locks to comb the short hair that
remains'; among 'Adorable Things', 'A young Palace page,
who is still quite small, walking by in ceremonial costume....
Duck eggs. An urn containing the relics of some holy person.
Wild pinks'; or among 'Things That Lose By Being Painted',
'Pinks, cherry blossoms, yellow roses. Men or women who
are praised in romances as being beautiful.'

One feels that some recent or hoarded experience is con-
cealed in every statement. Sei Shonagon thinks and talks
about the pleasure of receiving letters. 'An attractive woman,
whose hair tumbles loosely over her forehead, has received
a letter in the dark. Evidently' – and evidently Sei Shonagon
was watching, or was herself the attractive lady – 'she is too
impatient to wait for a lamp; instead she takes some fire-
tongs, and lifting a piece of burning charcoal from the

brazier, laboriously reads it by its pale light. It is a charming scene.'

Then, too, listing 'Shameful Things' (including abandoning a court lady after she becomes pregnant), she starts the list with a thief in the house; the thief becomes a particular thief: he has crept in, he is hiding in a nook where he can see what is going on – 'Someone else comes into the dark room, and, taking an object that lies there, slips it into his sleeve. *It must be amusing for the thief to see a person who shares his own nature.*' It is as if, again, Sei Shonagon herself had been the one thief, or the other.

Two centuries before this extraordinary woman was born, and before the climax of the extraordinary Heian culture she ornamented, a poet of the Nara period compiled the great Japanese anthology the *Manyo Shu*, or *Collection of Ten Thousand Leaves*, in which one poet writes of the way his dead lover had leant against him as the seaweed rests on the waves, another of being as close to his lover as the clothes of girls boiling salt on the shore fitted close to their bodies. I think that readers of *The Pillow Book* will be staggered by the extent and intensity of the Japanese feeling of a unity with nature, and the concomitant – and well-ordered – sense of the poignancy of life. I would say that in these islands we edged towards the same or a similar ideal in Ireland and Wales for a while in the Middle Ages, judging from translations of Irish and Walsh nature poetry. Then we edged nearer still in that balanced period – though we could not hold the balance – which produced Pope and Kent and Gilbert White, and the landscape gardens and the prospect-towers and Cotman and Constable and the Wordsworths, and John Clare, and William Cowper looking at the descent of the leaves of Buckinghamshire in 1790 and writing in one of his letters I quote to myself – and others – again and again: 'A yellow shower of leaves is falling from all the trees. . . . The consideration of my short continuance here, which was once grateful to me, now fills me with regret. I would live and live always.'

Sei Shonagon, too, would have wanted to live and live always. Consciously or unconsciously we have inherited enough from our own artists and poets to make me sure of one thing – that this *Pillow Book* will have an English public for years and years to come.

1967

2. *Stories by Kawabata*

Yasunari Kawabata is the most recent (and the first Japanese) winner of the Nobel Prize. I do not say that means anything. The large Nobel Prize, like all prizes, is at times given to dough which doesn't rise, at any rate to authors of a minimal artistry. It is a maximal artistry which strikes me first about Kawabata, even in translation. Artistry in fiction among other things means that a reader is never bored, also that he accepts, that he has to accept, the inevitability and instantaneous quality of the things described, the persons, the actions, the situations, being just so.

Novelists fumble, novelists are smart and add unnecessary touches. Or they smartly appear to be cutting everything down to a minimum which they hope will be effective and which really is no more than a manipulation of their own poverty. (I think myself that Hemingway – among Nobel prize-winners – was that latter kind of sentimental manipulator of only a little more than nothing.)

Inevitable, instantaneous. At once Kawabata establishes a situation. Sometimes in the very first sentence. *Snow Country*, an extraordinary study of love and sensuality which was the first of his books to be translated into English (some twelve years ago), began 'The train came out of the long tunnel into the snow country', a first sentence which the reader of the whole novel is unlikely to forget. And I remember that a chapter of *Thousand Cranes* (published in England in 1959) began 'Back in the bedroom after brushing his teeth, Kikuji saw that the maid had hung a gourd in the alcove. It contained a single morning glory.'

The title story in these new translations[2] begins with the same involving immediacy. A man in his late sixties has passed through the locked gate into the reception room of a

[2] *House of the Sleeping Beauties*, translated by Edward G. Seidensticker (1969).

peculiar house of assignation. The proprietress or rather manageress, who has a sharp knowledge of our secret life, provides old men with unattainable, though not untouchable, youth and beauty – or not to use such abstractions, they pay to pass the night, that and no more, with young girls drugged into unknowingness.

This is Kawabata's device – though 'device' suggests a trickiness or an apparent artifice very opposite to the reader's experience – for getting deep into the being of Eguchi. Old Eguchi finds himself drawn again and again to the house, as if in pursuit 'of a vanished happiness in being alive'. Each sleeping girl, by a feature, a movement, a tinge, a scent, revivifies moments, experiences, sensualities, secrecies in his past life. Perhaps, he thinks, the attraction of this house is 'the longing of the sad old men for the unfinished dream'; which is all we have in fact, the dream of what is never obtained, never obtainable.

Crudely or bluntly stated, the situation if not the theme of this *House of the Sleeping Beauties* sounds morbid or designing. In fact this is a story of subtle directness, of open secrecy, with no desire to catch readers by its peculiarity. It is dramatic, sad, and full of that poetic 'realness', which is so much more than 'being real'. Phrases, particular moments, particular touches, stick to the mind. One such moment is when another *habitué* first tells Old Eguchi of this strange house:

When Kiga had visited Eguchi, he had looked out into the garden. Something red lay on the brown autumn moss.
'What can it be?'
He had gone down to look. The dots were red acki berries. Numbers of them lay on the ground. Kiga picked one up. Toying with it, he told Eguchi of the secret house. He went to the house, he said, when the despair of old age was too much for him.

The touches – touches only, because Kawabata does not go on too long or say more than he needs to say – are like this opening to the last chapter: 'The new year came, the wild sea was of dead winter. On land there was little wind'; or like this upward glance: 'The dampness clouded the window, like a toad's belly stretched over it.'

As for morbidity – to a charge that he was morbid Kawabata could reply that he at times examines morbidity because it exists, as a condition of men.

I must mention the two briefer stories in the book. 'One Arm', which begins: '"I can let you have one of my arms for the night", said the girl. She took off her right arm at the shoulder and, with her left hand, laid it on my knee', reminded me of Gogol, though it is not a comparison I would press. The other, 'Of Birds and Beasts', about a man who prefers the contemplation of life in his pets or in women to its contemplation in other men, reminded me of Colette. There are things which Kawabata and Colette have in common, certainly. For example, a ruthlessness, and an honest realization that we are not creatures of undriven snow, and a regard for tastes and appetite, and for the colours of livingness. But I would think Kawabata has the greater range imaginatively.

A touch, a phrase – 'the dew of woman' – from the second story in this so far from usual or commonplace book:

> The outstretched fingers did not move. The arm was faintly white in the dim light. Crying out in alarm I swept it up and held it tight to my chest. I embraced it as one would a small child from whom life was going. I brought the fingers to my lips. If the dew of woman would but come from between the long nails and the fingertips!

The quality, or qualities, I have been indicating seem to me now dangerously undersupplied in western fiction, which will be useless unless man is still presented vis-à-vis man as someone *in* existence, and responsive to it; useless if his being in relationship is to be reduced or disembodied to his mere mental, individual nudity. Living needs its flesh, its clothes, its circumstances, its place, in art – at any rate in fiction and poetry – as in the successive actualities of the day. Different arts must not entirely infect each other. Neither fiction nor poetry are abstractable to music or to topographical and typographical whereabouts of items of wordage on the bare-ness of the white page, only a very few of us being abstracted cosmonauts in space and in space-suits.

1969

3. *A Heart on Paper*

Who was Li Ho? He was a young aristocratic poet of T'ang China, whom English readers do not know, who died young of tuberculosis, or of tuberculosis and too much drink and too many girls, in 817, when he was only twenty-seven. He left only about 230 poems, lyrical, satirical, reflective, and here they all are, in J. D. Frodsham's *Poems of Li Ho*,[3] in translation, explained, defended, and championed; and, the best of them, delightful to read.

The Chinese have thought of Li Ho as wild and peculiar. Westerners now talk of him as 'modern', colourful, enigmatic, as if something between a Rimbaud and a Dylan Thomas. Tu Fu, the greatest of Chinese poets, was a family friend; but that does less to explain Li Ho than a remark let fall by his mother. Unless he was in mourning or drunk, Li Ho was accustomed to go out every day on a colt, followed by a servant with a brocade bag. He would make up poems, and drop them in a bag (and perhaps work them up afterwards). 'His mother used to have her maid rummage through the bag. When she saw he had written so much she would exclaim angrily, This boy of mine won't be content until he has vomited out his heart.'

That about expresses the matter. Li Ho spread his heart on the paper. Words tumbled out, colourful, hard to understand sometimes, lacking in decorum and order, yet arresting and disturbing.

Clouds and mist gently intermingling cannot describe his manner; illimitable waters cannot describe his feelings; the verdure of spring cannot describe his warmth; the clarity of autumn cannot describe his style; a mast in the wind, a horse in the battleline cannot describe his courage, earthenware coffins and tripods with seal-characters cannot describe his antiquity; seasonal blossoms and lovely

[3] *The Poems of Li Ho*, translated by J. D. Frodsham (1970).

girls cannot describe his ardours; fallen kingdoms and ruined palaces, thorny thickets and gravemounds cannot describe his resentment and sorrow; whales yawning, turtles spurting, ox-ghosts and serpent-spirits cannot describe his wildness and extravagance.

A marvellous mixture of praise and blame, that description of Li Ho, by another T'ang poet, written fifteen years after his death.

If it is hard to make head or tail of some of the poems, hard to accept their imagery, others are splendid. Frontier poems, for instance. In his era of revolution and warfare and threat of invasion, that era like our own in which the ideal life seemed more than ever an illusion, Li Ho spent three years of his short life in a military border town. It is cold. 'Barbarian horns have summoned the north wind.' Life is full of threat.

> Where endless desert merges with white sky,
> We see, far off, red banners of the Han.
> They sit and play short flutes in their green tents,
> Mist soaks the painted dragons on their flags.

> We climb up on the walls as dusk is falling –
> Is something moving out there in the gloom?
> A wind is blowing, stirring the dead weeds,
> Our half-starved horses whinny in their stalls.

Ho uses again and again one particular image of doubt and unease. The Great Wall goes on and on over the hills,

> Along the Wall a thousand moonlit miles.

A road goes on and on, in the moonlight:

> Autumn whitens the infinite heavens,
> Moon bathes the highroad running past my gates.

Paths and vegetation and fruit express his feeling:

> Long, stony paths overgrown with rank grass,
> Bitter fruit of the wild pear dangles down.

(Think of poems and images of the road that goes on and on,

Catullus to George Herbert, to Christina Rossetti, to Hardy,
and Robert Frost, and Housman:

> White in the moon the long road lies,
> The moon stands blank above.)

He grows older, feels old, young as he may be, and the
'swallows chatter on rain-drenched beams'; and if orioles are
feeding their young, it is among 'the aging leaves of weeping
willows', when seed is raining down from the elm trees. The
good thing again and again is balanced – if balanced is the
word – with its death or its opposite – or its diminution; the
girl says that the beauty of her face will fade like the pink of
petals; in autumn the fireflies are torpid and fly near the
ground; he looks at a picture and thinks of green dawn in an
imperial park 'and palace ladies clad in gosling-yellow'.

Basically, Li Ho does seem a poet native, after all, to the
T'ang era, he does not seem quite so far out on his own limb.
And this is an enjoyable book, far more accessible to the
ordinary reader than the sight of a few Chinese characters
may suggest. It would have been still more enjoyable if the
English had been more that of a good hard English poet, and
less – if to say so is not too ungrateful – the English of a
university scholar.

1970

Browning and the Faces of Poets

The poet W. J. Turner entertained me when I was young to lunch at the Savile Club. Noticing that Yeats was in the club that morning, he said: 'You may see him going down the stairs.'

We were rightly placed. Yeats went down, slowly; the reflection of his height, of his white hair, of the ribbon drooping from his spectacles moved down with him slowly, from one mirror to the next.

It was a grand performance, no more than emphasized by the accident of the mirrors. The grandest poet then alive among the speakers and writers of English was expressed in his physical style; he confirmed, he did not contradict himself poetically; and I thought of his complaints about George Moore, 'a man carved out of a turnip, looking out of astonished eyes' who only discovered how to keep his pants from falling around his knees when a friend told him to put his braces 'through the little tapes that are sewn there for the purpose'.

I expect a consonance between a man and his work, and for good or ill, for pro or con, I think I have usually detected it among my contemporaries (though I realize that serious critics of the Cambridge school wouldn't care for this as a principle of selection and separation – nor would I).

Eliot – I recall the physical ways in which Eliot, in the semi-privacy of his publishing office in Russell Square, failed to parade his eminence or insist untowardly on himself; his smile would then *occur*, with a slight opening of his mouth, a slight sideways movement of his lower jaw; a smile in which he emerged, however briefly, and with which, however briefly again, he counted you in on the secrecies of having to do with verse (this may also suggest, not unfairly, a certain habit of qualification, or of escape down a parenthesis, in his later writings).

The unemphatic beauty of Bernard Spencer, the intriguing tall mop-headedness of Norman Cameron, the black aquilinity of Louis MacNeice not immediately or too easily responding, the pallid young authority and – not the eagerness which would be too ingratiating a quality – no, the vital inquisitiveness or quizzingness in the forward look and walk of Clere Parsons, the unemphatic movements of Edwin Muir and the lack of harshness or angularity in his quiet northern voice – these were all consonant with characteristics of their verse.

Then I have observed Roy Campbell stalking slowly and unsteadily along the pavement like a fat cassowary under sedation, holding a knobbed stick high against his chest – I have seen him drag the metal cap of a bottle of pale ale or tonic water, in an attempt to open it, across the polished veneer of a fine desk in the B.B.C. which through no fault of its own belonged to one of the controllers; I have observed, on television, our Poet Laureate[1] discoursing on Hardy, himself wrapped in the poetry uniform of a long cloak; I have seen and overheard, via the same medium, tubby Mr Lawrence Durrell remarking to a Paris bookseller: 'You gave me – remember? – my first book-signing session.'

Maybe the sight of a poet tells one more than the sound of him reading his poems. Maybe at Harvard and elsewhere they should collect, instead of their verse readings, a library of glimpses, a gallery of public and private faces. It is idle to suppose that a false face, a face assumed rather than awkward or evasive, doesn't hint at a falsity behind the face, at a tendency to be false in the work. Or the public and the private face may be identical – identically false.

I wonder if that isn't the case with Robert Browning, in whose work there is now a slight (I would say unfortunate) revival of interest. The question of Browning's public face and how far it agrees with the activity of his private person, with his work, is part of Maisie Ward's inquiry, as it should be, in the second volume of her new life of Browning.[2]

---

[1] The late Cecil Day-Lewis.

[2] *Robert Browning and his World: Two Robert Brownings?*, by Maisie Ward (1969).

His wife dies, he abandons Italy for England, again, for London; bit by bit he becomes known, he goes into society, he is lionized – an experience which seldom has to be endured by poets in our day – and he likes it. Miss Ward isn't the first to ask, Were there two Robert Brownings?

Her conclusion seems to be that there were not – that the real Browning 'hid behind the man of the world', who came to look, to be sure, rather stuffy and commonplace. Cecil Torr in his *Small Talk at Wreyland* recalled that he used to read Browning 'with interest and respect, if not with pleasure', until one afternoon when he saw him running after a bus at the end of Piccadilly – 'I could not stand his loftier poetry after seeing that.'

What he meant is to be seen as well in Max Beerbohm's cartoons, reproduced by Miss Ward. 'Browning brings a titled lady to call upon Dante Gabriel Rossetti': there he is on the carpet, short, wide, compact, neat-haired, neat-bearded, doffing his top hat to the snooty piece whom the maid shows into the room, and jerking his thumb in a common gesture towards Rossetti. Or 'Browning taking tea with the Browning Society' (which he never did, Miss Ward assures us) – the same frock-coated vulgar little object, balancing a teacup, and seated between his own umbrella and top hat and a female acolyte whose nose elongates in the direction of his elongated beard.

Cecil Torr added to his Browning anecdote that as a rule an author should be read and not seen. A good rule.

Yet what can a biographer do? He has to break it, he has to see his author; and Miss Ward sees Browning – through many eyes – till one is almost sorry for him. His hair was pomaded, he had a 'savour of sycophancy', 'he was a rich banker, a perfected butler'. The more intelligent, Miss Ward hurries to add, recognized that his exuberance and his loud voice 'were very different from vulgarity'.

But were they? I read on, I find and am unable to forget opinions uniting, or hinting at the union of, the outer and inner Robert Browning, social man and poet, ordinary man and 'genius'. Here is Henry James asking himself again and again what lodging the genius could ever have contrived 'in this particular sound, normal, hearty presence, all so assertive and so whole, all bristling with prompt responses and expected opinions and usual views'.

Here is Matthew Arnold calling him 'a man with a moderate gift passionately desiring movement and fulness, and obtaining nothing but a confused multitudinousness'.

I read extracts from his letters, and find words sounding thoroughly vulgar or false, in phrase after phrase – 'I lost my own soul's companion'. 'Pen's merry laugh' – the laugh of Browning's weak failure of a son – 'is never out of my ears.' 'I kept away when measles were to be apprehended . . . I minded worthy folk's fears', etc.

I read the poems – but not often now, I must admit – and recall the judgement of many excellent judges and in particular of that most truly seeing poet Gerard Manley Hopkins. In spite of good touches Browning's poems lack style, Hopkins declared. They have a wrong temper. Browning in his poems had 'a way of talking (and making his people talk) with the air and spirit of a man bouncing up from table with his mouth full of bread and cheese and saying that he meant to stand no blasted nonsense': he was not really a poet, Hopkins thought; he had 'all the gifts but the one needful' – 'the pearls without the string'.

The last is the ultimate criticism, the cruel sentence. It is the string – even if string is not the completest or the best possible image of the matter – which unites the pearls, which with them is essentially response and transformation; the new cohesion of the ordinary which becomes extraordinary; and is poetry.

Miss Ward swallows the poems, and discounts the mask. I cannot swallow them, except in bits, and I see the mask and the real face as one – I see Browning with Cecil Torr's eyes puffing after that horse-bus, I see him – what do you think – allowing lady admirers to snip off for themselves tiny locks of that pomaded hair. American Mrs Bronson to American Mrs Jack Gardner, in Boston: 'I enclose you, dearest, a tiny lock of hair – which dear Mr Browning allowed me to cut at Asolo . . . the thought flashed over me, he thinks this will be the last time anyone asks for his hair.'

Mr Larkin (bald as you may be), Mr Auden, Mr Eliot, Father Hopkins, Mr Blake, Master Dryden and Master

Donne, Master Chaucer, may I have a tiny lock of your hair?
  No, madam, you may not.

In a sour mood, ungrateful for some early pleasures, I
might say, having now read *Robert Browning and his World*,
that the grand interest of Robert Browning is really to be
found in his lack of interest, that his oddness is to be found
in his extraordinary ordinariness; in the way it was inflated
by himself and others. Certainly Miss Ward presents much
of the evidence by which we may see him as one of the last
century's gaudier balloons of art – a balloon still, even if in
appearance and reputation greatly full and floating.

1969

Seferis on Poetry

If you take a holiday in Greece, you take a risk, it is evident. You may not believe in witchcraft, but you are as likely as not to be bewitched by Greek light, and the revelations of that light. The spell does not easily lift, it can spread, from light, landscape, sea, and people, into Greek literature; and I mean less the classic literature we stumbled into at school, than the literature of the modern Greeks; of which there is more than a little now in translation, from Roides' wicked novel *Pope Joan*, so engagingly translated by Lawrence Durrell, to the poets, to Cavafy (though Cavafy belongs – as well as to the world – to urban Greece, or rather to Alexandria, to history, and the café, in the light of the Eastern Mediterranean), and down to George Seferis, who was given the Nobel Prize in 1963.

Now for the first time we can read some of the prose, as well as the poetry, of Seferis.[1] If you ask what interest English readers can have in a Greek writer writing, ostensibly at any rate, about other Greek writers, I shall say the obvious, that a notable poet is likely to have warming things to reveal in his prose, be it about anything.

Actually Seferis is not aways in Greece in these essays – in which he does comment on the light of his own country, and its effect on writing.

He is sometimes in grey London, a rather lost young man, savouring an absence of light and 'the sour taste of death in the fog, and the intensified circulation of fear in the arteries of the great city'. He thought that for Greeks in Greece death was 'a sudden wound', that for Londoners in London it was 'a slow poison'.

Then just before Christmas in 1931, he went into a bookshop in Oxford Street and came out with a book of poems by Eliot, and his poem 'Marina', printed as a kind of Christmas

[1] *On the Greek Style*, by George Seferis (1967).

card. What hit him, a Greek exiled from his Aegean ('for
many of us the bows of ships have a special place in the
imagery of our childhood'), was Eliot's

> ... water lapping the bow
> And scent of pine ...

It was the first 'spark of emotion' struck in him by English
writing, he had found the poet, or one of the poets, who
meant most to him, and who in his own good phrase, very
congenial to me, looked on human life with independence –
and he translated *The Waste Land* into modern Greek.

Fascinating as it is to read Seferis on Eliot, the important
thing is to read him on art and life – to find him saying, for
instance, that 'poetry, however marked by despair, saves us,
in some way or other, from the tumult of our passions', that
poetry is nothing if it is not 'deeply rooted in our bodies and
our world', that the better way of examining the personal
life of an artist is not by means of anecdotes and the like, but
by 'trying humbly to see how he incorporates his perishable
life in his work'.

He is a reverencing man, so you find him insisting that
there is no quarrel in the arts between old, or traditional, and
modern – 'there is no discrepancy between old and new
works of art, none whatsoever'; and if our 'modernism', our
'constant renovation of art forms could be stopped' – I have
known those who would like to have it stopped by a divine
thunderbolt or a deterrent sentence of thirty years – 'our
aesthetic perception would have come to an end also'. So far
as the arts go, Seferis looks for a public which 'can sometimes show a spark of emotional perception that is without
prejudice', and for critics who do not 'simply create a state
of personal litigation between the public and the work of
art. . . . No one, certainly, enters the kingdom of heaven in
this way.'

A good book, and the quotations will show how well it has
been translated by George Seferis's friends, Rex Warner and
T. D. Frangopoulos. In its more Greek content I was intrigued by the long piece describing the memoirs of General
Makryannis, hero of the War of Independence. He was an
illiterate who taught himself to write because he had some-

thing to say to the Greeks about freedom, justice, and human dignity. There is not a mention of Makryannis in any encyclopedia I possess, but the extracts given by George Seferis indicate a masterpiece waiting for its English translation and its English publisher, and its English public:

> When I was still in my mother's womb, she went one day to gather firewood in the forest. With the wood on her back, burdened and in the absolute wilderness, the pains came upon her and she gave birth to me. Alone and tired, she risked her life and mine. After the birth. she tidied herself, took up the burden of firewood, put some green leaves on top, laid me on the leaves and went back to the village.

Or towards the other end of his life, when he had worked for a constitution for Greece and been imprisoned under the new monarchy:

> When they let me out of prison, I went to my ruined house and my wretched family. My wounds began to torment me. They did so last Easter and the Easter before. I went to the grotto in my garden to get a breath of air. I could hardly make my way there and had to lean heavily on my stick and on my will. And then they began to throw stones at me and human excrement. They said, 'Eat that, General Makryannis, and fill your belly with it, you who wanted to make a Constitution!' The blows they gave me opened up new wounds. My flesh is rotting; I have worms in me. I reported all this to the authorities and they would not listen to me. This lasted until the even of the Day of our Saviour. . . . And on the day itself they beat me up badly. I was left for dead, and I could not feel whether I was dead or alive.

George Seferis was Greek Ambassador to London from 1957 to 1962. But it must be a long, long while since any English poet of distinction was appointed to such an office. There have been French poet ambassadors, South American poet ambassadors, among them Perse and Neruda. An English diplomat or two has been a pasticheur in the mode of the Nineties, but otherwise for an English diplomat of any stand-

ing as a poet I have to think back to Matthew Prior, and Sir
Henry Wotton, who is still worshipful in the words and
movement of

> You meaner beauties of the night
>   That poorly satisfy our eyes.

And before that, there was Chaucer.

Are there deductions to be made? About poetry? About
the Foreign Office? About poets? About respect for poetry in
England, or distrust of intellectualism? Are poets *ipso facto*
a 'security risk'? Or is this a matter in our tradition of the
self-respect of poets, for whose individuality becoming a
diplomat is hardly the career? Or perhaps we now and for a
while have suffered more than most countries from a divorce
between art and our men of place and influence?

1967

Poems by Robert Lowell

That poems by Robert Lowell should be reputed as they are, puzzles me. I suppose – to begin with some perhaps necessary conclusions – that a good poem is characterized by individuality of substance, by words which continue to be themselves (though inched a little in new directions) and all the same coalesce into a substance which is recognizably idiosyncratic, and agreeable. I suppose that a good poem requires to be interesting. It will be so – bother Olson and all – if its substance measures sufficiently well by sound, and if it is effective enough in the act of vocalization (hearing and vocalizing are not the same: effect in literature, especially in poems, has much to do with what occurs physically and processionally in the mouth, between tongue, palate, teeth, etc.); which is why poems need to be read aloud in their enjoyment (as in their making), by the enjoyer. You only slightly, or partly, experience a poem if it is being read to you or at you by someone else.

To be interesting the poem must also be well enough formed; and work enough by intimation, I mean as the product of *that* poet, that other one or special one of ourselves, in *this* world.

Poor verse, certainly, can do something by power of intimation (as by the power in isolation of any other of these qualities). I think of rather wobbly poems, without an equilibrium of intimation and other qualities, poems most obviously *about* this or that of proffering this or that – for instance, by George Barker or Ivor Gurney, or D. H. Lawrence, or by some early Tudor poets or by distressed and disordered small poets of the Civil War time such as Henry Bold or George Daniel. And I happen just to have come across a phonically and verbally conventional piece by Thomas Campbell, 'Hohenlinden' Campbell, which appealed to Hardy because it provokes or achieves interest, in spite of

itself, by its unexpected enough and genuine enough intimation. Campbell begins this once celebrated *Song* like any
other ordinary versifier of his time:

> How delicious is the winning
> Of a kiss at Love's beginning
> When two mutual hearts are sighing
> For the knot there's no untying.

He goes on to uncertainties of love, and its need to be free:

> Bind the sea to slumber stilly,
> Bind its odour to the lily,
> Bind the aspen ne'er to quiver,
> Then bind Love to last for ever.

Love is a fire, Campbell says, and what keeps it burning is
renewal of beauty, the poem ending like this:

> Can you keep the bee from ranging,
> Or the ringdove's neck from changing?
> No! nor fettered Love from dying
> In the knot there's no untying.

A conclusion is intimated, some images in this intimation are
nearly refreshed, or actualized just enough; in spite of the
general expectedness of substance, measure, and form, this
inferior poem just manages to achieve interest.

I think, in other words, that the supreme poem, whatever
else it may be about, must chiefly be about itself; and in
substance, measure, procession, vocalization, in the possible
constituents of interest, the poems I am aware of by Robert
Lowell are not, I consider, just wobbly, but worthless.

If that is so, some peculiarities of his three present collections[1] don't need to be examined. In *The Dolphin* there are
only new poems; in *History* there are eighty new poems with
287 poems, revised or rewritten, from the already revised
and rewritten *Notebook* of 1970; other recensions from *Notebook* entirely constitute *For Lizzie and Harriet*. I am not
going to analyse the uncertainty which is so revealed, and
which makes these monotonous, mostly equal length and
undramatic poems neither better nor worse. But I shall say

[1] *The Dolphin*; *History*; and *For Lizzie and Harriet* (1973).

that the reader of *History* may come straightaway on one or other of several poems which suggest, for a while, that a claim of worthlessness is extreme. The poem may be the one on page 89, 'Hugo at Théophile Gautier's Grave'. The intimation in this poem makes at once for interest:

> . . . we die. That is the law. None holds it back,
> And the great age with all its light departs.
> The oaks cut for the pyre of Hercules,
> What a harsh roar they make
> in the night vaguely breaking into stars –
>
> Death's horses toss their heads, neigh, roll their eyes;
> They are joyful because the shining day now dies.
> Our age that mastered the high winds and waves
> Expires . . .

Not bad, no. The reader may suspect – if he is not aware, and no one tell him – that Robert Lowell is perhaps up to a version. He is, he is borrowing from Hugo, from the closing lines of his piece on Gautier's death, the lines Valéry thought to be Hugo's finest writing, he is excerpting or devising a sonnet from Hugo's finest seventeen lines, leaving out their most magnificent closing images –

> Le dur faucheur avec sa large larme avance
> Pensif et pas à pas, vers le reste du blé;
> C'est mon tour; et la nuit emplit mon œil troublé
> Qui, devinant hélas! l'avenir des colombes
> Pleure sur des berceaux et sourit à des tombes

– and tacking on his own finale and introduction. If I won't say he is passing off the lines as Lowell, I will say he is offering them in contradiction of what he is able to manage on his own.

I will set against them lines in his norm, entirely, his stylistic norm:

> Unsheathed, you unexpectedly go redskin,
> except for two white torches, fruits of summer,
> Woman's headlights to guide us through the dark
> to love the body, the only love man is.

> Women look natural stripped to flesh, not man
> equipped with his redemptive bat and balls –
> Renoir, paralyzed, painted with his penis –

Endless, aimless consecutive sentences. The words do not coalesce into a good substance. They are difficult to say and knobbly to hear, their awkwardnesses are unconvincing, unjustifiable, they do not measure or move effectively, the interest arising from them, and in them, as substance, amounts to nothing – not to a good poem (if you add the six lines I have omitted), but to a scatter of vocables. Or if these vocables progress, they stumble and sprawl. But a scatter is the preferable image. I thought, as I wrote 'scatter' again, of old bits of stone, shapeless or shaped, occasional capitals, bases, or stumps of column, disconnected, pell-mell with orange peel, cigarette ends, tins, and plastic sweet coverings, across the headland site of a Greek temple, near a post of the United Nations force in Cyprus. Endlessly Robert Lowell's are the poems of a cultural and personal fragmentation, bits of everything, everything in bits. A good reader, I am sure, a frequenter of art galleries, a haunter of the past. I find a disorder of Orpheus, Marx, Mary Stuart, Verdi, the Sphinx, Diogenes, Plato, Juvenal, Heine, Abelard, Dante, Potter, Cuyp, Fra Angelico, Albert Pinkham Ryder, Maleherbe, Chidiock Tichborne, George Grosz, Henry Adams, Gongora, Ford Madox Ford, Conrad, Eliot, Louis MacNeice, Hopkins, Leopardi, Emerson, Flaubert, Bishop Berkeley, Sylvia Plath, Froude, Kokoschka, Claudel, Norman Mailer, Lévi-Strauss, Goya, Gramsci, I. A. Richards, Ernest Thompson Seton, Herman Melville, Ned Kelly, and Delmore Schwartz. I trail him to Torcello, Nantucket, Godstow, Killicrankie, Belsen, Florence, the Casentino, Bosworth Field, Kenyon College, and Saint-Denis, and on and on.

No, I don't call this showing off, I see it is the Lowell way, it is how he works; if as well it is rather American-poetical, in a nowadays less evident mode, which still, however, fits the greatest land of Earth-shifting Machine. In a European poet, whether he had been so much around or not, it would be a vulgarity; in an American, even from Harvard and Maine, even a Lowell, isn't it perhaps the extra need of the bright

Muses – or at least of the Museum – in the larger wilderness?

In an awkward 'Afterthought' appended to the *Notebook* of 1970 Robert Lowell declared: 'I lean heavily to the rational, but am devoted to unrealism.' I dare say. But it is not unrealism particularly which defines Robert Lowell's unreadibility, and has always defined it: among other faults, it is a verbal non-coherence, a verbal insensitivity. All the time he is appallingly able to write 'Like Henry VIII, Mohammed got religion', or 'dark harbor of suctions and the second chance', or 'bakes cracks in the slates of the Sixties piazza', or

> horsedroppings and drippings . . . hear it,
>   hear the clopping
> hundreds of horses unstopping . . . each
>   hauls a coffin.

Extraordinary. In one new poem he says critics should keep 'their sharpest tongue for praise':

> Only blood-donors retain the gift for words;
> blood gives being to everything that lives.

I accept the reproof. But someone must – it is high time – must admit, must declare the facts of this extraordinary case.

And this introduces a last, inevitable consideration. Can poems, book by book by book which have been so fervently praised in England and America, really deserve no praise at all? Can that be possible? Of course it can; though this example of a common happening is often half-acknowledged, and then evaded by casuistical argument. In a discussion which included Philip Larkin's poems as well, another poet argued with me the other day that Larkin was a 'great minor poet' and Lowell a 'great bad poet'. Those pronouncements I should call nonsense, and a not untypical substitution of conversational games for criticism: minor is minor, and bad is nothing else than bad. But at least I must remind adulators of Lowell that uncritical and appreciative delusion frequently occurs after the dying away of a powerful movement. Elderly pontiffs saw the movement continued in the young Lowell. He was their inheritor, pontifical hands were

laid upon him. Since then few have cared, or dared, to disagree. A case analogous to the present one might be, for
instance, that of Felicia Hemans (a collector of cultural oddments, by the way, disturbed in life and emotions), during
the slack after romanticism: she too was acceptable to her
elders, to Scott, to Lord Jeffrey, and to Wordsworth (who
called her a 'holy spirit', 'Sweet as the spring, as ocean
deep'); and attractive to Shelley, to Byron, and to Sainte-
Beuve who spoke of her, at any rate, as a poet 'tendre et
affectueux'. Felicia Hemans wrote her poor smooth verses
rather more skilfully than Robert Lowell writes his poorer
hiccuping ones.

1973

From Imagists to the Black Mountain

How convenient, though shaming, it would be, if we could feed various questions of literary value into the mouth of some red-throated calculating machine. It would hem, and cough, and come up at once with the comforting or discomforting answers, at any rate the final answers. The trouble is that English has been too successful. It does not split and divide fast enough. Our English-language community has become so huge that it is more open than in the past to delusions. We have no intellectual or cultural centre (certainly it is not the Institute of Contemporary Arts, or the University of Essex). If we like our space, our vacuum, to be starred all the time by a few literary heroes, we don't respect them, and we don't accept the judgements they make, a society of readers on the cheap, borrowing from the public library.

It is as if, historically, writer and reader have been able to decide together on what is good and what is bad only in a less extensive compass of taste and intellect; not homogeneous, but not large. The smaller, better-educated language community committed its gaffes, but it was perhaps better at identifying the ridiculous and disposing of it more quickly. So one believes, at any rate. A single review, a single criticism could snuff, extinguish, destroy. Problems by which we are nagged might in the past, we may fancy, have been solved by such a single fart of critical derision, heard and noted from end to end of the territory.

But not now. And we cannot do much but feed our doubts into time, and wait.

'Modernism' offers such problems. Years ago we had a revolution. Years ago we made fools of ourselves by rejecting many revolutionary products. We are not going to be caught

again. So we like everything and nothing. There is no sound
so soft, so determined, and so typical of our time as the steps
of art-officials advancing in fear of ridicule to accept the
ridiculous. What Wyndham Lewis so contemptuously and
prophetically called the 'advanced fool-farm', more than
fifty years ago, is populated as never before, with these art-
officials dispensing public money, with talkative office-
holders from the English departments of every new and
every old university, with recipients signing copies of their
unreadable subsidized works, and with literary lunchers in
ecstasy. 'And the pig' – since we are talking of a fool-farm –
'got up and slowly walked away.' At least that is what the pig
ought to be doing.

We could all name areas of exceptional confusion, and
perhaps hallucination. Not quite so popular today as yesterday is the area of the divinity of T. S. Eliot. Today's area, for
what examination would show to be many curious reasons,
is at last the proximate one of Ezra Pound, now overrun with
surveyors, stake-holders, and speculators. We could all name
particular questions in connection with this area. For instance, how sensible or silly or perverse – allowing that saints
can be silly and perverse – was Eliot in his persistent praise
of Ezra Pound? Ought we really to swallow all of that apparently humble dedication of *The Waste Land*, 'For Ezra
Pound/ *il miglior fabbro*'? (Though couldn't *fabbro* be a
trifle ambiguous?)

A late but entertaining example of Eliot divinely hedged –
so that the King and the new Kingdom, or Commune, of
Ezrael may be exalted – is now to hand in a small Penguin
guide to the poetry and the importance, or the significance
(to use a favourite word), of Imagism.[1] The reader may be
alerted by the fact that 72 pages of historically Imagist poems
– by Richard Aldington, H.D., John Gould Fletcher, F. S.
Flint, Amy Lowell, etc. – are embedded in 83 pages of editorial concern. Something must be afoot. Are we going to be
asked, at that length, to admire a number of, on the whole,
not very admirable poems? We are not. It isn't that kind of
anthology. On his first page, the editor, Mr Peter Jones, is
saying, These poems are bad. So why bother? Or at least,

[1] *Imagist Poetry*, introduced and edited by Peter Jones (1973).

round and round the mulberry bush, he is saying that
Imagism is beset with problems and paradox, that mani-
festoes and poems don't agree, that definitions of 'the Image'
by Imagists are not always identical: 'Perhaps the main
problem is that the poems the Imagists published as a group'
– in the end you do get to the mulberry bush – 'cannot
honestly be called to stand among the great achievements
of literature. Some are very fine, but many are weak by any
standards. And so why bother?'

Eighty-three pages of bothering, as well as the poems,
amount to an answer which is adumbrated, to begin with, in
two parts: 'Part of the answer lies in a statement made by
T. S. Eliot in an address on American Literature and the
American Language in 1953: "The *point de repère* usually
and conveniently taken as the starting-point of modern
poetry is the group denominated 'imagists' in London about
1910."' Not the most happily phrased statement in the run
of Eliot's prose. Even then it is marked by Eliot's not infrequent ambiguity. Look once, and he seems to say 'Modern
poetry began with Imagism'. Look twice and he says – no
more – that most people conveniently take Imagism in 1910
as the datum line or landmark which shows where modern
poetry began.

Mr Jones looks only once. Having an axe to grind, having
an historical cause to advance, he says immediately of the
Imagists, on the say so of Eliot, 'Their historical importance
is clear'. How not quite honest exegetes of holy writ can be.

Then Mr Jones comes to the 'other part of the answer'. In
preliminary shorthand this is discovered in a review in the
Times Literary Supplement in 1916. The reviewer was
noticing the second volume of Amy Lowell's *Some Imagist
Poets*. He wrote: 'Imagist poetry fills us with hope; even
when it is not very good in itself, it seems to promise a form
in which very good poetry could be written.' That gives Mr
Jones his green light, the Imagists may not have been very
clever, their poems may not have been very good, but – 'The
truth is that imagistic ideas still lie at the centre of our poetic
practice'.

The cat inched into view has really the sole features of
Ezra Pound. Eliot's Ezra helped to organize the Imagists,

Eliot's Ezra wrote them a manifesto of stylistic don'ts which Harriet Monro printed in *Poetry* in 1913, Eliot's Ezra (as things go, won't Eliot in the future have to be called Ezra's Eliot?) contributed some of the less weak (= 'very fine') poems to *Des Imagistes* in 1914, the first of the Imagist anthologies, the one which Ezra himself edited.

The cat so quickly out of the bag, by the second page of Mr Jones's long introduction, is nothing less than Ezra Pound's invention of modern poetry – modern poetry being 'our poetic practice', which in turn is that of the Ezraelites at large and by descent. Mr Jones's *Imagist Poetry* is a partisan exercise for the grander glory of Ezra and Ezrael.

It would be decent – before any further questioning of Mr Jones – just to look at the poems in the middle of his exercise. Are they as bad as he says they are, or as we remember them? Yes, they are, really. They reach at times an extreme of the apparently novel and the ludicrously old hat – for instance, in the poems of Frank Flint, 'one of the most dedicated and sincere of the Imagists,' as Mr Jones solicitously remarks, but not, as his poems and letters show (and as I remember him and his conversation), a man of very sparkling poetic intelligence.

'London, my beautiful', ends a poem he contributed to *Des Imagistes*, and is lucky, or unlucky, to have reprinted,

> I will climb
> into the branches
> to the moonlit tree-tops
> that my blood may be cooled
> by the wind.

Conrad Aiken, more sceptical than his compatriot and friend Eliot, or less affined to Ezra Pound, sent that poem up, in a 'Ballade of Worshippers of the Image' which Mr Peter Jones has obligingly exhumed from a New York newspaper of 1915: :

> You, whose meticulous clear lines run
>   In hideous insipidity;
> And you, forsooth, who shinned a tree
>   To keep with the gaping moon your tryst,

> Where in a score of years will you be
> And the delicate succubae you kissed?

Forsooth poets, tryst poets, they still were, most of them. At a remove a little something came into Amy Lowell's imagism (Amy-gism, according to Pound), into Pound's imagism as well, from the images of the Japanese masters of the *haiku*; but none of the Imagist poems – not a single one of them – ever achieves the emotional and image-inative drama which such as Bashō, Buson, Taigi, Issa, or Shiki contrived out of the strictness of their tradition in unison with the always surprising truth and exactitude of their sensual response. Mr Peter Jones does not mention *haiku* (just as well perhaps), but he does say that the Imagists 'were taking a *fresh* look'. They pretended to look, physically, and at the constituents of verse, but how fresh was William Carlos Williams exclaiming

> Agh! what
> Sort of a man was Fragonard

or 'Agh! petals maybe', or Ezra Pound ejaculating 'Haie! Haie!'? What they did, most of them (and Mr Jones passes it by, in his rather slight denigration; but he was awkwardly placed), was to write lines of Edwardian beauty-verse, of extreme unreality, and snip each line into two or three pieces, which were then strung down the pallid page, without rhymes. It was Frank Flint who seems to have been the first poet of Anglo-Saxony to reduce the capital at the beginning of each line to a lower-case letter, a trick which had, and has, its uses (he borrowed it from the French, but one which did not quite amount to a fresh look, or a decisive liberation. Possibly it is the feat for which he will be remembered.

Eyeing Flint and the Imagists, or Imagistes, he had assembled, Pound must have quailed. He must have recognized they were not, after all, a troupe it would be profitable – or reputable – to lead into a new land (in times ahead he would have to be content to have as disciples only later 'scarecrows of the advanced fool-farm' – that was his destiny). He divorced himself from his own creation.

Mr Jones puts Marianne Moore among proto-Imagists.

That wouldn't have pleased her, and she denied the influence.
She did not even indulge a contributor's flirtation with the
movement. Lawrence did. An Amy-gist, not an Imagist,
according to Pound, he contributed to the anthologies after
the well-to-do Amy Lowell had taken over. Two of his poems
were written in the first weeks of his elopement with Frieda
von Richthofen, Frieda Weekley, in 1912, and these two,
'Green' and 'Illicit', are imaged, not from Imagism but from
his own hypersensitized state, his own life – 'She opened her
eyes, and green/They shone' – in that first wonderful
Bavarian-Alpine experience. Lawrence surely realized, convenient as the anthologies may have been, that nothing tied
him to the insipidities of the movement, whether H.D.'s cold
filigrees of imitation Pentelic marble, Flint's niminy-piminy,
or Pound's wafer-like hedonism. He wasn't to be fixed in that
kind of *vers libres*, that kind or degree of liberation, or to be
found up the trees of poesy in Hampstead moonshine.

> I will get me to the wood
> Where the gods walk garlanded in wistaria.

Chinese gods?

Lawrence would get himself decidedly elsewhere. Lawrence on Pound, earlier in 1909: 'He is a well-known American
poet – a good one. He is 24, like me, but his god is beauty,
mine life.'
Subtracting this, that and the other, Mr Jones, as he in-
tended, leaves himself with his modern poetry, his 'poetic
practice' of our day, rooted not in poems, not in the renewed
imaginative life of poets, so much as in Pound's stylistic
injunctions contributed to *Poetry*, which in their school-
mastery Poundian slapdash were sensible enough, but not
unique, or exhaustive or exactly compelling. From there he
begins his descent into bathos, step by step, to William
Carlos Williams (who had contributed to *Des Imagistes*), to
Zukovsky, Olson, Creeley, Duncan, Basil Bunting, and all
the flatitudes of a particular modernism.
Of course Pound's injunctions of 1913 weren't original or
entirely his own. The rejection of the old idealism was every-

where around, and had been producing its new images, or
let us say its new image, in every art, writing, painting,
sculpture, music.

It would be idle or tiresome or too easy to pelt the representative Mr Jones with too many dates or instances, or to
argue with him too energetically that another 'modern
poetry' exists without benefit, by and large, of Ezra Pound,
though of the same ultimate ancestry, and little connected
with the insipidities and simple-simonism of the Ezraelitish
Commune ('kingdom', after all, won't do, the fool-farm is so
extensively American). Still, there are dates and facts which
Mr Jones and advocates of his kind mustn't forget, or must be
persuaded to remember.

Thomas Hardy. He will do for a beginning. Certainly
Pound respected Hardy's poems. Certainly three of Hardy's
collections, his *Wessex Poems* (1898), his *Poems of the Past
and Present* (1901), and his *Time's Laughing-stocks* (1909),
were in circulation before the young Ezra Pound posted
A Few Don'ts by an Imagiste from London to Chicago. Mr
Jones might go through that trio of books by Hardy for
images ('An "Image" is that which presents an intellectual
and emotional complex in an instant of time'), for the
features of style celebrated in *A Few Don'ts*.

Mr Jones might remember that Edwin Arlington Robinson
had been writing and publishing since the Nineties, that
Miniver Cheevy had been born, and *Luke Havergal*, as well
as such an animadversion as 'the small ink-fed Eros of his
dream' (which would describe more than a little of the early
Ezra Pound). Mr Jones might remember, might read, might
digest – as Pound must have done – Synge's preface to his
poems, written in 1908, and published in 1909: 'I have often
thought that at the side of the poetic diction, which everyone
condemns, modern verse contains a great deal of poetic
material, using poetic in the same special sense.' 'When
poetry came back with Coleridge and Shelley, it went into
verse that was not always human.' 'In these days poetry is
usually a flower of evil or good, but it is the timber of verse
that wears most surely.' 'It may almost be said that before
verse can be human again it must learn to be brutal.' Mr
Jones might remember (as Pound realized) that Edgar Lee

Masters in *Spoon River Anthology* (1915) wasn't all journalese: Pound to Harriet Monroe, January 1915, in Mr Jones's
own book: 'Masters hits rock bottom, now and again. He
should comb the journalese out of his poems.'

More than anything, when it comes to establishing a
pedigree for modernism (or identifying the modernism
which counts), Mr Jones might read – or if he has read it,
read again – Yeats's introduction to *The Oxford Book of
Modern Verse*: 'Then in 1900 everybody got down off his
stilts . . . Victorianism had been defeated.' 'My generation',
Yeats says, in his bizarre, perverse, but never to be neglected
document, 'began that search for hard positive subject-
matter.' And if in England, 'Victorianism' displaced, there
came temptations of facile charm and simplicity, 'Thomas
Hardy . . . made the necessary correction through his mastery
of the personal objective scene'. Assessing, not without
sympathy, the good and bad of Eliot (in whom he detested a
greyness, a coldness, a dryness, and a monotony of accent)
and of Pound (whom he reproves – in rather a sly passage –
for a 'loss of control common enough among uneducated
revolutionists', but 'rare – Shelley had it in some degree –
among men of Ezra Pound's culture and erudition', Yeats
more or less intimated that the throbbing effective continuity of English verse runs through neither of them.

Whether one should or shouldn't look for that continuity
in Yeats himself, in Hardy, in Graves and Ransom and Mac-
Neice and Auden (Herbert Read at times, as a disciple of the
other party, the other continuity or divergence, could be
heard at times regretting what he called Auden's betrayal
of *vers libres*), at least chronology denies any renewing
priority to Imagism. Sense will not exaggerate, and it will not
minimize, the influence of 'imagistic ideas'. These have had
their effects of tightening and brightening verse, of destroying the word 'like', and making verse more immediate – yes,
but they have been 'ideas' from all over the shop, and not
from one *ex post facto* formulation.

One hopes that teachers and taught, in universities – it
must be for them that Mr Jones intends his handbook, so
curiously directed to what it doesn't itself contain – won't
swallow the whole thesis. The facts have value. But then this

small book does conform to the new kind of scholiasm which goes so often with wholesale belief in works of the fool-farm and their promotion. Every article, every review on the topic – the past being so well indexed now – is looked up, excerpted, and employed, if convenient, no matter who the writer is or was, and no matter whether he possesses insight or authority. Scepticism is put out to grass, permanently.

To that, and to the unrealities of its case, readers of Mr Jones's book may also be alerted, in good time, by another characteristic, the carriage of its flotsam throughout on a surge of cliché, a surge of *thought which is on similar lines, states of poetry which are parlous,* and of *launchings which are full-scale.*

Such are the tides which usually convey the history or historical polemics of recent party literature.

1973

A Conversation[1]

INTERVIEWER: *You are, as you have rather ruefully pointed out in a recent essay, usually labelled as a Man of the Thirties. I wonder if there is any other twentieth-century decade that you would prefer to be identified with?*

GRIGSON: No. If things have to be divided into decades, as well to have 'belonged' to a decade in which you had Auden and MacNeice, and in which you were in full flight of feeling about *Prufrock* and *The Waste Land*. If you came to your twenties in the Thirties, you had a strong feeling of extraordinary things going on, of extraordinary painters about, of books about like *Tim and Western Man*. Hardy still alive, Auden coming up. One felt that everything was being done *de novo*, that fools were dying out rapidly on all sides – which they weren't.

People, I think, often have the idea of the Thirties poets as a rather matey gang. Did you meet with your New Verse *contributors very often, in a social way?*

GRIGSON: They were simply there – or elsewhere, Auden and MacNeice for instance, away teaching. I saw much of Norman Cameron, Dylan Thomas, and Bernard Spencer. Also Spender, Edwin Muir, and Herbert Read. Most of the people I knew well were artists. It was Henry Moore and Ben Nicholson I knew best in Hampstead.

How did it come about that you picked out Edith Sitwell as a kind of representative . . .

GRIGSON: Dummy in the social robes of art? I saw her once in my life, when she came down to Oxford to talk to the English Club. There she stood, with Tom Driberg, a very large emerald on one hand. She talked nonsense. She was

[1] With the Editor of *The Review*.

doing an act. At that age one doesn't expect poets to do acts.
I knew Margaret Lane at the time, she wrote a fulsome piece
about Edith Sitwell – about the meeting – in the *Oxford
Magazine*, which seemed to me more ridiculous than Edith
Sitwell herself, and I wrote a piece in reply.

So it started, as a reaction to the smart and fashionable
literary thing encountered, I suppose, by every generation of
undergraduates. About 1924–1927 the fashionable thing was
aesthetic, Firbankish, and upper crust; to do with Edith
Sitwell and *Wheels*; to do with Harold Acton (from Eton)
and Tom Driberg, among undergraduates. The fashionable
thing makes one feel awkward, one is out of it, one's a bit
envious, socially, yet one sees through it, reacts, and starts
looking for something genuine instead. The opposite thing to
seeing Harold Acton in his turtle-neck sweater prancing down
the High was finding poems in the *Oxford Magazine* or the
Cherwell by Auden. And when I left Oxford and found a job
on the *Yorkshire Post*, in London, I met Wyndham Lewis.

And Lewis encouraged your anti-Sitwell attitudes?

GRIGSON: Anti-Sitwellian, anti-aesthetic, anti-society-art attitudes, yes. He was wonderful to know, intellectually generous, more so than anyone I have met. I never understand the
talk about Lewis as monster, the Herbert Read talk; the
Hemingway talk about the 'most evil' man he'd ever come
across.

*It does strike one as odd, though, that you – well known as
editor of the leading verse magazine of a period which is
ordinarily viewed as peculiarly political and left-wing –
should have had this total admiration for a figure like Lewis.*

GRIGSON: But you see politics were his after-cloak. One grew
up to think of Lewis as the hammer of the effete, in days of
ridiculously correct Sunday journalism of the half-mind. And
the *London Mercury*. And Bloomsbury. And Edith Sitwell
making a public monkey of herself in order to be celebrated.
So Lewis seemed very sane, very serious, and modern; laying
propositions down in front of you. He was a phrase-maker. It
was more useful than you'd think to have Strachey at that

time described as 'a girlish if bearded patriarch', or Chester-
ton located in his bar-parlour as 'a fierce foaming toby-jug'.

Lewis flirting with fascism is a Lewis I don't know and
don't recognize, whom Lewis himself didn't recognize after
a while. He was disgusted with a break-up of intellectual
categories, he had come to a despair – it was partly personal.
He was pushed for the next week's cash. After his stupendous
start, he may have despaired of finding room and time for his
intellectual strength. Perhaps that was the explanation. I
never thought of him as political. For me Lewis was the
accessible great man. Who else was I don't know.

Was Eliot?

GRIGSON: Not for me. Another matter, I'm sure, if you liked
him, or he liked you. There was something prissy about Eliot.

*There again, of course, it might be thought odd that you and
your* New Verse *contributors should have appeared so often
in* The Criterion, *and that you should have written about it
so respectfully when it folded.*

GRIGSON: At the time Eliot seemed turning queerer about
God, or the C. of E., than about politics. But, again, you have
to think of Eliot as another revolutionary leading us out of
the self-conceit of provincial writing, another revolutionary
hero who had revolted against the old rhetoric, in a time
when no deviation was readily approved. So one didn't notice
what he was up to politically in *The Criterion*; or it was too
early to care. I realize he was more right-wing, probably, and
more sly about it than Lewis. I had the feeling that slightly
mincing Eliot might once have strangled a housemaid in
Camden Town with one of her stockings, and kept creeping
back to gaze into the area basement. I knew that large,
bawdy, elegant-minded Lewis would have laid the housemaid, and come back for more, if she'd been attractive. But
they were high priests of art, all the same – of art, not
aesthetics.

On the question of New Verse, *you have written – to my
reading – somewhat ambiguously, or shall we say ambivalently, on the one hand regretting the billhook and yet on the*

*other seeming rightly gratified by the magazine's achieve-
ment. And you have, of course, gone on using the billhook.*

GRIGSON: One comes to feel uneasy about negation. I remember Empson saying once, 'Oh well, the trouble about Grigson
is that he never attacks on principle; he attacks because he
attacks'. *Touché*, because I was attacking on literary grounds;
I wasn't clear enough in my ideas.

*But this is what seems to me to be good, that you were
attacking on literary grounds.*

GRIGSON: Yes, but I should have done it better. I should
have expressed more positives. I should have been more
selective, and billhooked only the importantly bad.

Is there anybody you wish you hadn't attacked?

GRIGSON: Only those – only those books or poems – whose
badness was too unimportant to be worth attacking. In any
case, as one grows older one sees that there is more of the
piebald about good writers than one supposed.

*And yet I think that for a lot of people one of your chief
qualities is that as you have grown older you haven't become
part of the flabby Establishment scene.*

GRIGSON: I prefer to be able to look at myself in the morning
– and not be entirely disgusted. On the face of it, it is simpler
to like everything. If I can't like everything, and if I would
like everyone to like me, I would have to do calculation sums
all the time. I'm not good at calculation.

In New Verse *you had an almost Popeian view of the literary
scene as packed with dunces and racketeers and back-
scratchers of one sort or another. Has this continued to be,
for you, the way things seem to work?*

GRIGSON: I was a student of *Peri Bathous or Martin Scrib-
lerus his Treatise on the Art of Sinking in Poetry*, a treatise
I recommend with confidence to Alvarez, and to the selectors
of the Poetry Book Society. Isn't the 'literary scene' always

ridiculous? Perhaps today the centres of the ludicrous have shifted a little bit; perhaps more poets have a chance of being observed, if only because more critics or literary editors fear to be caught out. 'The taste of the Bathos is implanted by nature itself in the soul of Man', all the same.

Do you feel that if New Verse *had not championed Auden his reputation would have taken much longer to establish itself?*

GRIGSON: Probably it wouldn't have made a great deal of difference. Auden was so obviously a powerful writer that it wouldn't have mattered for long if there had been fifty *New Verse* pro and fifty Leavises or *Scrutinies* against.

But there was some resistance, surely?

GRIGSON: There was. I think I would say fortunately, because resistance does help – if no more – like support. I mean, with a reputation. Perhaps it helps a talent as well. Auden was helped and supported most of all, I would guess, by the approval of Eliot. From the first Eliot admired the drama in his poems. You've questioned the approval of rightish Eliot or Wyndham Lewis in a leftish situation. I shall remind you that neither Eliot nor Lewis failed to approve of Auden because of a divergence in politics.

Eliot didn't appear in New Verse?

GRIGSON: Once – he appeared once in a number about poets and the theatre. I was chary of asking him, from a blend of reverence and antipathy – a personal antipathy which I suspected was mutual, much as I had to do with Herbert Read.

Eliot's lieutenant.

GRIGSON: Eliot's lieutenant, who thought that Auden had betrayed free verse. Lewis's *bête-noir*.

A number of New Verse *poets have faded out, haven't they? People like Madge and Allott spring to mind. Has this surprised you?*

GRIGSON: Every period or movement has its persuasive

phantom poets, its self-advanced simulacra without fuel or furnace, who are deceptive, and then lapse into professorships, esotericism, or attending writers' conferences. I am surprised that as many good poems were printed in *New Verse*.

New Verse didn't show much interest in American poetry, apart from John Crowe Ransom.

GRIGSON: Apart from one out of the very few good poets in America. There is an American sprinkling through *New Verse*, Allen Tate, Theodore Spencer, Macleish, Roethke. I would have liked poems from Marianne Moore. Or from Léonie Adams. Norman Cameron was always saying I should ask Léonie Adams. It was too late for Ransom, for more than one poem – he was dry by the time *New Verse* was going. There was almost a Ransom cult – 'I pernoctated with the Oxford students once' and *Captain Carpenter* – due to Robert Graves, who introduced his poems to England.

So you did know what was going on in the States, but didn't particularly like it?

GRIGSON: Every American poet with a claim to readers had been on sale in Harold Monro's Poetry Bookshop. I bought Stevens, Tate, Marianne Moore, Cummings, Jeffers, Hart Crane, Aiken, at the Poetry Bookshop – and *The Fugitive*, and Ransom, book by book. There was no chance of not knowing. And I had an American wife. And I edited a poetry magazine, and I wanted poems.

A thing that has puzzled me over the last twenty years is the resurgence of American poetry one knew long ago was turgid and lifeless, or thin and lifeless. All of Hart Crane, for instance, most of William Carlos Williams. The universities at work. I was reproved a year or two ago by Jonathan Williams, who said to me, in a pained way, 'There have been American poets since Ransom.' How many?

And how many English poets have there been since Auden?

GRIGSON: Larkin, at any rate, making words cohere in his own way, so that you have to remember them even if you've read the poem only once

Give me your arm, old toad;
Help me down Cemetery Road.

Not the dream-poet of the 'advanced fool-farm', I suppose.

New Verse's *attitude to Surrealism strikes one, looking back,
as having been –*

GRIGSON: Half-hearted. You remind me of the opening of the
Surrealist Exhibition in London. Herbert Read's opening
speech: 'Ladies and gentlemen, this is an historic occasion'.
He might have been opening a first international show of
five-legged poodles. It was, in the event, most unhistoric.
Whose quip was it that dear good Herbert, indeed saintly
Herbert, was always present at the birth, never at the death-
bed of movements?

But New Verse *was fairly hospitable to the movement?*

GRIGSON: I was being fashionable, not critical. I wanted to
see, and saw quickly enough. The best things about Surrealism were the Surrealist annexations; Surrealism made one
look at Victor Hugo's drawings, at Arcimboldi, Seghers,
Desiderio, at Chirico's early mysteries. In *New Verse* I enjoyed having David Gascoyne's version of *Poem in Seven
Spaces* by Giacometti – a spatial-verbal companion to his
wonderful *Palace at 4 a.m.* Surrealism was better for painting. It didn't go very well into English, or with England of
the Thirties.

One does see traces of it in Auden.

GRIGSON: One does see in Auden parallel elements of the
fantastic, or the kind of fantasy the Surrealists annexed.
Iceland, dwarfs, trolls, Auden of *The Witnesses*, or *Paid on
Both Sides*, before he knew about the formularies of surrealism.

In English art you have, already had, in the Thirties a nice
balance between Henry Moore, shaping an almost local surrealism of his own in those heavy shapes cohering on the
ground, and Ben Nicholson, being severe and clear in an
unsurrealistic mystery of tones, areas, and layers. Somewhere
between the two, possibly, lay the secret egg. But the secret
egg was approached only by Auden among the new poets.

How would you define your political position during the Thirties?

GRIGSON: A natural supporter of the under-doggishness in myself and others. Or a natural opponent of the agreed and settled average. Or a natural private socialist. Traumatically you discover that truth isn't always where it ought to be entertained. I was luckily unendowed with money, I could never be an Edward Boyle Tory or a hedging Liberal.

Nor it seems – during the Thirties – could you have filed an application for your C.P. card.

GRIGSON: I was tempted. I think I wrote once, naïvely, and had no answer, which was sensible of the Communist Party. I dislike orthodoxy.

Day-Lewis was the only one of the noted poets who did join the Party, wasn't he?

GRIGSON: I have no secret knowledge, either way. I have supposed that to be so. He must have been a very mild member. Between Moscow and Rome, I have always preferred the untidy free area of independence in which ideas might be set against ideas, without dogma, to produce new ideas, or in which sensibility might work. The Thirties was not a period for accepting beliefs – facts, certainly. Not beliefs.

And yet it is thought of now as a period when, of all periods, the issues were clear cut and one knew where the enemy lay.

GRIGSON: I knew perfectly well where the art enemy lay.

One of the striking things about New Verse, *which came out until 1939, is that one can read it without being aware, very precisely, of what was going on politically. In some ways it was a peculiarly, shall we say, aestheticist periodical.*

GRIGSON: No. Its journalism apart, *New Verse* was a poem periodical. Aestheticism is for aesthetes, like the Sitwells or Cyril Connolly or Harold Acton, whose father had five villas and who went off to be an aesthete in Peking. I've just read the second volume of Harold Acton's memoirs. I thought I

was reading the memoirs of the wife of the President
Emeritus of the Literary Society of New Barnet. Aestheticism
was exclamation and thrill and wriggle: it was effect. Profounder than politics, I hoped a good poem was 'life'. Also I
was in a queer position between newspapers and politics. I
saw that the poets who inclined to party membership were
the ones weak in talent, looking for a belt or a brace, or a
built-up shoe; and I edited the book pages of a Tory newspaper, I had the trivial stink of 'news-value' up my nose all
the time, Tory-slanted news. I had to contemplate elderly
journalists, too. They're the most denatured, depersonalized
people in the race of man, like scampi shells. So, between
journalists and communist poets, what about a real round
poem?

Publishing real round poems, if discoverable, could be paid
for, nearly, and ironically, by the sale of the literary editor's
perks, the unreviewable review books.

Why did New Verse *come to an end?*

GRIGSON: It had done its job, and I hadn't a job. My paper,
the *Morning Post*, disappeared down the throat of the *Daily
Telegraph*. No more review copies by the taxi-load. We were
just about in the war. I was alone, without a job, without a
wife, and with a child.

*I wanted to ask you one or two questions about Now rather
than Then. Do you feel that the poet today works in a more
hostile, a more culturally hostile atmosphere than, say, thirty
or forty years ago?*

GRIGSON: No – which isn't a good thing. I have the feeling
that it's better to have to work in a culturally hostile atmosphere. A painter I knew, who came here as an exile from
the Nazis, used to say 'In a way I'd rather paint in secret
under the Nazis'. He was exaggerating, but it was indifference he was stifled by. In the past, oppression – but without
the card-index of the political police – has so often been the
situation of the artist. Without going that far, I think a
strong, militant, dominant vulgarity concentrates the purpose, and the pride.

And you feel we don't have this vulgarity today?

GRIGSON: We have a different one, supine, on its back, having its belly tickled, accepting everything, never objecting. The approval of the *New Statesman*, the *Spectator*, the *Observer*, the *Sunday Times*, the *New York Review of Books*, is probably poison for the young, and should be felt as poison, along with selection for a prize and the cash support of the Arts Council. A culturally hostile atmosphere also helps to define and locate what is genuine – if you're looking for it. Take Leavis, our recent Gosse or J. C. Squire or St John Ervine inside out. How helpful his approval or disapproval has been. His blessing defined the vorthless, his dismissal defined the meritorious. Or Alvarez.

A valued contributor of ours. Which writers now do you find valuable?

GRIGSON: I'd swop five John Berrymans and three Robert Lowells for one Ginsberg, in a way.

Ginsberg?

GRIGSON: He *does*. I like big rejection of the abrasive and nasty, rather than crawly rejection.

I'm surprised by your hostility to Lowell. He does seem – at least in theory – to be the kind of poet you might admire.

GRIGSON: This hostility to Lowell – no, to the Lowell effect, the reputation of Lowell, reviewer's Lowell – goes back to your misstatement of the 'aestheticism' of *New Verse*, to my correction about real round poems, or real cubic ones, or real oblong ones, three-dimensional. Watching the dog-act to the sprawling and clumsy, the inexact, the unexacting, revolts me, if it fascinates me too.

And Ginsberg?

GRIGSON: I talk of Ginsberg as a situation, as an extended man, a situation of enormous sympathy. Others – actual writers – have possibility in Ginsberg, Mo., or Ginsberg, Ill., or wherever. In Lowell, Mass., I see no situation, only response. One is asked to admire a poet, this time, with no edges, no style, no tendon. In a poet I don't ask for the fake academic tendon, contracted, of some forgotten imitator of early Eliot or of a *New Lines* Donald Davie using neat rhymes to show that he's looked at Juan Gris, or understands the meaning of 'diastasis'. I look for style as reverberant sinew of expressive words: I don't find it in Lowell, though a strong style in that sense has made so much American poetry, expansively with a clean edge in Whitman, precisely in Ransom or Robinson, or Eliot, or Marianne Moore. I buy Lowell's books, one by one, in hope. I haven't found a stanza of the good in one of them, only postures. Still, when he was asked about poetry in England he praised Larkin.

So, in the end, it is back to Larkin.

GRIGSON: I don't want to die away with a long tirra-lirra in that direction. But Larkin is – or was – the kind of poet Betjeman ought to have been, at least.

Larkin, of course, probably thinks that Betjeman is the kind of poet he ought to have been. I was going to ask you earlier about the intervening period between the Thirties and New Lines, The White Horsemen.

GRIGSON: Unbraced, un-bra'd, no body belt, saddles slipped under the belly. Dead guts instead of empty shell. A revelation of sprawl.

I think if I were to select a hero poet, an exemplar poet, I would erect Pasternak: the apocalypse of extraordinary delight where delight is possible and just – judging from translation. I miss that, between the edges and in the substance of style, in anybody now writing, anybody that I know of. There was much of it in Louis MacNeice. But he was behind defences here and there. He wasn't reckless. Justified critical exuberance, it's rare. An embracing simultaneity. All nature, of man, of his words, of his senses. With Pasternak I think I would couple Wen-I-to.

On the subject of your own poetry, it seems to me that in your last two books you have evolved something very distinctive – a tone, a voice. I wonder how you would characterize your own development as a poet.

GRIGSON: I don't know. Obviously one is conscious of becoming older, and having less and less time to live. What moves me is what I was saying about Pasternak. I would like to establish the best of what I enjoy in existing.

There is, though, a gravity and a sorrow in many of the poems. And these qualities seem to me to conflict somewhat with, well, with the way you have been taught to make poems, a way which puts the stress on intelligence, exactitude, wit, and so on.

GRIGSON: I repeatedly thought at one time of a deep lane down which water ran over white and red quartz. Most uncommonly exquisite flowers, rare ones, in great health, grew on one side of the lane. But I was there alone. A year or two ago I found that letter of Cowper's in which he watched yellow leaves falling from willows all over his county and rejected a short earthy continuance, and heaven, and avoidance of hell, and wished instead to live for ever and ever. It's a very mixed situation we live in: I would hate to go off in one direction only. The whole situation is in front of us, in all its compartments, all the time. We can hold nothing, we can – perhaps – construct a word-equivalent. But a strong sense of things having vanished before we are conscious of enjoying them, of enjoyment being posthumous to the event – is saddening, I think. I've put this better in *Notes from an Odd Country*, a book – not of poems – coming out this summer or autumn. Intelligence, exactitude – possibly about inexactitude – and wit and the whole of sensibility can co-exist in poems; it is not an impossible dream.

I asked you an impossible question.

GRIGSON: You would be suspicious if I could give a clear answer. Not writing – either having a clear answer, like a convert, or having only the other animals' consciousness, might be restful. A restful idiocy – almost. I hate extinction, I hate the selfishness of being only an aesthete.

1970

Fourteen Remarks[1]

The place for writers of poems to appear, in relation to themselves as writers of their poems, is in their poems.

Exegi monumentum is acceptable, if rashly said, in a poem.

Five paragraphs or a single paragraph beginning I believe, I do not wish, I am, I write because, are unacceptable. They are pornography.

Poetry is, Poetry will become, are presumptuous.

The pronouncements I play in a mountain corner on a scrannel pipe and I play with myself in my confessional box without a curtain so that everyone can see the spasm on my face are self-advertising, equally.

And no astrologizing, no warlocking.

Attaching to one's public self an abbreviated proletarian form of a Christian name is writing your advertisement or wearing your Order of Merit at an art auction where your own pictures are being sold.

At a Poetry Festival or a Writers' Conference Hesiod and Coleridge and Pasternak are unlikely to be encountered.

Poetry, poem – each in regard to oneself inclines to presumption. Even more so poet.

I regret – but not much – a snobbery in these remarks.

I regret such relation as these remarks have or must have to

[1] For a *Bulletin* of the Poetry Book Society.

the I myself of the poems which the selectors of the Poetry
Book Society are recommending.

If I could concisely or extensively explain I myself or my
poems, or writing them, I should not write them.

Do I claim to be consistent?

The poets who talk as if they were Apollo, or Thersites–
Apollo – whereas, say the Muses,

ἴδμεν ψεύδεα πολλὰ λέγειν ἐτύμοισιν ὁμοῖα,
ἴδμεν δ’, εὖτ’ ἐθέλωμεν, ἀληθέα γηρύσασθαι.

– we know how to tell lies which seem the facts, but when
we wish, how to tell the things which are true. It does us no
harm to recall the Muses, on Helicon. And their shining
dancing-floors.

1969